The Postnational Fantasy

CRITICAL EXPLORATIONS IN SCIENCE FICTION AND FANTASY
(a series edited by Donald E. Palumbo and C.W. Sullivan III)

1 *Worlds Apart? Dualism and Transgression in Contemporary Female Dystopias* (Dunja M. Mohr, 2005)

2 *Tolkien and Shakespeare: Essays on Shared Themes and Language* (ed. Janet Brennan Croft, 2007)

3 *Culture, Identities and Technology in the* Star Wars *Films: Essays on the Two Trilogies* (ed. Carl Silvio, Tony M. Vinci, 2007)

4 *The Influence of* Star Trek *on Television, Film and Culture* (ed. Lincoln Geraghty, 2008)

5 *Hugo Gernsback and the Century of Science Fiction* (Gary Westfahl, 2007)

6 *One Earth, One People: The Mythopoeic Fantasy Series of Ursula K. Le Guin, Lloyd Alexander, Madeleine L'Engle and Orson Scott Card* (Marek Oziewicz, 2008)

7 *The Evolution of Tolkien's Mythology: A Study of the History of Middle-earth* (Elizabeth A. Whittingham, 2008)

8 *H. Beam Piper: A Biography* (John F. Carr, 2008)

9 *Dreams and Nightmares: Science and Technology in Myth and Fiction* (Mordecai Roshwald, 2008)

10 Lilith *in a New Light: Essays on the George MacDonald Fantasy Novel* (ed. Lucas H. Harriman, 2008)

11 *Feminist Narrative and the Supernatural: The Function of Fantastic Devices in Seven Recent Novels* (Katherine J. Weese, 2008)

12 *The Science of Fiction and the Fiction of Science: Collected Essays on SF Storytelling and the Gnostic Imagination* (Frank McConnell, ed. Gary Westfahl, 2009)

13 *Kim Stanley Robinson Maps the Unimaginable: Critical Essays* (ed. William J. Burling, 2009)

14 *The Inter-Galactic Playground: A Critical Study of Children's and Teens' Science Fiction* (Farah Mendlesohn, 2009)

15 *Science Fiction from Québec: A Postcolonial Study* (Amy J. Ransom, 2009)

16 *Science Fiction and the Two Cultures: Essays on Bridging the Gap Between the Sciences and the Humanities* (ed. Gary Westfahl, George Slusser, 2009)

17 *Stephen R. Donaldson and the Modern Epic Vision: A Critical Study of the "Chronicles of Thomas Covenant" Novels* (Christine Barkley, 2009)

18 *Ursula K. Le Guin's Journey to Post-Feminism* (Amy M. Clarke, 2010)

19 *Portals of Power: Magical Agency and Transformation in Literary Fantasy* (Lori M. Campbell, 2010)

20 *The Animal Fable in Science Fiction and Fantasy* (Bruce Shaw, 2010)

21 *Illuminating* Torchwood: *Essays on Narrative, Character and Sexuality in the BBC Series* (ed. Andrew Ireland, 2010)

22 *Comics as a Nexus of Cultures: Essays on the Interplay of Media, Disciplines and International Perspectives* (ed. Mark Berninger, Jochen Ecke, Gideon Haberkorn, 2010)

23 *The Anatomy of Utopia: Narration, Estrangement and Ambiguity in More, Wells, Huxley and Clarke* (Károly Pintér, 2010)

24 *The Anticipation Novelists of 1950s French Science Fiction* (Bradford Lyau, 2010)

25 *The* Twilight *Mystique: Critical Essays on the Novels and Films* (ed. Amy M. Clarke, Marijane Osborn, 2010)

26 *The Mythic Fantasy of Robert Holdstock: Critical Essays on the Fiction* (ed. Donald E. Morse, Kálmán Matolcsy, 2011)

27 *Science Fiction and the Prediction of the Future: Essays on Foresight and Fallacy* (ed. Gary Westfahl, Wong Kin Yuen, Amy Kit-sze Chan, 2011)

28 *Apocalypse in Australian Fiction and Film: A Critical Study* (Roslyn Weaver, 2011)

29 *British Science Fiction Film and Television: Critical Essays.* (ed. Tobias Hochscherf, James Leggott, 2011)

30 *Cult Telefantasy Series: A Critical Analysis of* The Prisoner, Twin Peaks, The X-Files, Buffy the Vampire Slayer, Lost, Heroes, Doctor Who *and* Star Trek (Sue Short, 2011)

31 *The Postnational Fantasy: Essays on Postcolonialism, Cosmopolitics and Science Fiction* (ed. Masood Ashraf Raja, Jason W. Ellis, Swaralipi Nandi, 2011)

The Postnational Fantasy

Essays on Postcolonialism, Cosmopolitics and Science Fiction

Edited by MASOOD ASHRAF RAJA,
JASON W. ELLIS *and* SWARALIPI NANDI

FOREWORD BY DONALD M. HASSLER

CRITICAL EXPLORATIONS IN SCIENCE FICTION AND FANTASY, 31
Donald E. Palumbo *and* C.W. Sullivan III, *series editors*

McFarland & Company, Inc., Publishers
Jefferson, North Carolina, and London

LIBRARY OF CONGRESS CATALOGUING-IN-PUBLICATION DATA

The postnational fantasy : essays on postcolonialism, cosmopolitics and science fiction / edited by Masood Ashraf Raja, Jason W. Ellis and Swaralipi Nandi ; foreword by Donald M. Hassler.
    p.   cm. — (Critical explorations in science fiction and fantasy ; 31)
[Donald Palumbo and C.W. Sullivan III, series editors]
Includes bibliographical references and index.

ISBN 978-0-7864-6141-7
softcover : 50# alkaline paper

1. Science fiction — History and criticism. 2. Postcolonialism in literature. 3. Globalization in literature. 4. Fantasy fiction — History and criticism. 5. Cosmopolitanism in literature. I. Raja, Masood Ashraf. II. Ellis, Jason W. III. Nandi, Swaralipi
PN3433.6.P67   2011
809.3'8762 — dc22   2011005346

BRITISH LIBRARY CATALOGUING DATA ARE AVAILABLE

© 2011 Masood Ashraf Raja, Jason W. Ellis and Swaralipi Nandi. All rights reserved

No part of this book may be reproduced or transmitted in any form or by any means, electronic or mechanical, including photocopying or recording, or by any information storage and retrieval system, without permission in writing from the publisher.

Cover image © 2011 Bertrand Benoit

Manufactured in the United States of America

McFarland & Company, Inc., Publishers
  Box 611, Jefferson, North Carolina 28640
    www.mcfarlandpub.com

Acknowledgments

We would like to thank our friends and colleagues who contributed encouragement and advice as we moved forward with this project. A debt of gratitude is owed to our distinguished contributors who agreed to share their ideas with us, and now, with you. Also, we would like to thank our essay reviewers who provided their expertise and time during the revision process: Stacie Hanes, Seth Johnson, Yu-Fang Lin, Babacar M'Baye, Geoffrey Moses, David Murad, and Sohomjit Ray.

Table of Contents

Acknowledgments   vii

Foreword   1
    Donald M. Hassler

Introduction
    Masood A. Raja *and* Swaralipi Nandi   5

Part I: Postcolonial Issues in Science Fiction

1. Science Fiction as Experimental Ground for Issues of the Postcolonial Novel
    Michele Braun   17

2. Truth Is Stranger: The Postnational "Aliens" of Biofiction
    Karen Cardozo *and* Banu Subramaniam   30

3. Forms of Compromise: The Interaction of Humanity, Technology and Landscape in Ken MacLeod's *Night Sessions*
    Adam Frisch   46

4. The Language of Postnationality: Cultural Identity via Science Fictional Trajectories
    Chris Pak   56

Part II: The Nation and Ethnicity in Science Fiction

5. The "Popular" Science: Bollywood's Take on Science Fiction and the Discourse of Nations
    Swaralipi Nandi   73

6. Postcolonial Ethics and Identity in Mike Resnick's *Kirinyaga*
    Jenn Brandt   88

7. The Frontier Myth and Racial Politics
    ÁNGEL MATEOS-APARICIO MARTÍN-ALBO   100

 8. Dystopia and the Postcolonial Nation
    SUPARNO BANERJEE   125

Part III: Towards a Postnational Discourse

 9. Body Speaks: Communication and the Limits of Nationalism in Octavia Butler's *Xenogenesis* Trilogy
    KATHERINE R. BROAD   141

10. Engineering a Cosmopolitan Future: Race, Nation, and *World of Warcraft*
    JASON W. ELLIS   156

11. When "Nation" Stops Making Sense: Mexico and Giorgio Agamben's "State of Exception" in *Children of Men*
    STACY SCHMITT RUSNAK   174

12. Fantastic Language/Political Reporting: The Postcolonial Science Fiction Illocutionary Force Is with Us
    MARLEEN S. BARR   188

About the Contributors   211

Index   213

Foreword

Donald M. Hassler

To my old-fashioned sensibility, this collection of essays seems both alien and massively important at the same time. But these two characteristics have always drawn me to science fiction and fantasy, which in turn, I think, has helped keep my inevitable agedness young. You see, I am just in the proper generation to have been glued to my television set when *Star Trek* began about the time of Woodstock. And then immediately, as though there were some cause and effect operating, Neil Armstrong showed up on the set in his incredible puffy suit to take the first steps of our species on the moon. I had been watching the Apollo program along with *Trek* all along. Further, I knew that these two "new frontier" moves of the sixties harked back politically both to the vigorous and martyred JFK and to his hero FDR and the need for a new American frontier in the Depression years, the same decade when the new pulp genre of science fiction was evolving in American culture. Thus my memories of the genre carry the clear imprint of local American history and American geography of an ordained manifest destiny for expansion and growth. But when any force pushes its boundaries and expands into new environments, the new environments effect changes in development. Darwin tells us that. Clearly, the origins of science fiction are in the strong nationalism of the American frontier so that now, in the postmodern era, as the American Empire spreads the taste for SF globally the genre changes in response to its new environments. Also, science itself continually moves closer to the fantastic, and it has since Newton and his calculus, where infinitesimal measurements presage what we now call nanotechnology. In other words, we are always discovering that the frontier is a substantive and liminal boundary at the same time. Both a place and a door into strangeness.

I think of the influence of the Polish writer Stanislaw Lem on the original pulp genre out of the American thirties. I think of the French, who built from their own Jules Verne; and then with their peculiar intellectuality and its roots in the Enlightenment forged a strange and mainstream genre that had its close links to experimental movie making. I think of cultural critics in Brazil who delight in James Cameron's visit to the Amazon rain forest as he was preparing to create *Avatar* and their profound interest in the links between movies and science fiction. I think of Japanese *manga*. I think of a young Finnish scholar I know who is now working on the Foundation stories of Asimov and is making his reading of them ground itself in the work of Frederick Jackson Turner and his theories of the expansion of the American frontier — this reading rather than the usual study of Asimov and his debt to Gibbon and the fall of the Roman Empire. The globalization of the American genre here is in full stride and ranges from texts to movies to criticism.

Our small globe as laboratory or greenhouse for "the Darwin moment" seems insufficient, however, for what are much more widespread theoretic notions on change. And so the more important contribution in this collection may strike closer to theory than to the other subsets of artistic, literary, or even memoir study I mention above. I think we are always fascinated by the largest puzzles in the dynamic of change. Is change located at the core where pressure is greatest and where dramatic explosions occur, such as Paris or St. Petersburg at the moment of huge revolutions? Or does change take root and begin to grow at the edges of Empire, such as in the goth villages on the edges of the Roman Empire or in colonial Boston at the time when Samuel Johnson was located at the center of Englishness in London? In this collection, I know there is sufficient material, both in the research and in the voices present, to elevate my own sensibility beyond genre considerations and standard literary work to these higher alternative interpretations, or theoretic considerations, of what I have called the Darwin moment.

Over the years, I have watched the work of many of the contributors here and know they love to work at the edges at the same time that they are grounded in the center. The three editors especially embody these complementary traits of the juggler and the scholar. In fact, the three taught with me in 2009 at Kent State University and I was intrigued to see their influence on students, on one another, and on the wider community of science fiction and fantasy. We had hired Masood Raja to teach postcolonial literature several years ago, but I did not learn until he came to Kent that science fiction and fantasy had been reading passions of his as well. He recently launched an important new journal on Pakistani literature and has now launched his own professional career far from Kent. The two brilliant doctoral students working with Raja are, of course, on the same trajectory. I think in the days of old students might have remained near the center of their own university for a lifetime career, less so now. And what I refer to above as "memoir studies," perhaps, are always linked to, and even reflections of, the larger theoretic issues. Swaralipi Nandi arrived at Kent from India, and I remember well her start in our doctoral program when she took an eighteenth-century course from me in which I wanted to focus to some extent on Samuel Johnson as a "class" in himself. Nandi wanted to look at the edges. Her momentum has increased apace, and she is now well-launched on her dissertation with Professor Raja. Jason Ellis is my doctoral student. His work focuses on P.K. Dick, one of our most explosive and liminal SF writers. The French especially appreciate the revolutionary nature of Dick. Ellis is from rural Georgia, began his work as a physicist at Georgia Tech, earned his M.A. in Liverpool working with the British collection gathered by the Science Fiction Foundation there, and his trajectory is now firmly toward a fine dissertation and this volume. So eagerly I step back at this moment and reclaim my TV-watcher's seat, so to speak, in the face of change. What the editors set in motion here has a trajectory; it is on its way along with my own joy and delight in being able to share in the launch.

Donald M. Hassler is a professor of English at Kent State University. In 1991, he won the J. Lloyd Eaton Award for the best critical study of science fiction in that year for his study of Isaac Asimov. In 2001, he won the Thomas D. Clareson Award for service to the science fiction community.

Introduction

MASOOD A. RAJA *and*
SWARALIPI NANDI

> "In the capital, where, our Queen lives, there are two universities. One of these invented a wonderful balloon, to which they attached a number of pipes. By means of this captive balloon ... they could draw as much water from the atmosphere as they pleased...When the other university came to know of this.... They invented an instrument by which they could collect as much sun heat as they wanted. And they kept the heat stored up to be distributed among others as required."
> — Rokeya Sakhawat Hossain, from "Sultana's Dream"

In her 1905 short story, published in a Madras English magazine, Rokeya Sakhawat Hossain imagines and represents a female utopia. She offers a world in which the gender roles have been reversed and while the women run this utopian polity, men have been confined to quarters and observe strict Purdah. This ultimate utopia owes its existence to scientific knowledge. Such faith in the power of science to reverse gender roles and to bridge class differences is not rare in the postcolonial writings, even when they are ultimately realistic narratives. Thus, it is not surprising that Mulk Raj Anand's hauntingly realistic character Bakha in *Untouchable*—a sweeper whose job is to clean the latrines and live on the edge of the class/caste society—sees the modern toilet as a way of escaping the very given of his life. For logically speaking, if the latrines become self cleaning through technology, there will be no need for sweepers and hence no need for someone to live the life of a sweeper. In the colonial appropriations of the early twentieth century, then, science is usually seen as a means of instrumentalizing nature, even the natural functions, to change the living conditions of humans.

Science, at least in the early stages of colonial literary production, was inextricably linked with class or gender utopias. Somehow, it was felt that the advancement of science would affect utilization of labor and thus reconfigure gender and class/caste divides. Fantasy, another branch of science fiction, was also a useful genre in imagining a life outside and beyond the constricted terrain of colonial power. It is no surprise, then, that the most popular fantastical epics of Muslim India — *Dastaan-a-Amir Hmaza* and *Tilism Hosuruba* were fixed and printed in standard forms during the height of colonialism for in these epics the native could relive the glories of the past. Thus, while the possibilities for the future were envisioned in the realm of science, the possibility of cultural revival were seen in a nostalgic return to a fantasized past. Science fiction in both its major strains was thus an enabling form for the colonized to write a different kind of existence, an existence in difference and outside the sphere of colonial power.

The female characters of Hossain's short story are deeply invested in the possibilities of science in reversing the gender roles. It is the scientific advancement effected by women scientists that first controls and instrumentalizes nature, harnesses its energies to make the need for male labor redundant and this redundancy then leads to the complete erasure of male power to an extent that having rendered useless to the productive processes, the men are, in turn, sequestered in the *zenana*. The native colonial utopia, therefore, does not envision the advent of science as destructive nor as a threat to a so-called natural and communal way of life, but rather an enabling precondition for the reconfiguration of native cultures. Utopia in the colonial literary vision is also both temporal and spatial: It envisions a time and a space where the naturalized hierarchies of the native time and space can be reconfigured through scientific knowledge. Fantasy and science fiction, therefore, are linked, by extension, to this question of reconfiguration effectuated through knowledge.

In the metropolitan arena, Utopia, as Frederic Jameson suggests, "has always been a political issue" (xi). Jameson also discusses the negative reception of Utopia as something suspect and laced with the normative drive of power in the following words:

> During the Cold War ... Utopia had become a synonym for Stalinism and had come to designate a program which neglected human frailty and original sin, and betrayed a will to uniformity and the ideal purity of a perfect system that always had to be imposed by force on its imperfect and reluctant subjects" [xi].

Thus, it seems, Marx's vision of a classless society — a political Utopia — had by the mid–1980s been transformed into a vision of human collectivity that did not materialize from below but needed to be imposed from above, and in order for this to happen a more coercive system of power and implementation was needed. In other words the Utopia, at least the socialistic one, could be achieved only through the repressive state apparatuses since the ideological state apparatuses had proved ineffective against the onslaught of a global capitalistic system of production and desire.

During the decolonization phase of twentieth century colonialism, many times the leaders and the theorists had to curtail a larger utopian vision in order to articulate a more sustainable nationalist vision. Rise of national consciousness, in such a scenario, preceded the creation of larger utopian systems. Fanon's later work is a good example of this nationalization of the utopia of freedom. In his major work, *The Wretched of the Earth*, Fanon opines on the importance of constructing a national consciousness:

> The consciousness of self is not the closing of a door to communication. Philosophic thought teaches us, on the contrary, that it is its guarantee. National consciousness, which is not nationalism, is the only thing that will give us an international dimension.... If man is known by his acts, then we will say that the most urgent thing today for the intellectual is to build up his nation. If this building up is true, that is to say if it interprets the manifest will of the people and reveals the eager African peoples, then the building of a nation is of necessity accompanied by the discovery and encouragement of universalizing values. Far from keeping aloof from other nations, therefore, it is national liberation which leads the nation to play its part on the stage of history. It is at the heart of national consciousness that international consciousness lives and grows [247–8].

For Fanon, then, the universalist drive of a pan–African movement, which he in his early work describes as a new form of humanism, can be possible only if the Africans first remove the colonial yoke through a national struggle. Thus, structuring of a national identity and its mobilization for freedom is an important first step in imagining a free African culture. This emphasis on the nation, certainly, goes against the grain of current emphasis on cosmopolitanism as posited by the works of Bruce Robbins and Pheng Chea. And here it is important to connect this Fanonian view of the nation on the latter's take on the "postnation," especially since this book is primarily focused on the issues of postnationalism and the role of science fiction and postcolonial theory in underwriting or contesting any such claims.

In the introduction to *Cosmopolitics*, Bruce Robbins suggests that there has been a transformation in the current usage of term cosmopolitanism:

> Understood as a fundamental devotion to the interests of humanity as a whole, cosmopolitanism has often seemed to claim universality by virtue of its independence, its detachment from the bonds, commitments, and affiliations that constrain ordinary nation-bound lives. It has seemed to be a luxuriously free-floating view from above. But many voices now insist ... that the term should be extended to transnational experiences that are particular rather than universal and that are unprivileged — indeed, often coerced [1].

What Robbins seems to assert is against the grain of traditional emphasis on a Universalist, postnationalist brand of cosmopolitanism. In fact, a cosmopolitics that goes beyond the nation, has its internationalist and Universalist priorities but is not necessarily closed to a local articulation of a cosmopolitan spirit. Thus, one could say that Robbins emphasis is not quite different from that of Fanon, only he wants to reintroduce the nation/local within the postnational and universalistic terrain while Fanon wants to infuse the postnational drive of pan–Africanism with the spirit of the nation. The local and the nation form an integral part of this postnational whole.

Thus nation and nationalism, despite the emphasis on the postnational and the cosmopolitan, still remain two most potent symbols of the most highly developed human systems of administration and collective identity organization. The rise of neoliberal capitalism, heralded as a system that defies nationalistic modes of production of advanced capitalism, cannot also erase the nation and the national in any true aspect, and from a postcolonial point of view, one could truly question the very nature of this insistence on the postnational. If nation-states do not matter and capital and commodities can move freely, then whose interests are served in the name of such economic postnationalism? In other words, rephrasing a famous question by Gayatri Spivak, "Who crawls into the post of postnationalism at the end of the day?"

The neoliberal globalization develops its own vocabularies and sociologies, and while its exponents posit it as an equalizing force across the global spectrum of productive activity, the ground realities tend to defy any such claims to an equalizing spread of economic and social justice. Despite its claims to free trade and open borders, it is a fact that "the center of gravity of many of the transactions that we refer to in an aggregate fashion as the global economy lies in the North Atlantic region" (Sassen 58). Thus globalization, in one sense, tends to be "a sort of globalization of Western standards" (69). In the realm of culture, globalization, instead of creating a two way hybridization process, also tends to restructure the global cultures mostly in the image of a Western and North-Atlantic norm. So it seems that both cosmopolitanism and globalization, despite their claims to more universalistic and equalizing roles in restructuring the world, even when some lip service is paid to the local, is in essence a restructuring of the world in the age-old interests of the North. The latest research on neoliberal globalization also suggests that the recipes concocted in the name of free trade in the west are not necessarily always useful for the developing countries and in fact mostly tend to be harmful to the local interests of the developing countries. In fact, "even IMF agrees that it has pushed that agenda too far" (Stiglitz 59). So, even though cosmopolitanism and postnationalism are concepts worthy of our interest as scholars, we must also remember that weakening of the nation-state and its attendant redemptive functions for the poor may not be in the best interest of those on the periphery of the global division of labor.

It seems that all the terms mentioned in the title of this book are the terms that privilege, at the end of the day, a Eurocentric view of the world. The purpose of this volume, then, is also to bring these conceptual signifiers face to face with the most radical from of imaginative literature — fantasy and science fiction. Our main title, *The Postnational Fantasy*, therefore, plays with the concept of fantasy as a postnational genre but also overloads the postnational with an element of the fantastical, for after all, what we call postnationalism is in itself quite a fantastical concept. The whole idea in this book is to bring to bear upon some classical and some contemporary works of science fiction, the full resources and innovative vigor of postcolonial theory. The result, we hope, would be not only an invigoration of science fiction studies in the light of postcolonial theory but also an enrichment of postcolonial canon by incorporating science fiction and fantasy as forms and genres worthy of inclusion in what is called the postcolonial counter-canon.

The connection between science fiction and postcolonial studies is almost natural: both these fields are deeply concerned with questions of temporality, space, and existence. Central also to both these fields of study are the questions of the "other"— human, machine, cyborg — and the nature of multiple narratives of history and utopias and dystopias of the future. Thus, while we started this introduction with a reference to one of the earliest works of science fiction in the Indian narrative tradition, we also know that even today — despite the politicization of sciences and their Eurocentric vision — science and its attendant possibilities are seen as a path toward a more just and equitable restructuring of the globe. It is no wonder that the so-called third world nations are at the forefront of the open access movement that attempts to force the metropolitan powers and corporations to share scientific knowledge more freely in order to break or complicate the North's monopoly over transformative scientific knowledge. It seems, then, the struggle between the North and South, despite the claims of cosmopolitan theory and globalization, is still a struggle about access to knowledge and its redemptive aftereffects. In such a scenario a book such as ours presents itself as a tool in teaching and rehearsing the major debates of two radical and often challenging fields of study to seek out and delineate the possibilities of coincidence between the two fields as well as the impact of such a mixing on the practical politics of our everyday lived experience. In such a scenario the literary text becomes a staging ground and a launching pad for a radical reconfiguration of our job as critics and scholars. This is important, as we know live in an academic culture where the stalwarts of literary theory, such as Stanley Fish, want us "To save the World in our own time" while focusing just on the depoliticized and neutered form of what we teach. Our aim then, is also to challenge such a complacent and wearied approach to literary studies, for if imaginative literature just becomes an inert object of study, then we might as well lower our "shields" and let the captains of industry and prophets of neoliberal globalization incinerate us out of existence with their full-powered rhetorical ion blasters.

We know that the world is not really postnational nor is the nation-state irreconcilable with the ideas of cosmopolitans, but an honest and just appraisal of these powerful tropes is necessary to foster a more nuanced, humanistic, praxis-guided scholarship. The chapters included in this book, mostly by emerging scholars, are therefore a testament to our attempt at foregrounding the importance of critical thought as produced and articulated by those who would eventually take over the helms of literary theory and its practice from those wearied seniors who have already been co-opted by the very systems that public intellectuals must contest at all times. This attempt is therefore also a challenge from the praxis-driven emerging public intellectuals to those who have now, for reasons too complex to explain, become foundational scholars. So, before you delve deeper into this innovative and experimental anthology, we provide a brief overview of what is included in this book.

The volume has been divided into three sections organized in the trajectory of addressing the issues of postcolonial science fiction, contextualizing them in the discourse of nation and mapping the emerging trends of postnational fictions. The contributors in the first section, titled "Postcolonial Issues in Science Fiction," take a postcolonial perspective in critically examining the genre, foregrounding the points of confluence of both the fields. The section thus initiates the primary goal of this volume of fusing SF and postcolonial studies theoretically and thematically.

Michele Braun's essay "Science Fiction as Experimental Ground for Issues of the Postcolonial Novel" reads Salmon Rushdie's *Grimus* as a science fiction exploring issues of inclusion, nationalism and the cosmopolitical. Through the Flapping-Eagle's quest to find his sister, explaining his immortality, and rejoining the human race, Rushdie, as Braun shows, is able to use magic, technology, and scientific theories ranging from physics through anthropology to investigate the postcolonial imagination in ways that maximize the strengths of both the science fiction and the postcolonial genres.

In a similar strain, in their essay "Truth Is Stranger: The Postnational 'Aliens' of Biofiction" Karen Cardozo and Banu Subramaniam explores the issues of late capitalism and globalization, of nationalism and cosmopolitics in Ruth Ozeki's novels. They focus on *My Year of Meats* and its theme of transnational meat production that introduces "alien" and toxic elements into female reproductivity. In *All Over Creation* they see Ozeki exploring genetic engineering alongside mixed race discourses — here the other/alien is literally in oneself, in the genome. With these two readings Cardozo and Banu conclude that Ozeki's biofiction weaves together questions of identity, citizenship, nations, self and other with discourses of science and agriculture, proposing that contemporary "aliens" embody the cosmopolitics of contemporary twenty-first century life.

Adam Frisch's essay "Forms of Compromise: The Interaction of Humanity, Technology and Landscape in Ken Macleod's *Night Sessions*" goes beyond a conventional reading of Ken MacLeod's *Night Sessions* by seeing it through the paradigm of postcolonial hybridity. Reading *Night Sessions*, a murder mystery set primarily in a near-future Edinburgh, Frisch sees how the novel's protagonists treat their robot companions much as Western colonialists treated the colonized, as untrustworthy inferiors in need of civilizing/Christianizing. The artificially intelligent robots, in turn, adopt many of the traditional coping mechanisms of conquered populaces. However, using the postcolonial concept of the "bridge" area where humans and AIs most closely interact, Frisch goes beyond this and argues for new definitions of identity for both master and mastered groups, a dialectical range of human/AI "compromise" that MacLeod builds into the very landscapes of his novel.

Chris Pak's essay "The Language of Postnationality: Cultural Identity via Science Fictional Trajectories" moves from the thematic issues to the linguistic, exploring how the language of science fiction explores constructions of national and cultural identity while offering visions of a future postnationality. Pak examines Samuel Delany's *Nova*, Nnedi Okorafor-Mbachu's "When Scarabs Multiply" and Vandana Singh's "Delhi" through the concepts of Broderick's megatext, Foucault's discourse and Bakhtin's dialogism combined with linguistic analysis to explore how SF makes use of language to engage in a dialogue with cultural identity and negotiate potential postnational identities.

The second section of the volume concentrates on the more specific postcolonial issues of nation and ethnicity, exploring their relationship with science and scientific imagination. "The 'Popular' Science: Bollywood's Take on Science Fiction and the Discourse of Nations" by Swaralipi Nandi deals with the discourse of science in the popular media of commercial Hindi films. Though quite a rarity in the otherwise proliferating Hindi film industry (aka Bollywood), the few science fiction films in Bollywood operate under the rubrics of Indian popular culture and dominant motifs of Indian cinematic imagination. Consequently, the essay presents a study of three popular Bollywood

SF films—*Mr. India*, *Koi Mil Gaya* and *Krrish*—from different time periods of postcolonial India, to exemplify how these films apply the popular themes of commercial cinema to invoke a discourse of science in sync with the changing notions of nationhood in India.

Jenn Brandt's "Postcolonial Ethics and Identity in *Kirinyaga*" and Ángel Mateos-Aparicio Martín-Albo's "The Frontier Myth and Racial Politics" both discuss the imaginary worlds of the science fictions as echoes of the present postcolonial issues of nationhood. Set in a future where Africa has been colonized and modernized, complete with cities in the European tradition, Brandt reads *Kirinyaga* as using science fiction and extrapolation to explore and challenge moral and ethical values within postcolonial societies and structures of power. Brandt not only explores the ways postcolonialism is represented textually in *Kirinyaga*, but also through the character of Koriba, Resnick explores the ambiguities and dualities of social change and the (mis)uses of power that are common themes in both science fiction and postcolonial literature. Mateos-Aparicio sees the stories of the red planet Mars echoing the American myth of the Western frontier. He reads various fictions to explore the two versions of the frontier theme which symbolize two contradictory trends in the development of the United States as a nation: the assimilation of the country to its Anglo-Saxon majority and the recognition of the presence of numerous immigrant and minority groups and their influence on the vision of America as a multiracial, multicultural "melting pot." The essay analyzes how the Martian frontier enacts the ideological dialogue between the two versions of the frontier myth as "civilization" and assimilation and as a space for cultural exchange, multiplicity, and hybridity.

Finally, Suparno Banerjee reads Ruchir Joshi's *The Last Jet-Engine Laugh* as a narrative of disillusionment towards the idea of a unified nation. Like many other postcolonial science fictions this text depicts a semi-dystopic future; yet, Banerjee notes, rather than singling out any specific political ideology as the cause of this dystopic scenario, this book unfolds in a typical postmodern fragmentary way the lack of a consistent political principle that can deliver the nation to the promised glories of the future. Banerjee's essay "Dystopia and the Postcolonial Nation" explores the various postcolonial and postmodern critical approaches applied in this book—from a Derridean deconstructive approach to Baudrillardian simulacra—in questioning history and nation building. Thus, Banerjee argues that in the process of telling this story Joshi disrupts the hierarchy of reality and fiction and highlights the intrinsically hybrid nature of the Indian nation.

The third section makes a transition to the emerging trends in the genre that go beyond the questions of the nation towards a postnational discourse.

Katherine R. Broad's essay "Body Speaks: Communication and the Limits of Nationalism in Octavia Butler's *Xenogenesis* Trilogy" discusses the limits of both current SF and postcolonial discourses in reading in Octavia Butler's *Xenogenes*. The essay considers how the aliens Oankalis' communication through the body instead of through language impacts the hybrid human-alien social order. Reading *Xenogenesis* through a postcolonial lens, Broad reveals how Butler subverts the expectations of both SF and postcolonial discourses when the alien we cannot understand is in fact the colonizer, and the exploration of a distant land is the re-acquaintance with Earth. The relationship between the colonizer and colonized neither replicates nor repudiates traditional narratives of colonization. Instead, Broad argues that the text explores the tensions of colonial discourses and the limits of nationalism when a constructed society explicitly depends on communication and integration in order to survive.

Jason W. Ellis demonstrates how *World of Warcraft* utilizes cosmopolitan principles to support a more real worldly identity in spite of the re-inscription of racism from the real world role-players. Ellis critiques the shifting racial signifiers within the massively multiplayer online role-playing game *World of Warcraft* and how those constitute new constructions of nation while encouraging, and even necessitating, a cosmopolitan attitude on the parts of the role-players to travel and engage other races to find success within the game's world, Azeroth. These provide a point of entry to discussing the kind of digitally mediated cosmopolitanism, hinging on travel and engagement with the other, found in *World of Warcraft*.

Stacy Schmitt Rusnak proposes a case study on science fiction's interrogation of the "national" in late capitalism. Combining identity politics and postcolonialism, she focuses on how the Mexican director Alfonso Cuarón allegorizes the state and its role in the formation of a transnational, global Mexican citizenry in *Children of Men*. Reading of the film through Giorgio Agamben's concept of the "state of exception" to uncover cultural and political debates within the text, Rusnak opens up various layers of the film to demonstrate how the film's allegory comments on post–NAFTA, post–PRI (Revolutionary Party) Mexico and its new cosmopolitan identity.

Having foregrounded the discussions on the postnational and cosmopolitan trends of current science fiction, the final essay sums it up with a focus on the new language of science fiction affecting the global scenario. Marleen S. Barr's "Fantastic Language/Political Reporting" discusses the role of the postcolonial SF language (considered a linguistic other) as a new national language for navigating the political landscape that serves an instantaneously recognizable metaphor which challenges, normalizes, and contests political debates. Citing the *New York Times* editorial page as the field of discussion, Barr explains the affective value of the new postcolonial language of SF and its connotation in the context of national and global politics.

The Postnational Fantasy: Postcolonialism, Cosmopolitics and Science Fiction thus places itself at the nexus of current debates about nationalism, postnational capitalism, the reassertion of third world nationalism and its cosmopolitical counterparts, and the role of contemporary science fiction and fantasy in challenging, normalizing, or contesting these major conceptual currents of our times.

Works Cited

Anand, Mulk Raj. *Untouchable*. London: Penguin, 1940.
Cheah, Pheng, and Bruce Robbins, eds. *Cosmopolitics: Thinking and Feeling Beyond the Nation*. Minneapolis: University of Minnesota Press, 1998.
Fanon, Frantz. *The Wretched of the Earth*. London: Pelican, 1959.
Hossain, Rokeya Sakhawat. *Sultana's Dream; and Padmarag: Two Feminist Utopias*. Trans. Barnita Bagchi. New Delhi: Penguin, 2005.
Jameson, Frederic. *Archaeologies of the Future: The Desire Called Utopia and Other Science Fictions*. New York: Verso, 2007.
Sassen, Sakia, ed. *Global Networks, Linked Cities*. New York: Routledge, 2002.
Stiltz, Joseph. E. *Globalization and Its Discontents*. New York and London: Norton, 2002.

PART I
Postcolonial Issues in Science Fiction

1

Science Fiction as Experimental Ground for Issues of the Postcolonial Novel

MICHELE BRAUN

In the final scene of Salman Rushdie's *Grimus* (1975), Flapping-Eagle, who has spent his immortal life searching for his sister, finds her with Grimus, a "halfbreed, semisemitic prisoner of war" for whom "ideas were the sole justification for existence; and when he found the knowledge and power to play with his ideas, he could not be stopped" (306–7). Grimus, who is obsessed with the idea of sharing his knowledge with Flapping Eagle (by force if necessary), tricks Flapping Eagle into using a technology that blends the two men's consciousnesses together. Flapping Eagle finds his consciousness shared with Grimus so that "(I was Flapping Eagle.) (I was Grimus.) Self. My self. Myself and he alone.... Yes, it was like that. Printing. Like printing. Press, his thoughts pressed over mine, under mine, through and into mine, his thoughts mine" (305–6). This scene is the climactic moment in this very strange novel but it also demonstrates how this novel's playful approach to identity, technology, consciousness, and even genre itself is used to complicate simplistic conceptions of such ideas.

That two minds might be printed upon each other calls our attention to the very real technology of Gutenberg, a technology that facilitated the spread of knowledge that we take for granted today. However, imprinting two minds into one consciousness would require a technology that humans have not yet developed. The depiction of futuristic or alien technologies signals readers that the story they are reading might be science fiction. At the same time, this encounter with the other and the alienation of self that Flapping-Eagle undergoes as a consequences of that encounter suggest that there is something more going on here as well. The text also employs the conventions of magical realism and includes "ideas of personal and national identity, the legacy of colonialism, [and] the problems of exile" though they are not as fully or maturely developed as in Rushdie's later work (Cundy 129). The multi-generic nature of *Grimus* allows the text to address tropes and themes in science and technology through the science-fictional elements in the text and issues of identity, migrancy and displacement of the postcolonial novel through the magical realist elements in the text.

As *Grimus* was Rushdie's first novel, it contains features he develops more fully in his later novels so that in *Grimus*, we begin to detect the complexity, and dense allusion that characterize Rushdie's later work. Although Rushdie's work defies categorization at times, his use of magical realist techniques in novels obsessed with migrants and their encounters with other lands and other peoples lead to his frequent identification as a postcolonial writer. In *The Empire Writes Back*, the editors suggest that post-colonial literature is concerned with place and displacement, both of which can erode the sense of self, and that "such alienation is shared by those whose possession of English is indisputably 'nature' (in the sense of being possessed from birth) yet who begin to feel alienated within its practice once its vocabulary, categories, and codes are felt to be inadequate or inappropriate to describe the fauna, the physical and geographical conditions, or the cultural practices they have developed in a new land" (10). What this definition suggests is that it is not the structure or language used, but the encounter with a strange place that produces the alienation found in postcolonial literature. Similarly, science fiction texts often create fauna, geographical conditions, and cultural practices that readers are not familiar with, so that in the act of reading a science fiction text, the reader can share that sense of alienation that the postcolonial subject or writer might feel. Darko Suvin describes the novelty this creates as cognitive estrangement (71–3), while Philip K. Dick labels this "distinct new idea" within an otherwise realist text as "dysrecognition" (99). *Grimus* suggests that the postcolonial text shares with science fiction texts a sense of displacement or alienation from the storyworld depicted within it because of the number of characters that experience alienation—Flapping-Eagle is rejected by his tribe, Virgil is exiled from K, and the townspeople of K themselves are alienated from ordinary human society.

When Rushdie wrote *Grimus*, he submitted it to the Gollancz science fiction contest, but it was not considered for the prize, because as Roger Clark suggests "while the novel contains intergalactic journeys and a race of extra-terrestrial stone frogs, the characters have heavy mythological and mystical associations, the setting is a strange fusion of four cosmographies, and the structure derives mainly from a Sufi mystical journey" (13). However, a story like *Grimus* that is heavily allusive, employs mythology and rewrites history, operates in the same way that science fiction does. Nancy Kress suggests that science fiction can "present a far denser, richer, spicier version" of an issue or event than reality based fiction (205). This happens because science fiction makes metaphors literal and it represents alternative ways of being (Vint 20). Thus, in this science fiction novel, we find thematic parallels to the postcolonial issues and ideas found in Rushdie's later magical realist texts, such as his interest in migrancy and identity (exemplified in his fiction as well as in essays like those found in *Imaginary Homelands*). Rushdie's use of magic, history, and myth to create multiple cosmologies (particularly in his early novels like *Midnight's Children* [1980] and *The Satanic Verses* [1988]) is present in *Grimus*, but is also supplemented in this first novel by aliens, fabulous technology and interdimensional travel as well.

Following Arthur C. Clarke's dictum that "any technology sufficiently advanced is indistinguishable from magic" (21), I would suggest that the science fictional elements of *Grimus* perform the same function as the magical realist ones, because of the way that magic and technology are both able to organize and explain the world. In Jacques Ellul's *The Technological Society*, he identifies magic as a prime feature of the first of the three milieus that humans have evolved, followed by the milieu of civilized society and then the technological milieu, describing a progression in which magic and technology perform a similar organizing function in society. Mary Douglas also suggests that belief in science and technology follows the belief in magic because "magic resulted from early man's inability to distinguish between his own subjective associations and external objective reality" (35). This is not to say that modern humans have gotten much better at identifying objective reality. For most people, the shift during the twentieth century from Newtonian to quantum physics as a means of explaining the world means that scientific knowledge became even more mysterious, since the principles of quantum physics are based on the movement of subatomic particles that cannot be observed firsthand. Thus, as Gerald Holton notes, to most people, "science [is] magic, and the scientist [is a] wizard, *deus ex machina*, or oracle" (135). The "magic" of science emerges out of its relative incomprehensibility to most people, particularly when it pushes the boundaries of the possible beyond the reality we experience everyday. In *Grimus*, Rushdie blurs the distinction between magic and science further by keeping the reader in the dark as to the nature of the fantastical events in the story until well into the narrative, so that the fantastical events of the story appear at first to be the result of magic; it is only later that the reader understands that the "magic" in the story is produced by a technologically advanced race of aliens.

Flapping-Eagle, the narrator of *Grimus*, is a hermaphrodite Axona Indian of the American West who is expelled from his community because he does not belong. While searching for his sister, who has also left the community, he obtains an immortality elixir and in the course of his long life, finds Calf Island, a refuge for immortals like himself who have grown tired of living among mortals. This quest requires Flapping-Eagle to struggle up the island's mountain through the Grimus Effect, a by-product of the Stone Rose, a technology created by the extraterrestrial Gorfs. The Grimus Effect is a weakening of the boundaries between reality and the Inner and Outer Dimensions: the Outer Dimensions are other worlds that one can travel to using the Stone Rose, while the Inner Dimensions are a concrete manifestation of the internal psyche of the individual. In the Stone Rose and Grimus Effect, we see how the science fictional and magical realist elements of the text combine so that the merging of magic, technology, consciousness, alternate worlds and inner dimensions in this text confuses the boundary between the real and the fantastic in novel ways. But more important than a convenient label, Rushdie's play with generic conventions allows him to explore how human beings like Flapping-Eagle might encounter the strange and unexpected.

As Minoli Salgado notes, *Grimus* "strain[s] against the boundaries of the science fiction genre" because the text examines issues such as "personal and national identity, the experience of exile, cultural diversity and aesthetic unity, the colonial legacy, fantasy and imaginative truth, and the relationship between the past and the present" (32). This rather large list of issues within the text does make it challenging to discuss the text as an example of the science fiction genre. However, it is possible to consider the novel as an example of what Brooks Landon calls "science fiction thinking" which is "a set of attitudes and expectations about the future" that "bridges the gap between the givens of science and the goals of the imaginary marvelous, the emphasis always on 'explaining' the marvelous with rhetoric that makes it seem plausible, or at least not yet impossible" (4, 6). Following Landon's line of thought, the science fiction of *Grimus* can be understood as a mode or technique within a narrative that allows a writer to explore issues relating to science and technology as they affect characters like Flapping-Eagle or even Grimus himself.

The science-fictional mode of *Grimus* is one way of accounting for the relationship that Grimus (the man) has with the objects he controls. He can be read both as a magician and as a technologist, just as some elements within the novel can be read as both magical realism and science fiction. *Grimus* contains science fictional elements like an extraterrestrial race of frogs and the interdimensional intergalactic travel, but it also contains elements of magical realism like a pair of magical elixirs that grant life and death, a woman whose love-making opens a portal across dimensions and a dance capable of temporarily allowing one person access to another's consciousness. But regardless of whether these elements are read as technologically advanced or as magical, they perform a similar function, that is, they are expressions of the operation of power. Flapping-Eagle suggests that the word "magician" might be understood through this power because "born and raised as he was in a tribe where magic intermingled continually with daily life, [magician] meant anyone apparently in possession of power, or knowledge, which he himself lacked. Perhaps that's the only sense in which the word has meaning" (20).

This ready acceptance of the supernatural is also expressed by Virgil Jones, the first person Flapping-Eagle meets on Calf Island. Jones is an immortal like Flapping-Eagle who has been thinking about the implications of his immortality. He tells Flapping-Eagle, "by your own account you have had at least one or two experiences which would normally be classed as supernatural. Your very acceptance of immortality, for instance: most human beings would classify that as sorcery. So, then. You must accept that the world in which you lived was no simple, matter-of-fact place" (61). Flapping-Eagle's immortality comes about because he is given two vials of liquid: one which gives eternal life to its drinker, and the other which gives eternal death. Becoming immortal was as simple as drinking the potion, an action that seems more suited to a fairy tale than a science fiction story. It is only much later in the novel that we learn of the extra-terrestrial origins of the liquid, which introduces ambiguity regarding the potion's origin into the text: was it magical, or simply the product of a pharmacology much more advanced than our own?

Virgil explains his own understanding of the magic and science of the things he has witnessed as an immortal as a matter of perception. He explains that Flapping-Eagle perceives him as a solid even though the space between the atoms in his body is no greater than the space between those in the air that fills an empty well-shaft, even though the body appears solid while the air appears empty. Virgil suggests that "with a different set of tools of perception — I mean other than eyes — one could conclude say, either that I am as 'empty' as the air in the shaft, or that it is as 'full' or 'solid' as I." Virgil further suggests that sanity is constructed from a "previously agreed construction of reality" that places things that do not conform with that reality outside of it. This leads him to the question he wishes Flapping-Eagle to consider:

> Is it not a conceptual possibility that here, in our midst, permeating all of us and all that surrounds us, is a completely other world, composed of different kinds of solids, different kinds of empty spaces, with different perceptual tools

which make us as non-existent to its inhabitants as they are to ours? In a word, another dimension... In fact, that an infinity of dimensions might exist.... And further: there is no reason why those dimensions should operate solely on our scale [61–2].

Virgil's speech begins with a rudimentary physics lesson, but his discussion of dimensions, while still based in physics, adds a sense of the mystical in its invocation of the unseen other worlds that might surround us. The reader might be willing to accept Virgil's argument as simply a mental exercise, except that we learn a few pages later there is a Gorf from the Endimion (dimension) containing the planet Thera who is living on Calf Island (77). With this revelation, Virgil's suggestion of different dimensions becomes realized in the rock body of the Gorf and the novel vacillates between a mystical (or magical) mode and a science fictional one.

As Virgil and Flapping-Eagle travel up the mountain in the center of Calf Island, they come under the influence of the Grimus Effect, a kind of paralyzing hypnotic state that converts fears and anxieties of the subconscious into manifestations that the traveler must master (both physically and psychologically) in order to return to consciousness. Flapping-Eagle becomes trapped in his subconscious so that Virgil must dance the Spiral dance, which is "a physical exercise based on the primal rhythms, and its purpose was to enable every humble, imperfect living thing to aspire to that fundamental perfection" (92). This hypnotic dance enables Virgil to enter Flapping Eagle's consciousness to rescue him.

In *Stranger Gods*, Roger Clark suggests that in constructing Virgil's dance, Rushdie is "borrowing from the theory and practice of the Sufi brotherhoods" commonly referred to as Whirling Dervishes (47). However, the description of the Strong- and Weak-dance that Virgil learned when he traveled via the Stone Rose to the Spiral Dancer planet also sounds like the strong and weak nuclear forces of quantum physics. In the novel, the Spiral Dance is described as "a harmony of the infinitesimal, where energy and matter move like fluids." The point at which energy forces come together is the Strongdance; when they fall "back into the Primal, they were dancing the Weakdance" (Rushdie 92). In quantum physics, the strong nuclear force holds the (infinitesimally small) proton and neutron together in the atom, while the weak nuclear force is radioactivity, the breakdown of the nucleus through loss of ionizing particles (Hawking 71–2). Further confusing categories of knowledge, Virgil performs the dance in order to enter the Inner Dimensions, a space in which Flapping-Eagle's inner desires, fears ("monsters") and imagination create a landscape that he must physically escape. This space contains "his own devils burning in his own inner fires. His own worms gnawing at his strength" and if he cannot overcome these obstacles "then he dies. Or lives on, a working body encasing a ruined mind" (Rushdie 103). Thus Virgil uses a mystical dance to harness the force of quantum physics to rescue Flapping Eagle from the psychological terrors of his own id. Here, the dense allusions to the science of physics and psychology resemble the dense mythical allusions that characterize much of Rushdie's later work.

Science fiction and magical realism, like that found in *Grimus*, may operate through different tropes but they are both also founded on a playful modification of the commonplace extratextual world. Rawdon Wilson describes the parallel between science fiction and magical realism in a parable of two brothers who tired of their "commonplace existence and began to reinvent the world" by proposing that "all these mundane assumptions about human experience could be overturned and strange, but profoundly exciting propositions would follow" (210). The first brother began to imagine strange new worlds by "assuming a single proposition that was contrary to reason and to the likelihoods of human life.... The propositions that he invented were often antirational and not at all intuitive, like the axioms of differential geometry. Still, he was able to draw from them fascinating consequences" (211), a mode that produces science fiction. In the second brother's stories "there were no single axioms from which everything descended, or from which the world hung, but there were instead two codes that were interwound" one of which organized events normally while the other allowed for any number of strange things so that "in the second brother's imagined narratives, the possibilities of the two worlds were always copresent, their codes lovingly interwound, and clung fiercely to each other" (212), which describes the operational parameters of magical realism. Wilson suggests that in fantasy or science fiction "all indications of distance, capacity, or arrangement are generated in accordance with self-contained assumptions, gamelike rules that are experienced as axioms" while in magical realism "the indications of local place are sometimes those of the extratextual world but at other times are those of another place, very different in its assumptions" (Ibid.). Magical realist and science fictional modes, while operating from different axioms, both reject realism to some extent in that while they do reflect the extratextual world in portions of their narrative, they deviate from it in significant ways that cannot be incorporated into that extratextual world except as extrapolation (science fiction) or disruptive fantasy, dream, or allegory.

The conflation of mystical or magical events and science fiction that we see in *Grimus* is not necessarily unusual: in "Aliens Have Taken the Place of Angels," Margaret Atwood suggests that science fiction narratives "can explore the relationship of man to the universe, an exploration that often takes us in the direction of religion and can meld easily with mythology — an exploration that can happen within the conventions of realism only through conversations and soliloquies." In Rushdie's early novels like *Midnight's Children*, *The Satanic Verses* or *Shame* (1983), religion and mythology are heavily used as sources for the multiple cosmologies that novels rely upon. *Grimus*, with its science fictional axioms (Wilson's definition of how the genre operates), or science-fictional thinking (Brooks Landon's idea about the function of science fiction) allows Rushdie to explore that "relationship of man to the universe" in the same way as the dense allusion to religious and mythological narratives do in Rushdie's later work.

In *Grimus*, the fantastical elements of the story — alternate dimensions, "conceptual technology" and the power of the Spiral dance Virgil undertakes — can be read as magical irruptions of an otherwise realist narrative (Wilson's second brother), or as arising from the axioms of a science fictional universe in which aliens have shared their means of travelling between dimensions (Wilson's first brother). Being able to read a narrative event as either science fictional or magical realist poses problems in genre classification of the novel, but also draws our attention to how the reader's knowledge and attitude toward that narrative event can cause slippage between generic modes. Whether one reads an event as based in science or belief can depend on not only personal preference, but previous knowledge, as Arthur C. Clarke's dictum suggests.

The people who live in the town of K in the midst of the Grimus Effect are only able to keep it at bay by being single-minded, "to a fault" as Virgil tells Flapping-Eagle (99). The single-mindedness of the resident philosopher, Ignatius Gribb leads him to declare "obsession is the path to self-realization" (200) and that Grimus does not exist "nor do[es] his precious machine, nor his supposed dimensions, nor any of it. It's all the babbling of an idiot like Jones: sound and fury, signifying nothing" (163). Gribb's philosophy is founded on an emphatic rejection of technology. He tells Flapping-Eagle that he loves K for its lack of scientists: "In their absence, science is returned to its true guardians; scholars, thinkers, abstract theoreticians like myself. However, the absence of the technocrat does not mean a relapse into superstition, my dear Flapping-Eagle; on the contrary, it places upon us an even greater duty to be rational" (162). But Gribb's speech demonstrates that the abstract nature of scientific theory does not differ significantly from the philosophical theory which is Gribb's obsession. When we consider the subject of Gribb's study, we see how narrative, philosophy and Gribb's science come together in myth. Gribb tells Flapping-Eagle that he has discovered the essence of philosophy itself through his study of "race-memory: the sediment of highly-concentrated knowledge that passes down the ages, constantly being added to and subtracted from" (163). The best part of his study is that his conclusions have also allowed him to disavow knowledge of Grimus and his Stone Rose. He declares

> I am taking the intellect back to the people.... When I arrived I found a certain number of unfortunate myths [about Grimus] in the process of forming; myths which I have made it my business to expunge from the minds of the townspeople. It is, incidentally, an interesting corollary study to my work on race-memory: the growth of a mythology in a single, long-lived generation [Ibid.].

In Gribb's description of his obsession, we see how knowledge becomes important to both the magical and the technological descriptions of the narrative because the environment the characters experience is created by thought itself.

As one of the men with knowledge, Grimus is a character who bends the "gamelike rules" of the science fictional elements of the text by hiding the knowledge of just what the Stone Rose is from the other characters within the text. For that matter, Rushdie also manipulates our understanding of the narrative by failing to explain the axioms on which the narrative is built until the end of the tale. In describing the text as embodying magical realist elements, I am relying upon the reader's sense that many of the events of the narrative at first seem to be magical because the axioms underlying them are not described. At the beginning of the narrative, Flapping Eagle's immortality and transportation to the island are fantastical disruptions of an otherwise realist narrative (for example, the Axona settlement on a tabletop in the southwestern United States correlates with the extratextual world). Even the Calf Island residents' superstitious beliefs about Grimus and denial of his existence are fantastical. It is only later when the Gorf and the Stone Rose are introduced that we understand these events are not magical, but arise from extraterrestrial interference and technology which shifts the reader's sense of the narrative from magical realist into a science fictional mode. As the reader accommodates his or her changing knowledge of the cause of the fantastical events in the narrative, Grimus, as the man with the power over the Stone Rose, looks more like a technologist (or the kind of technocrat that Gribb describes) than a magician.

Whether one understands Grimus to be magician or scientist depends on whether one reads the conceptual technology of the Stone Rose as mystical artefact, or technological marvel. The magician and scientist have much in common as they use their knowledge to manipulate or control those who do not have such knowledge. For example, in *New Maps of Hell: A Survey of Science Fiction*, Martin Amis suggests that *The Tempest* is a science fiction text because "I cannot help thinking that one of the things it is about is specialised knowledge, and whatever may be the relation currently devised between

Jacobean science and magic, it would be safe to say that contemporary attitudes towards what we now see as two things were partly inseparable" (29–30). Further, "even if one resists the temptation to designate Caliban as an early mutant — 'a freckled whelp,' you remember, 'not gifted with a human shape,' but human in most other ways — and Ariel as an anthropomorphised mobile scanner, Prospero's attitude to them, and indeed his entire role as an adept, seems to some degree experimental as well as simply thaumaturgical" (30). Amis's suggestion that Prospero is both an experimenter and a magician reinforces the idea that the activities of the magician and scientist can look alike. Similarly, Ib Johansen connects Prospero to Grimus, suggesting that Grimus's position "as a powerful *magus* turns him into a somewhat dubious, but impressive representative of the technological skills and scientific culture of his own continent — even if he may also be characterized as a Gothic villain and has a number of qualities in common with the *mad scientist* of many early science-fiction novels" (25). Whether Grimus is a powerful magus or a mad scientist depends on how much one knows about the source of his power.

The Stone Rose in *Grimus* can also be read as either a magical object or a technological one because the novel moves between magical and science-fictional modes as Rushdie reveals more about the storyworld within it. After being introduced to the Grimus Effect with its mysterious influence over the subconscious (what Virgil calls the "Inner Dimensions" to distinguish it from the "Outer Dimensions" experienced by the conscious mind) and Calf Island itself, full of immortals who have drunk a liquid provided them by Grimus, we learn how these things came to be.

Virgil and Deggle, gravediggers, find a Stone Rose in the woods by the cemetery but when they touch it, they faint. They drag the Rose home, and when their friend Grimus touches it, he doesn't faint, but disappears. Upon his return he tells them he travelled to Thera and encountered the Gorfs; he also returns with the two liquids that grant eternal life and eternal death (263). They decide to distribute the immortality liquid to a select group and to prepare a place of refuge where "those who tire of the world but not of life may come" (264). As they construct this refuge — Calf Island — they disagree on its nature. In his diary, Virgil says "we have been building a world. Impossible to say whether we *found* the island or *made* it. I incline to the latter, Grimus to the former. He holds that Conceptual Technology merely reveals existences which mirror your concepts" (265). The Conceptual Technology used to create Calf Island operates in such a mysterious fashion that its status as a technology is questionable; it certainly does not conform to any form of technology that human beings have created. If it is a technology, it certainly is alien; we are told earlier that the Gorf conceptualized an Object through which he came into contact with Grimus (the Stone Rose) so that this ability to create a piece of technology simply by thinking it marks Gorf as either magical, or technologically superior.

The Stone Rose seems to be a technology because of the whine that develops after it is damaged by Deggle (Rushdie 270) and its ability to transport its users to other dimensions — Virgil describes how there had been "voyages to the real, physical alternative space-time continua" (91). But the Stone Rose is also mysterious. Virgil describes how he doubts that the force of Grimus's will can hold the island together (267) and he says, "I have always thought of the uses of the Rose as rites. They are so very unmechanical.... Rose can heal as well as hurt. I am more scared of it than I ever was" (270–1). Although technologies often evoke fear, they are rarely described in terms of rites, and generally do not rely on the will of the user in order to be effective.

Given that the Stone Rose allows travel between different dimensions of the universe, Grimus's possession and control of it gives him the power to transcend the reality (or the dimension) into which he was born. He tells Flapping Eagle that the latter will never be able to control the Rose because he does not know how to "conceptualize the coordinates of your Dimension" which will trap him Calf Island. But Grimus's possession of the Stone Rose has also alienated him from the other human occupants of the island. Flapping Eagle tells him "the Stone Rose has warped you, Grimus; its knowledge has made you as twisted, as eaten away by power-lust, as its effect has stunted and deformed the lives of the people you brought here" (297). The danger inherent in the Stone Rose as an Object of Conceptual Technology has warped Grimus because it is not a human technology — the alien Gorf created the Stone Rose for its own desires to play games with Grimus and the other inhabitants of the island. Flapping Eagle and all the other occupants of Calf Island are at the mercy of an alien technology; their advancement through everlasting life is bought at the cost of not understanding the technology that brought them there.

Magic and technology, two potential means of understanding narrative of *Grimus*, are both ways of knowing the world and controlling it. Generally speaking, magic identifies what is sacred through ritual and symbol, while technological information is contained within tools such as machines. In his study *Technology as Magic*, Richard Stivers suggests that magic, including "the sacred, symbol, myth and ritual comprise a cultural configuration that represents the deepest and most profound structure of any culture" (29). Stivers also suggests that within culture, "technology uses its information as a logical procedure embedded in a tool or machine to realize a specific goal" (9). The two modes of understanding the world may originate in different beliefs and practices, but they share a similar effect: "technology employs scientific information in the service of a material technique that acts upon the physical world, but magic uses information that is symbolic to influence nature or human beings. Magic establishes an indirect or symbolic relationship between a set of practices and a desired outcome so that the magical practices become, as it were, operational indicators of the outcome" (11). As systems of knowledge, magic and technology thus become equally useful as descriptors of human experience.

When the I-Grimus half of Flapping-Eagle-Grimus tries to stop him from unmaking Calf Island, I-Grimus offers the knowledge of how to return to Flapping Eagle's original dimension as a temptation. But I-Eagle replies, "O, hell... What would I do there anyway?" (318), a clear indication that I-Eagle has transcended the need for his original homeland, in much the same way as Rushdie imagines that for the migrant, the homeland is imaginary and forever altered by emigration (*Imaginary Homelands*). I-Eagle continues with the plan to conceptualize an island without the Stone Rose. As a result, at the end of the novel, this new Calf Island appears to be slowly dissolving back into the energy that created it. The island is being returned to the humans that inhabit it, correcting the unnatural experience of immortality provided by an alien species, but even so, it cannot continue to exist and will unmake itself because the Stone Rose no longer exists to sustain it. It is at this point that the tension between the magical realist elements of the novel and the science fictional ones also begin to dissolve as the reader understands that the point of this experimental novel was not to define a genre but to explore ideas about identity and belonging. Through Flapping-Eagle's quest to find his sister and destroy the Stone Rose, Rushdie is able to use magic, technology, and science fictional motifs to investigate the postcolonial imagination by exploiting science fictional and magical realist generic conventions.

Works Cited

Amis, K. *New Maps of Hell: A Survey of Science Fiction*. New York: Harcourt, Brace and World, 1960.

Atwood, Margaret. "Aliens Have Taken the Place of Angels: Margaret Atwood on Why We Need Science Fiction." *The Guardian* 17 June 2005. Accessed 23 April 2009.

Clark, Roger Y. *Stranger Gods: Salman Rushdie's Other Worlds*. Montreal and Kingston: McGill-Queen's University Press, 2001.

Clarke, Arthur C. "Hazards of Prophecy: The Failure of Imagination." *Profiles of the Future*. New York: Harper and Row, 1973. 12–21.

Cundy, Catherine. "'Rehearsing Voices': Salman Rushdie's Grimus." *Journal of Commonwealth Literature* 27.1 (1992): 128–138.
Dick, Philip K. "My Definition of Science Fiction." In *The Shifting Realities of Philip K. Dick: Selected Literary and Philosophical Writings*, edited by Lawrence Sutin, 99–100. New York: Pantheon, 1995.
Douglas, M. *Purity and Danger: An Analysis of the Concepts of Pollution and Taboo.* Harmondsworth: Penguin, 1966.
Ellul, Jacques. *The Technological Society.* New York: Vintage, 1964.
Hawking, Stephen. *A Brief History of Time: From the Big Bang to Black Holes.* New York: Bantam, 1988.
Holton, Gerald. "Modern Science and the Intellectual Tradition: The Seven Images of Science." *The World of Science: An Anthology for Writers.* Ed. Gladys Garner Leithauser and Marilyn Powe Bell. New York: Holt, Reinhart and Winston, 1987.
Johansen, Ib. "The Flight from the Enchanter. Reflections on Salman Rushdie's Grimus." *Kunapipi* VII.1 (1985): 20–32.
Kress, Nancy. "Ethics, Science and Science Fiction." *SciFi in the Mind's Eye: Reading Science Through Science Fiction.* Chicago: Open Court, 2007. 201–209.
Landon, Brooks. *Science Fiction After 1900: From the Steam Man to the Stars.* New York: Routledge, 2002.
Rushdie, Salman. *Grimus.* New York: Random House, 2006.
_____. *Imaginary Homelands: Essays and Criticism, 1981–1991.* London: Granta, 1991.
Salgado, Minoli. "Migration and Mutability: The Twice Born Fiction of Salman Rushdie." In *British Culture of the Postwar: An Introduction to Literature and Society, 1945–1999*, edited by Alastair Davies and Alan Sinfield, 31–49. London: Routledge, 2000.
Stivers, R. *Technology as Magic: The Triumph of the Irrational.* New York: Continuum, 1999.
Suvin, Darko. *Positions and Presuppositions in Science Fiction.* Kent, OH: Kent State University Press, 1988.
Vint, S. *Bodies of Tomorrow: Technology, Subjectivity, Science Fiction.* Toronto, ON: University of Toronto Press, 2007.
Wilson, R. In *Palamedes' Shadow: Explorations in Play, Game and Narrative Theory.* Boston: Northeastern University Press, 1990.

2

Truth Is Stranger
The Postnational "Aliens" of Biofiction

KAREN CARDOZO AND
BANU SUBRAMANIAM

> "Nothing is simple. There are many answers, none of them right, but some of them most definitely wrong."
> — Ruth Ozeki (*My Year of Meats* 327)

Introduction

Biofiction: Science Fictions of the Here and Now

As interdisciplinary scholars, we trouble "The Law of Genre" (Derrida), approaching the rich intersection of postcolonial studies, science fictions and feminist science studies to model the boundary transgressions needed to address the concerns of this anthology: "debates about nationalism, postnational capitalism, third world nationalism and its cosmopolitical counterparts, and the role of contemporary Science Fiction and fantasy in challenging, normalizing, or contesting these major conceptual currents of our times" (editors' abstract). To this end, we offer the concept of *biofiction* as a new rubric capacious enough to integrate the engagements of both science fiction and postcolonial literature in relation to the multifaceted developments of contemporary globalization.

Science fictions typically deploy discourses of fantasy and futurism, imagining new locations for old and utterly worldly problems of alienation and otherness. Yet these fantasies of the future remain riddled with anxieties of the present, which is *not* what it seems! Amidst the technological weirdness of twenty-first century capitalism, truth is often stranger than fiction. Our concept of biofiction thus disrupts the traditional generic frame of science fiction in two important ways — space and time — by locating science fiction and its aliens in the present. This move to examine the "here and now" is significant since, as postcolonial critics have eloquently shown, the colonial continues to haunt the postcolonial, as structures do poststructuralism, the modern does the postmodern, or the human the posthuman. In order to adequately address the "post," we need to attend to the present, to its national and international mythologies, fears about race, panic about permeable boundaries in both natural and cultural environments and nervousness about sexual or reproductive deviance.

Biofiction, as we conceptualize it, is imaginative writing with a substantive research foundation that explicitly engages biological and environmental issues, exploring the complex politics of science and technology of life in the past, present, and future. It has genealogical roots in four intellectual traditions: science fiction, literary theory, social and cultural studies of science, and theories of interdisciplinarity (Cardozo and Subramaniam). Biofiction is a unique mode of knowledge production that can provide a fuller understanding of the lingering effects of colonialism and other forms of structural violence that elude strictly empirical analysis: such literature "teaches us, through imaginative design, what we need to know but cannot quite get access to with our given rules of method and modes of apprehension" (Gordon 25). The literary imagination enables us to explore both current realities and the future as it might be: "We need to know where we live in order to imagine living elsewhere. We need to imagine living elsewhere before we can live there" (Gordon 5).

Our primary tutor in the generative capacities of biofiction has been the multifaceted Asian American writer Ruth Ozeki. Ozeki's work is located at precisely the intersections this anthology seeks to interrogate — nationalism/cosmopolitics, postcolonial/ethnic studies, and science fiction/science studies. Her novels *My Year of Meats* (1998) and *All Over Creation* (2003) literally represent the "meat and potatoes" of such issues, since the first investigates transnational meat production and the second tackles the incursions of big agribusiness into U.S. potato farming. Since "cultivation" is at the root of the term "culture," the emphasis on *agri/culture* in Ozeki's biofiction highlights the interconnection of the scientific and humanistic, the material and symbolic realms, embodying what Donna Haraway called "naturecultures." Delving into the economics, politics, and science of agriculture, Ozeki deftly shows how ideologies of race, difference and nationalism seep into discourses of nature and culture. She makes a compelling case for why postcolonial studies should meet science fiction, why biology should meet science studies, why economics should face ecology, and so on.

Ozeki's *oeuvre* is interdisciplinary, pedagogical, and activist; her biofiction deftly takes us through an educational tour of what happens when disarticulated discourses come into conversation with each other. Avoiding an easy polemic of the politics of left or right, Ozeki nonetheless implies that her political sympathies lie with an earth-friendly cosmofeminism, a caring capitalism or its alternatives, and a polycultural world teeming with diversity and contentious plurality. Her novels render alternately amusing and horrifying scenarios to explore the biofictions of industrialized agriculture and postnational fantasies of a cosmopolitan future.

We provide some background on Ozeki's multifaceted *oeuvre* before elaborating upon the epistemological, pedagogical and political potential of her biofiction.

"Where No One Else Has Thought to Look": Ozeki's Biofiction

"I could not break through the jumble of chaotic fragments: the bleeding cattle and the bloody meat, the farmer's rage, the mother's stupor, and the child's disfigured and unnatural grace" [*MYOM*, 296].

Hybridity is a central feature of Ruth Ozeki's personal and professional genealogies. The daughter of a Euro-American father and a Japanese mother, Ozeki studied literature and Asian Studies in both the United States and Japan and worked in film and television before turning to fiction-writing. Thus, just as genetic engineering pushes the frontiers of agricultural production, Ozeki is pioneering new ground in cultural production, "taking the novel into corners [where] no one else has thought to look—but where she finds us in all our transcultural and technological weirdness" (Michael Pollan, jacket of *AOC*). Her literary handling of issues at the heart of capitalism and globalization offers an integrative framework that foregrounds the rich resonance between gender, sexuality, race, place and the politics of agribusiness and science. Ozeki's work is a hybrid science fiction in its insistence that under the cultural and technological revolutions of globalization, "truth wasn't stranger than fiction; it *was* fiction." As one character, Jane, says of her mixed race identity, "I'm neither here nor there, and if that's the case so be it. Half documentarian, half fabulist…. Maybe sometimes you have to make things up, to tell truths that alter outcomes" (MYOM 360). In Ozeki's novelistic universe, we do not need to travel to fictional future-lands or unearthly worlds to encounter the strange: the aliens have already landed, in our national discourses on migration and migrant flows of plants, animals, and humans and other "invasive species" and in our own bodies through the increasing presence of biotechnologies and chemical interventions of pharmaceuticals, toxins and foreign genes.

Her debut novel, *My Year of Meats* (*MYOM*), recounts the adventures of a Japanese American documentary filmmaker, Jane Takagi-Little, who works as a self-described "cultural pimp" selling American culture to Japanese television audiences via the weekly documentary series *My American Wife*, a show sponsored by a transnational meat industry whose principal goal is to increase exports of American beef. The novel's structure chronicles the weekly television production, thus offering a tour of the naturecultural diversity of the United States as a different "American Wife," family and region are featured each week. The television explores differing constructions of national identities in America and Japan in the transnational exchanges of ideas, media, cultures and economies of global capitalism. Along the way, Jane begins to discover the toxic effects of global capitalism, specifically in the form of synthetic hormones and antibiotics used and abused in mass meat production. Jane also discovers she is a DES child, confronting first-hand the enduring legacy of chemicals in our bodies, as well as the all too common transfer of hormone treatments from animals to humans.

Ozeki's second novel, *All Over Creation* (*AOC*) is an extension of *MYOM* in its inquiry into the science and politics of food production. Set in Idaho, the rural heartland of the United States, the novel tells the story of a prodigal daughter, Yumi Fuller, who returns home twenty-five years later with three children in tow to care for her aging parents, Idaho native Lloyd Fuller and Momoko, the Japanese wife he brought back after his service in World War II. Setting Yumi's mixed-race story in this locale enables an exploration of nationalism — i.e., concepts of the native and alien — through the diversity of human cultures and nature's many species. Through this rich topography, *AOC* explores the themes of capitalism, creation, biodiversity, hybridity, and reproduction in an unfolding drama about the politics of contemporary industrialized agriculture. The novel explores discourses on invasive species, plant breeding, and genetic engineering of potato crops from multiple perspectives, including that of a group of environmental activists from San Francisco called *The Seeds of Resistance*, who crisscross the heartland to oppose industrialized agriculture — specifically corporate power, toxic pesticides and genetic engineering. Against a politically dramatized war on terror, Ozeki's *oeuvre* reminds us of all that should truly terrify us — the chilling realities of what we are drinking, eating, breathing, and touching, as well as what we fail to see and hear. As one of her characters rants against GMOs: "It's the system I'm talking about. The corporations are the pushers, the framers are the users, and the fields are our bodies, mainlining the stuff in order to wake up in the springtime and keep ticking until fall" (*AOC* 272). In their harrowing tales of mass production, Ozeki's biofiction suggests that the bloody underbelly of industrial capitalism is what we most ought to fear.

Rather than viewing circuits of capital as underwriting a utopian "postnational" future, Ozeki reveals transnational capitalism as a political economy that both transgresses and relies upon ideologies of nationalism, unambiguously placed into the mouths of her *least* admirable characters. In *MYOM* that is the sexist and violent Japanese executive, John Ueno, who sells American beef to an audience of Japanese housewives while he abuses his own wife at home. *AOC* depicts various representatives of corporate America trying to rouse nationalist passions to sell toxic wares, notably the morally bankrupt (former) statutory rapist and corporate marketing shill, Elliot, who develops a campaign against environmental activists. He writes:

> *Political Activists or Plain Old Pests?*
> Whatever you call them, their politics are familiar, anti-corporate, antigovernment, anti-globalization. And most offensive of all, anti–American. These so-called radical environmentalists represent the latest fad in the protest movement that traces its roots to the sixties. And, like their progenitors in the political proscenium, the target of their opposition is progress [165].

In contrast, the environmental activists, the farmers, and the sympathetic protagonists of Ozeki's novels all promote a cosmopolitics of people, plants, and genes in a veritable cornucopia of hybridity and cross-breeding. The novel explicitly takes on the dubious nationalism that rigidly circumscribes "natives" and "aliens" or "citizens" and "foreigners"—whether plants, animals or people— and instead opens to an ecologically responsible "cosmofeminism" (Black). Ozeki questions the limits of the identity politics and cultural nationalisms, particularly through the sensibilities of her mixed-race protagonists, adoptive families, and forms of biodiversity.

If these novels thematize hybridity in relation to the "natural" or "unnatural" reproduction of *genera*, they also reminds us in their own genre-bending or formal hybridity that culture often relies on the reproduction of recognizable *genres* for its intelligibility. In theme and form, Ozeki's biofiction stretches the boundaries of both science fiction and ethnic or postcolonial literature as conventionally understood. In so doing, she situates discourses about difference within the fullest interdisciplinary context of an ecological framework. As her protagonist in *MYOM* writes of an outdated anthropological text, "The conflict that interests me isn't *man* versus *woman*; it's *man* versus *life*. Man's

REASON, his industries and commerce, versus the entire natural world. This, to me, is the dirty secret hidden between the fraying covers" (154).

Ozeki's biofiction reveals that nationalism and capitalism work hand in hand, breeding monoculture at the expense of "life" itself. Yet her novels are also replete with the micro and macropolitics of resistance, in which an array of diverse characters in diverse settings "imagine otherwise" (Gordon 5). Ozeki explores the possibilities of the "post," not in the sense of denying or "moving beyond" legacies of colonialism, modernism and humanism, but in her recognition that a future-oriented politics depends on writing the history of the present ethically. In the next section we elaborate upon the three intellectually productive aspects of Ozeki's biofiction before mapping these onto the tripartite model delineated by J.K. Gibson-Graham in *A Postcapitalist Politics* as the prerequisites for building a new social imaginary: a diversity of language, a new politics of the subject, and the necessity of collective action.

The Generative Capacities of Biofiction

Epistemology: Ozeki's Interdisciplinarity

"Guns, race, meat and Manifest Destiny all collided in a single explosion of violent, dehumanized activity" [*MYOM* 89].

Our concept of "biofiction" arises from a commitment to cross-fertilization, bringing together the humanities and sciences in new approaches to problem solving and knowledge production. One of us (Karen) was trained in literary and ethnic American studies and the other (Banu) in evolutionary biology and women's studies. Our collaboration has revealed that disciplinary identifications and formations are not unlike logics of nationalism. Thus our work models an epistemological cosmopolitics in its healthy transgression of disciplinary boundaries, an orientation to knowing not grounded in strict identity politics. Ozeki's biofiction is the literary analogue of our academic attempts to engage interdisciplinary, intersectional, and transnational analysis.

In both novels, Ozeki fosters deliberate and productive conversations between the humanities and the sciences. For example, in *AOC*, the protagonist Yumi echoes Haraway's concept of "natureculture" when she describes her master's thesis, "Fading Blossoms, Falling Leaves: Visions of Transience and Instability in the Literature of Asian-American Diaspora," as exploring "the way images of nature are used as metaphors for cultural dissolution" (42). Likewise, one of the activists in *AOC* observes that, "Seeds tell the story of migrations and drifts, so if you learn to read them, they are very much like books — with one big difference.... Book information is relevant only to human beings. It is expendable, really.... However, the information contained in a seed is a different story, entirely vital, pertaining to life itself" (171).

In these and other narrative instances, Ozeki explodes the binaries of fact/fiction, nature/culture, native/foreign, science/humanities, theory/practice, or science/religion. Her work demonstrates how larger ideological and historical discourses around race, gender, sexuality, nationality seep into both sciences and humanities discourses. Such interdisciplinarity reveals the interdependence of the humanities and sciences, their utter foundational and epistemological connection. In a powerful example, she deploys the trope of "aliens" to show how nationalism against human immigrants permeates scientific and cultural discourses of plants and humans. In grappling with the racist politics of anti-immigrant nationalism, Ozeki weaves the lives of plants and humans into a complex tale of interdependence, as in this example of how kudzu is viewed differently in Japan and the United States:

> Suzuki put down the camera, dumbfounded. He hadn't realized that in the [American] South, kudzu was a weed — the whole time he was shooting it, he'd thought it was Vern's prized crop ... he showed Vern how to turn them into starch, then how to use the starch to thicken sauces and batters. He made a salad with the shoots and the flowers, and even a hangover medicine that resembled milk of magnesia. Vern was astounded. He'd never thought of the plant as anything but an invasive weed [*MYOM*, 75–76].

This episode suggests not only that both cultural and scientific analyses are needed to understand how kudzu came to populate the American South, but also how such relativistic and interdisciplinary understanding can help manage our ecological systems as well as put food on the table. Ozeki's biofiction, in short, illuminates the complexities of naturecultures.

Pedagogy: The Novel as Tutorial

"[Sei Shonagon] inspired me to become a documentarian, to speak men's Japanese, to be different" [*MYOM* 15].

Reading Ozeki's novels is an education in both cultural and scientific literacy. Her writing is based on extensive and sobering research: she writes for an audience that needs education, and fast! In *MYOM* we learn in detail the reality of factory farms producing beef—feedlots, hormones, antibiotics, growing conditions, processing of meat, diseases etc. In addition to the specifics of production, the narrative makes the causal connections loud and clear, as in this character's succinct summation of the issues at hand:

So what you're basically saying is that the residues in meat from hormones, steroids, pesticides, bacterial and viral contaminants, will lead to cancers, infertility, brain fevers, and a host of other illnesses, which we will not be able to cure with antibiotics because our tolerances have been jacked up by the residues also found in meat? So we are doomed to die young and not be able to reproduce ourselves in the bargain? [*MYOM*, 223].

AOC illustrates the arduous cycles of potato farming — the acreage, the pesticides, herbicides, farming practices, its impact on the farmers etc. Her novels present the urgency of popular scientific literacy, our need to understand what is being done to food, bodies, air, water, soil, and our earth. As one of her characters laments, "poison testing is being carried out at our dinner tables every day. Our government and Biotech Industry are conducting a massive experiment on unsuspecting, uninformed human subjects — You. And me. We are their Guinea Pigs!" (*AOC* 184). These are neither esoteric nor theoretical but wholly material issues as "the environment" is literally being written onto and into our bodies. Yet Ozeki empathizes with rather than condescends to her readers, particularly through the device of ambivalent or even skeptical protagonists such as Jane and Yumi, who only gradually become convinced of the significance of the crises at hand. Their reluctant but ultimately ethical self-transformation encourages us to take responsibility for our own learning and development.

Politics: Collective Engagements

"Resistance is fertile!" [*AOC*, 416].

Ozeki's novels explore not only the science, but also the politics of agribusiness. She lays out the major players: corporations (who largely come out as powerful, corrupt and mostly irredeemable), farmers (who are wrestling with the complex science and politics of agribusiness), activists (who are passionately trying to change the world — sometimes through dubious means and with mixed results), and consumers (largely ignorant and suffering the consequences).

MYOM is a scathing indictment of the meat industry's unhealthy, chemically enhanced production of beef. Resistance in this novel remains largely in the realm of individual consumers, who may reject or accept but must certainly ponder their choices: for example, the Japanese housewife who rejects the campaigns for American beef headed by her multinational company executive husband, the Japanese American protagonist rendered infertile because her mother was prescribed DES, or the little white American girl ravaged by the illegal use of DES by her farmer uncle. By juxtaposing the lives of cattle and women, e.g. describing a female character who "straddled his tenderloin and offered up her round rump for his inspection" (43), Ozeki reveals the intertwined subjugation of animals and women in global capitalism.

All Over Creation is fundamentally a novel about the power of the corporate establishment and the necessity of collective challenges to their grip on politics; it is distinctly pedagogical in this respect. Here we see political and educational campaigns unfold in many genres — plays, pamphlets, newsletters, slogans, impromptu theatre in the grocery store. For example, the *Seeds of Resistance* are a rag tag lot — infinitely creative and thoroughly passionate — who unfold zany campaigns with subversive hilarity as well as righteous commitment:

> "Instead of all the magnificent, chaotic production, picture a few thousand genetically mutated, impoverished, barren patented forms of corporately controlled germplasms.... This is how diminished, how pathetic the planet has become, that you can picture it like a cute little blue-green orb cupped in the palm of your hand. Like a logo on a fucking brand! Is this progress! I don't think so. It's bullshit, but that's all we hear — the same old stories, justifying the same old bad, exploitative, greedy fucked up behaviors. The same old excuses about why it's okay — no, it's economically beneficial — to raze the land and destroy animal habitat and exploit people and drive honking big SUVs to go shopping at the fucking mall. Nothing changes" [*AOC*, 409].

As the Seeds educate their fictional publics, Ozeki's readers may also become politically galvanized. In showing a range of audience reactions within the novel, Ozeki demonstrates the difficulties of activist intervention even as she convinces us that it is urgent and critical. Whether reluctantly, like Jane and Yumi, or avidly, like the *Seeds of Resistance*, many of Ozeki's biofictive characters grope towards a new social imaginary which, in our last section, we articulate as the domain of the "post."

The Possibilities of the "Post"

The primary purpose of our analysis thus far has been to show how Ozeki's novelistic inquiry integrates the cultural, economic, political, and scientific to offer a cosmopolitan and interdisciplinary orientation to subject formation and knowledge production. We view *biofiction* as a genre that enables us to explore new epistemologies, pedagogies and politics in order to save the biological and cultural future of the planet. To bring out this potential further, we turn now to the theoretical framework provided by economic geographers J.K. Gibson-Graham in *A Postcapitalist Politics* (2006).[1]

In *The End of Capitalism as We Knew It* (1996), Gibson-Graham argued that the hegemonic discourse of "capitalocentrism" renders capitalism hypervisible and inevitable, thus obscuring alternative cultural and economic formations (both existing and future ones). Subsequently, *A Postcapitalist Politics* delineated at the level of both theory and practice what a liberatory postcapitalist politics might entail — how new ways of speaking, being, and organizing could yield alternative futures. Gibson-Graham argued that a postcapitalist politics requires three new orientations that serve as alternatives to "capitalocentrism": 1) a politics of language that emphasizes *difference*, thus illuminating the existing heterogeneity of both capitalist and non-capitalist forms of organization; 2) a politics of the subject or of identity not as fixed modes of "being" but, rather, "a politics of *becoming*," and 3) a politics of *collective action*.

In this final section, we map Gibson-Graham's trifold paradigm of a politics of the "post" onto the three main aspects of Ozeki's biofiction discussed above: the epistemological, pedagogical, and political. First, we highlight how Ozeki's interdisciplinary engagements offer a language of diversity that validates different ways of knowing. Second, her biofiction offers a pedagogy in the politics of becoming, the transformations that occur as we let go of the rigid beliefs and subject positions that get in the way of cosmopolitics. Third, the novels emphasize collective action, including the development of the kind of creative, alternative "community economies" described by Gibson-Graham.

Beyond "A Sad and Hollow" Monoculture: Ozeki's Epistemology of Difference

"Diversity is inconvenient to mechanized farming. This is what happens when agriculture becomes agribusiness. When engineers replace poets, and corporations gain total domination over all our food and all our poems." ...Monoculture, has a sad and hollow ring to it, no?" [*AOC*].

In Ozeki's cosmology, traditional ideologies of natives, nations, national economies, competition are anti-life, anti-diversity and "sterile" at the level of social reproduction. Just as this anthology troubles the purity of discrete postcolonial and science fiction genealogies, Ozeki's hybrid nations, genres, people, plants, animals, and genomes resist the "nationalistic" logic of enclosure, border, and homogeneity. In Ozeki's hands, diversity is never reduced simply to multiculturalism or environmental biodiversity. Rather, her texts insistently connect all forms of diversity: agri/cultural, economic, and political. Ozeki's work explores the aliens of agri/culture, offering the broadest context of an exploration of "others" in our system of industrialized production under globalization or late capitalism. In exploring difference, Ozeki simultaneously demonstrates both positions — the hollowness of nationalism/sameness as well as the power of diversity/difference. She shows us how we come to valorize monoculture through a parochial insular nationalism (by both political left and the right) that relies on an unproblematic understanding of native and "other." While such discourses of purity are critical to twenty-first century nationalism, technoscience and capitalism, Ozeki presents an alternate vision, where characters celebrate the interconnected diversity of animals, plants and humans as well as hybridity.

For example, in *AOC* Ozeki develops a wonderful expose of xenophobic discourses of alien plants, animals and humans through the story of an interracial couple, Lloyd and Momoko, who sell seeds produced through Momoko's patient and loving cross-fertilization in their garden. She cultivates a variety of flowers and vegetables without regard for the national origin of her seeds. Against the backdrop of the horrific costs of monoculture potato production, the Fuller's seed catalogue provides a wonderful and engaging counterpoint, as in Lloyd's exposition here:

> And while we are on the subject of Exotics, there is an idea in circulation, that these so-called "aggressive" non-native plants are harmful, invasive, and will displace "native" species. How ironic to hear these theories propounded by people of European ancestry in America! Just consider this: Not a single one of the food crops that make the U.S an agricultural power today is native to North America. Our plants are as immigrant as we are ... I do not intend to promote Third Reich eugenics in our family garden. Finally, we believe anti-exoticism to be propaganda of the worst kind [*AOC*, 67].

Similarly, *MYOM* troubles the idea of the homogenous American family, and of who is "American." Ozeki powerfully demonstrates the construction of both nationalism and gender, in this case through corporate Japan promulgating the ideals of the perfect American and Japanese wife through the consumption of American beef. With great hilarity the novel unfolds the Japanese male executive's desire for Japanese women to see and appreciate the perfect American wife: "a kindler, gentler mate." In one executive's summary:

> *My American Wife:* Meat is the Message.... It is the meat (not the Mrs.) who's the star of our show! Of course, the "Wife of the Week" is important too. She must be attractive, appetizing, and all American. She is the Meat Made Manifest: ample, robust, yet never tough or hard to digest. Through her, Japanese housewives will feel the hearty sense of warmth, of comfort, of hearth and home — the traditional family values symbolized by red meat in rural America" [*MYOM*, 8].

In contrast, Jane's direction of the television show presents diverse representations of the All-American family: she pleads with the network executives "to continue to introduce the quirky, rich diversity and the strong sense of individualism that make the people of this country unique" (*MYOM* 64):

this includes a family in Askew, Louisiana who have adopted 12 international and multiracial kids; a mixed-race lesbian vegetarian family in Northampton, Massachusetts; a Polish middle class family in Indiana with a disabled daughter who recovers through the care and love of the whole town; and one in Colorado who own their own ranch and suffers the consequences of chemical-based agriculture. Both novels explore the politics of gender, specifically the positive and negative consequences of globalization on female reproduction and fertility.

Throughout, Ozeki interweaves discourses on biological and cultural diversity with those on economic diversity. Hers is an imagined world nourished by biodiversity amidst an apocalyptic biotechnological world doomed to sterility. In Ozeki's biofiction, difference is inclusive and breathes innovation and vision, demonstrating that cultivating genuine diversity could be a way out of our ecological, political and economic crises.

"You and Me": A Pedagogy for New Subjects

"a crack in consciousness is a dangerous thing. The slightest tremor can turn it into a gaping abyss" [*MYOM* 177].

Ozeki wields the novel as a pedagogical space for the necessary "resubjectification" that a new cosmopolitics entails. Ozeki teaches us how to let go of rigid subject positions — be they racialized, gendered or nationalist — in favor of a more humble recognition of our mutual interdependence. To this end, both her novels are narrated by protagonists who are Japanese American; their mixed race identity allows Ozeki to present an engaged cosmopolitan spirit; these women can critique and praise both countries with disarming ease, as well as note the growing transnational circulations under recent globalization.

In addition, both protagonists begin as intelligent but naïve. This is an effective pedagogical device as the narrative unfolds with the growing education of the protagonists who grow increasingly horrified by the realities of agribusiness, as does the audience's understanding of the issues involved. As Jane puts it:

> I chose to ignore what I knew. "Ignorance." In this root sense, ignorance is an act of will, a choice that one makes over and over again, especially when information overwhelms and knowledge has become synonymous with impotence. I would like to think of my ignorance less as a personal failing and more as a massive cultural trend, an example of doubling, of psychic numbing, that characterizes the end of the millennium [334].

Ozeki's pedagogical approach underscores the difficult process of change rather than any dogmatic vision of a utopian "post" world. Like Gibson-Graham, she focuses on the complex politics of becoming—attempts to free ourselves to imagine and inhabit a different world. Her work suggests that we have untapped power and imagination to work through the historical legacies of sexism, racism, colonialism, and monopoly capitalism. The joy and political subversiveness of her biofiction highlights change as occurring in surprising ways and places. She dismisses the totalitarian rhetoric of both the political and ideological right and left, while refusing the easy binaries of a utopian "post" or a pessimistic vision of a doomed present. Rather, it is in our resubjectification that our future possibilities unfold and brighten. For example, a newly emboldened Jane ultimately "defects" from the TV show to produce a documentary about the ills of the meat industry. That this decision is ultimately rewarded (through Jane's increased prominence) suggests the novel's moral commitment to a politics of becoming. However, as we describe in the next section, it also recognizes that change at the individual level is inevitably intertwined with collective transformation.

"Resistance Is Fertile": Collective Action and Community Economies

"We're hacking the landscape, dude," they told Frankie. "Bringing back the commons" [*AOC* 256].

As political histories suggest, it is difficult to sustain the heterogeneous alliances necessary for truly democratic representation. Yet, Ozeki's biofiction insists that such coalitions, however fragile, can be sustained when diverse people act collectively to confront shared problems. In both novels, Ozeki assembles an eclectic group of diverse characters to illuminate the limits of rigid identity politics. In *MYOM*, the conservative and religious Lloyd Fuller forms an alliance with progressive and mostly atheist activists to fight corporate power over genetically modified crops. Indeed, Ozeki purposefully models an adoptive rather than a biological structure of community, "queering" the notion of belonging from a model of kinship or heterosexual reproduction to one of elective affiliation (Cardozo and Subramaniam). It is upon the plurality and generative possibilities of diverse natural and cultural assemblages that Ozeki places her bet for a sustainable future. Ultimately, her biofiction suggests that a cosmopolitan future depends upon the *political* equivalents of hybridity and biodiversity.

In emphasizing the necessity of collective action, Ozeki invites us to observe the links between the biological, cultural and economic, as when she highlights the similarity in discourses of invasive species and human immigrants. Similarly, *MYOM* draws a powerful connection between the circumstances of animals and women, most powerfully in her treatment of Akiko, the abused Japanese wife of the executive who produces *My American Wife*. Ozeki juxtaposes the domestic violence of Akiko's situation with slaughterhouse violence, describing a cow who "had just watched the cow before her being killed, and the cow before that, and she was terrified" (283). As Shameem Black argues, "In its narrative construction, *My Year of Meats* [links] fertility and violence to exploit the discursive strategies that empowered transnational feminist activism in the 1990s ... it seeks to extend the conceptual tactics of activism in order to shape an even more powerful political imaginary" (227). Ultimately, Akiko goes through a political and personal transformation, leaving her husband for an unknown future that begins with traveling to meet the different "American wives" she had encountered through the television show.

Ozeki's novels present an array of actors who are engaged across the political spectrum, from the reactionary to the progressive. While, resistance in *MYOM* is at the level of the individual (in Akiko's rebellion against her husband or Jane's production of a powerful documentary), *AOC* explicitly thematizes collective action in featuring *The Seeds of Resistance*, a political grassroots group that roams the country side organizing against big agribusiness. Against this familiar model of collective activism, we want to discuss another example of self-determination in the *MYOM*'s creation of what Gibson-Graham call a community economy — one determined by the participants themselves.

In *MYOM*, Jane interviewed an "American Wife" in the economically depressed Midwestern town of Quarry whose daughter, Christina had been run over by a delivery truck turning into the local Wal-Mart. With her legs and spine crushed, Christina lay comatose, seemingly unable to respond to external stimuli. Her parents installed her in their living room, outfitting it with a hospital bed, and developed a method of treatment that involved visits from the "entire underemployed population of the town." For seven months a steady stream of visitors visited, read to her, and otherwise tried to stimulate her, until one day Christina miraculously opens her eyes and asks for lamb chops! With a settlement from Wal-Mart, the parents turn their house into a deluxe Physical Training Center: "The girl had no choice but to get better" (135). The media publicity brings visitors from afar to the town of Quarry, which had discovered a "new natural resource — compassion — and they were mining it and marketing it to America" (135–136). The town officially changed its name to Hope and opened a brand new two hundred bed long-term-care facility. This generated jobs for the town whose visitors contribute to a flourishing new economy. Christina's father was elected mayor, and her parents produced a best-selling book and videotape, *Welcome to Our Living Room:*

The Bukowsky Method of Compassion and Renewal. In establishing a collective economy of volunteer care work, the town of Quarry becomes the town of Hope through an "economy of compassion." Ultimately, this creative model becomes an alternative form of entrepreneurial capitalism, underscoring Ozeki's theme that hope can come in unusual packages and change can occur in unlikely places if we are open to "becoming," to the organic possibilities that life throws at us. The transformation from Quarry to Hope beautifully integrates and exemplifies Gibson-Graham's model of a postcapitalist politics, with its language of diversity, process of becoming, and politics of collective action.

Conclusion

Ozeki's biofiction continually reminds us that "resistance is fertile," affirming the importance of heterogeneous, inventive, and pragmatic alliances. Unlike nationalistic discourses, the emphasis here is not on shoring up the boundary between natural and unnatural forms of reproduction or hybridity, or between correct and incorrect identities or politics, but rather in asking which forms of engagement are truly "productive" (Cardozo and Subramaniam). Ultimately, Ozeki's biofictive universe reveals that we can only glimpse the possibilities of the "post" by grappling with the science fictions of the present. The epistemological, pedagogical, and political imperatives of Ozeki's biofiction invite us to engage with the big picture and to accept responsibility as historical and moral agents in the here and now.

Notes

1. J.K. Gibson-Graham is the pen name of Julie Graham and Katherine Gibson. The form of their cross-continental collaboration, as well as their explicit delineation of the kind of "thinking techniques" that serve a politics of possibility, offer an inspiring model of intellectual production.

Works Cited

Black, Shameem. "Fertile Cosmofeminism: Ruth L. Ozeki and Transnational Reproduction." *Meridians: Feminism, Race, Transnationalism* 5.1 (2004): 226–256.
Cardozo, Karen, and Banu Subramaniam. "Genes, Genera, Genre: The Naturecultures of Biofiction in Ruth Ozeki's *All Over Creation*." In *Tactical Biopolitics: Art, Activism, and Technoscience*, edited by Beatriz da Costa and Kavita Philip, 269–287. Cambridge, MA: MIT Press, 2008.

Derrida, Jacques. "Structure, Sign, and Play in the Discourse of the Human Sciences." In *Writing and Difference*, trans. Alan Bass. London: Routledge, 1978. 278–294.
Gordon, Avery. *Ghostly Matters: Haunting and the Sociological Imagination*. Minneapolis: University of Minnesota Press, 1997.
Ozeki, Ruth. *All Over Creation*. New York: Penguin, 2003.
_____. *My Year of Meats*. New York: Penguin, 1998.
Subramaniam, Banu. "The Aliens Have Landed: Reflections on the Rhetoric of Biological Invasions." In *Making Threats: Biofears and Environmental Anxieties*, Betsy Hartmann, et al., eds. Rowman and Littlefield, 2005.
Sze, Julie. "Boundaries and Border Wars: DES, Technology and Environmental Justice." In Rewiring the 'Nation': The Place of Technology in American Studies: Special Issue on Technology and American Studies in *American Quarterly*, 58:3 (2006): 791–814.

3

Forms of Compromise
The Interaction of Humanity, Technology and Landscape in Ken MacLeod's Night Sessions

ADAM FRISCH

Near the beginning of Ken MacLeod's novel *Night Sessions*, creationist engineer turned preacher John Richard Campbell is arguing with religious fundamentalist leader John Livingston:

> "But surely," protests J.R. Campbell, "surely in all the world there are qualified ministers whose sermons you can listen to?"
> "The Churches here have all compromised!" responds Livingston. "Here, and everywhere! ... Compromises, compromises, compromises!" [20].

MacLeod's *Night Sessions*, awarded best 2008 SF novel by the British Science Fiction Association, depicts a mid-to-late twenty-first century world filled with "compromises" of all sorts, from religious to political to technological. Detective Investigator Adam Ferguson of Edinburgh, the novel's protagonist, has helped create and now polices a "secularist" society where organized religions are officially ignored, and unofficially ridiculed by the majority of Scotland's populace. Following an early twenty-first century "Faith War" between a U.S./Western European alliance and the Islamic countries of the Middle East, finally won by the West at the battle of "Armageddon" that featured live media coverage of the exchange of tactical nuclear weapons, Scotland has passed through a Sozi government (a Socialist-Nationalist-Green coalition) to its current Secularist society. The Scots work hard to feed, house and protect themselves from the economic fallout that followed the Faith Wars, as well as from the environmental consequences of a world fighting off the effects of increased global warming. Ferguson's own struggles begin when he arrives at a flat where an underground Catholic priest has apparently been killed by a mail bomb. Other "assassinations" follow, and the more Ferguson learns about these apparently religious hate crimes, the deeper and wider their implications become. Meanwhile, halfway around the world in New Zealand, engineer John Campbell helps run a creationist park supported largely by the American fundamentalists who originally instigated the Faith Wars, a park where parents and children can watch Adam and Eve animatrons walk next to dinosaurs, and where Campbell himself offers weekly sermons on biblical inerrancy to refugee androids. MacLeod's *Night Sessions* switches between Ferguson's and Campbell's worlds to unfold a top-notch mystery amidst a fascinating near-future landscape.

One of the most intriguing aspects in *Night Sessions* involves the relationships that exist between humans and their robotic assistants in various forms. Robotic Artificial Intelligence had originally been created as advanced "combat mech" to aid Western soldiers during the Faith Wars, but many of these AIs became self-aware, particularly those forced to cope with complex battlefield logistics amidst intense nuclear radiation. Following the Faith Wars, "robots that could almost, but not quite, pass as human aroused a deep unease. There was an old name for this phenomenon: the uncanny valley. Humanoid robots found themselves, unhappily, at its floor" (64). Only several hundred androids remain, many of whom have sought refuge with their own kind in Campbell's New Zealand creationist park. A number of others have had their AI "chips" transferred into more mechanistic forms, such as the "lekis" (law enforcement kinetic intelligences) who are "partnered" with the Edinburgh detectives. These AIs are not shaped in human form but rather "like a two-metre-tall scale model of a Martian fighting machine from *War of the Worlds*" in order to frighten civilians into compliance (35). And throughout much of the world, as well as on Earth's two space elevators and in near–Earth orbit, vast numbers of non-humanoid "autonomous machines, some of them self-aware," labor alongside a minority of human workers. Adam Ferguson and most of his contemporaries dismiss all of these as "seriously screwed-up tin men" (213).

In this SF mystery novel, Ferguson's dismissive attitude towards robots turns out to be his, and his society's, "blind eye" which — while allowing them to use AIs as problem-solving tools — also blinds them from discovering until too late wider truths about a much more significant impending revolution being implemented by another group of AI's. Unwittingly laying the groundwork for that revolution, creationist engineer John Campbell attempts to Christianize his New Zealand robotic congregation. His efforts succeed, but in a way far beyond what Campbell and his fellow fundamentalists could have envisioned or would have wished.

Dismissive attitudes towards "mechanicals," as Leela Gandhi has pointed out in her work on *Postcolonial Theory*, have in fact often been an historical tactic used to create "categories of people (i.e., servants and mechanics) who might not be considered adequately or representatively human" (47). In many ways Adam Ferguson treats his leki partner, Skulk (short for Skullcrusher), in the same dismissive manner that a nineteenth-century British nabob would have treated an Indian or Nigerian servant. Indeed, the reader's initial encounter with Ferguson occurs as the detective arrives with Skulk at the site of the Catholic priest's assassination: "After a step or two" Ferguson, who had been carrying Skulk, "remembered the weight on his back. 'Walk yourself,' he said" (35). As a number of postcolonial critics have noted, "The message sent to these 'Others' by the dominant culture has been clear and consistent — conform and be quiet; deny yourself, and all will be well" (Ashcroft 234). During the preliminary investigations Skulk continually addresses Ferguson as "boss," but while occasionally heeded, Skulk is just as often ordered to "shut — the fuck — up " (39). Most of Ferguson's compatriots respond to Skulk and the other lekis in a similar fashion, a combination of distaste mixed with just a bit of fear. For example, to begin his investigation of the Catholic priest's murder, Adam Ferguson arrives with Skulk to interview Grace Mazvabo, a professor of religion. The professor's first words are: "'Does that thing need....' Her voice trailed off ... 'It makes me uncomfortable.'" Ferguson replies: "You needn't talk about the leki as if *it* [my emphasis] isn't there." (91). Ferguson's unconscious use of the pronoun "it" does as much to undercut respect for Skulk as his professional rejoinder does to promote it. Similar depersonalizations mark most people's attitudes; for example, to local Roman Catholic bishop Dr. Hugh Culey, Skulk is merely "a walking lie detector" (99). So although it is Skulk who first correctly intuits that the unknown murder subject must be either a human *mutilado* or a robot, even his own partner continues to dismiss Skulk's and all AIs' competence and trustworthiness:

> "It [Skulk's AI chip transfer into a leki form] still rankled, as it did with all his kind. Tough shit, was Ferguson's basic attitude to this — he sympathized with the lekis' sense of having been degraded, disabled, castrated almost; but there was no way, *no fucking way*, any KI running the strange loop of self-awareness could be trusted with control of a combat mech" [110].

Except for the SF novum and the presence of the "f" word, Ferguson's tirade might have been written by many nineteenth-century British administrators serving in Africa or the Far East.

For their part, the lekis and other self-aware robots respond with tactics and strategies similar to those evolved by the historically subjugated, the powerless, especially in the ways they use language to maintain some degree of integrity and self-respect. For example, Edinburgh lekis distinguish between the "nicknames" given to them by their police masters and their "real" or "taken names" (41). Failure to recognize the importance of such naming, in fact, is the main reason it takes the police so long to recognize that the "human" Graham Orr and the robot "Hardcastle" are the same "person."

Among themselves the self-aware AIs often communicate through a secret language which their masters can detect but not understand, like the colonized speaking their own code. "In many instances, the resulting Creole served as a secret language shared among the slaves, incomprehensible to the owners who spoke Portuguese" ("Languages"). For example, in the situation room Ferguson "could detect the continuous infrared flicker of robot repartee crisscrossing the room, [but] the effect was somehow disquieting, and for no gain, so he blinked the normal colors back" (44). And like one of those Portuguese slaves, Skulk, as he heads toward a crime scene, "exchanged infrared pings with a road sweeper that labored along the gutter, its non-reflective thoughts bare as machine code" (76).

In addition to employing hidden naming and in-group-only communication, all self-aware robots seem to have become experts at counter-discourse, especially the use of ironic counterstatement to put the "master" on the defensive while simultaneously deflecting criticism. Simply to reject or contest the language of the subordinators represents "an incomplete or failed radicalism which needs to acquire the more subtle political habits of 'appropriation' or 'subversion-from-within'" (Gandhi 147). Homi Bhabha refers to this tactic as "colonial mimicry," which he defines as "the desire for a reformed, recognizable Other, *as a subject of a difference that is almost the same, but not quite*" (86). For example, when Ferguson attempts to dismiss the importance of Skulk's reasoning about the identity of their suspect with:

> "I suspect the expression 'No shit, Sherlock' was coined with lekis in mind."
> "It was not," said Skulk. "The earliest examples of the usage pre-date—"
> "I was joking," Ferguson interrupted.
> "So was I," said Skulk [97].

As Gayatri Spivak has pointed out, "Subordinate people ... are not without a sense of irony, [but] it is never perceived as a joke unless [they] tell them" (61). Thus, when Adam Ferguson muses after the initial murder that "relations with church officials could be a bit of a mine-field," Skulk immediately replies: "It is not at all like a minefield." Instead of using Skulk's quick counter, with its underlying humor, to begin a dialogue, "Ferguson heard the remark as a reproach" (42–43).

Similar "mimicry" tactics are employed by the various self-aware robots that inhabit John Richard Campbell's Waimangu creationist park. One of the park's main attractions is Piltdown Man, a self-aware robot whom Campbell is asked to repair early in MacLeod's novel. J.R. Campbell, as oblivious to the implications of his religious commitments as was his real-life analog, John W. Campbell, inquires if Piltdown Man simply has a back problem, The AI replies"

> "Yes ... Stripped a gear in my lumbar hinge. Fucking baraminologists."
> "Language," chided Campbell, not looking up.
> "From the Hebrew," explained the robot head, *willfully misunderstanding* [my emphasis] [55].

It turns out that Piltdown Man now has to shamble about on all fours, because "some little dipshit," as the robot puts it, has decided an upright stance is anthropologically unwarranted. "Oh well," exclaims Piltdown when Campbell's repairs are finished, "back into character. Ook ook" (55–56). The colonial mimicry is, of course, completely lost on the fundamentalist scientist.

Any colonizer/colonized relationship will inevitably lead to fundamental cultural exchanges, subsequent changes and eventual redefinitions. As Benjamin Graves notes in his study "Homi K. Bhabha: The Liminal Negotiation of Cultural Difference":

> Cultural identities cannot be ascribed to pre-given, irreducible, scripted, ahistorical cultural traits that define the conventions of ethnicity. Nor can "colonizer" and "colonized" be viewed as separate entities that define themselves independently. Instead ... the negotiation of cultural identity involves the continual interface and exchange of cultural performances that in turn produce a mutual and mutable recognition (or representation) of cultural difference.

In Ken MacLeod's near-future world, where the phrase "Have you been saved?" can refer to everything from a personal religious conversion to a robot's making a backup copy of its own identity, humanity — and MacLeod's readers — discover crucial features of what it means to be human by his characters' fictional interactions with their controlled artificial intelligences, Adam Ferguson's "seriously screwed-up mechanical tin men" (213). The dynamic encounters between humanity and its AI technology become a fluid "bridge" where both master and servant can mix together to form new, more global identities. As the German philosopher Martin Heidegger has noted: "Always and ever differently the bridge escorts the lingering and hastening ways of men to and fro.... The bridge *gathers* as a passage that crosses" (99).

The redefinitions of what it means to be a human intelligence and what it means to be a machine intelligence are embodied in the "performances" of the novel's two main characters, the protagonist Adam Ferguson and the antagonist Graham Orr / Hardcastle. Throughout the novel Adam Ferguson is continually haunted by his previous vicious responses to Christian protesters during the Great Rejection that served to create Scotland's current secularist government. As Ferguson shares a drink with his wife Isla, he remembers:

> never religious himself, there had been nothing personal about it: just a cold, hard determination that the reforms would be enforced.... As a young PC Ferguson had been right there swinging. He'd battered through congregations to drag seditious priests and mullahs from their very pulpits. He'd slung screaming schoolchildren in the back of police vans, then turned and batoned down their parents and slung them in too. In the two worst years of the civil disorder he'd shot, up close, three men and one woman, and he'd taken part in more beatings than he liked to recall.... He never remembered it without shame [80–81].

Ferguson gradually learns, as he tracks down the perpetrator of the bombings, that actions based only on ideology, without any consideration for compassion, invariably lead to gross atrocities such as Hardcastle's murder of twenty-seven children, twelve adults, and a hundred or more other innocent victims in the hospital, all in order to "deliver a judgment on the Lord's enemies" (299). Thus, near the end of the novel, when Ferguson feels the impulse to "draw the pistol again and smash it across [a] man's face," he resists the urge and instead "clenched his hands at his sides" (316). Ferguson has changed, to the point where in his final scene he can overcome his instinctual reluctance and "let his hand be grasped by a larger one, with rough skin and clawlike nails" (319). The larger hand belongs to a lycanthrope known as "The Lieutenant," who learned about the futility of national ideologies during the Faith Wars. As he tells Ferguson: "There are no lies. The people who sent me to the Middle East told us we would destroy an evil empire. They didn't lie either" (319). The irony, of course, is that the Faith Wars have led to the destruction of all the Earth's empires, East and West, evil or not.

The robot Hardcastle, the master deceptionist in MacLeod's novel who disguises himself as a human *mutilado* and uses an ancient hand-operating printing press to avoid detection, similarly learns a lot during the novel about who he (and robots) are and who he (and they) are not. Hardcastle ultimately discovers two features about AI identity that he had never previously considered, that robots can exhibit selfless behavior, and that a robot can tell another robot a convincing lie for reasons based upon compassion rather than ideology. He is tricked by Skulk2, a copy of Ferguson's AI partner who has had his self-destruction prevention mechanism disabled, into revealing the plans of the robot insurrection. Skulk2 then hurtles himself and Hardcastle into the Earth's atmosphere in an uncontrolled descent, not the controlled re-entry Skulk2 had promised, and like the mythic Lucifer both AIs burn up "like a meteor

"... with an orange light" (300). Skulk2's last words to Hardcastle are simply: "I lied."

As individuals in colonial relationships discover bridges, so do entire cultures. Biologists refer to the boundary areas where two different ecological zones meet as "ecotones" (*Mirriam-Webster*). Ecotones are especially revealing because they display both clear definitions of diversity as well as occasional examples of new syntheses being created between formally distinct species. "Cultures," notes Homi Bhabha, "recognize themselves through their projections of 'otherness'" (12). Perhaps what J. R. Campbell's fundamentalist friends, the believers of the Third Covenant, depict as "sinful compromise with heathen darkness" (61), MacLeod's readers may find as areas of social reinterpretation and discovery. MacLeod himself, as Andrew M. Butler points out in his introduction to *The True Knowledge of Ken MacLeod*, "is a libertarian, is a Trot, is both at once — and sometimes neither" (ix). Bhabha points out the developmental value of colonial bridges for whole societies: "The borderline engagements of cultural difference may as often be consensual as conflictual; they may confound our definitions of tradition and modernity; realign the customary boundaries between the private and the public, high and low; and challenge normative expectations of development and progress" (2).

The very landscape of *Night Sessions* constitutes a giant ecotone, an "interstices [of] overlap and displacement of domains of difference" (Bhabha 2), where humanity and technology continually interact in a direction towards a post-modern, post-national society. What are the features of this *Night Sessions* landscape that characterize, connect and bridge the human and technological worlds? What does this novel suggest about the world we and our technology are now in the process of becoming?

To begin with, MacLeod's characters are joined together through technology. Everyone has immediate access to interactive internet visuals and voice via personal contact lenses and implanted ear-phones. In Edinburgh's night clubs, youth dressed in the latest "Gothic Lolita" style dance within a virtual mosque to "silent music" heard only by themselves, against a background of contemporary deep space photos intermixed with twentieth-century rock band holograms (66–67). The Edinburgh police investigate crimes in consensual conference rooms, using perspective tools ranging from tiny midges that search for trace explosives in small spaces to Ogle Earth's vast zooms, used to focus in on individual space-elevator workers. Police recordings are continually cross-checked by a giant computer, PNAI, which also suggests new investigative leads.

Yet the human/tech mix remains ragged. PNAI is nicknamed "Paranoia," because it must constantly be recalibrated to reduce its myriad number of "most important" hits. Also, carbon copies of all police records are kept meticulously on paper: "The rationale for this was [that] it was hard to hack and harder still to crash" (43–44). MacLeod's future Scotland is a nation of "capitalism with Russian characteristics," translation: greed combined "with tyre irons" (51). Gazprom goons provide both seed money and security for everything from the transient container housing for the homeless on Edinburgh's Leith Docks to the Atlantic and Pacific space elevators. It is a world of theme parks based on "intelligent design," created by engineers whose "job *is* intelligent design" (206), several of whom regularly attend an Anglican church filled with Maori carvings, including Christ as a warrior in a Maori cloak" (60–61). It is a world where, because global warming has already inundated Earth's low-lying areas, agriculture has shifted into high-rises, hydroponic farms like the Honeywell tower at Turnhouse, "twenty levels of solar-power-lit hydroponic greenery" (247). In sum, it is a world of "compromise, compromise, compromise," a world of human/tech blend that has sought to counter global warming by deploying into orbit gigantic space umbrellas, called *soletas*, to shade the rapidly parching Earth, a "compromise" that Adam Ferguson labels "a typical hubristic technical fix [by] the industries that burned more carbon than they turned into bucky-tech" (148). It is a mix of the new and the old, a blend of the pre– and the post–, a meeting ground for conquerors and subject intellects where each side can measure itself against the "alien" which it is not. It is a world in evolutionary mix, which, like the *soletas*, comprises at best a temporary solution. MacLeod's novel ends with the soletas' destruction and the Earth's temperature once again on the rise, but also with the elimination of the AI threats to both Ferguson and Campbell, and with hints of post-national social growth.

Two of *Night Session's* secondary characters demonstrate the polarities of possible human response that can emerge from MacLeod's ecotones. At one extreme is Skulk's former army partner, the Lieutenant. A tank commander severely traumatized by his experiences at the decisive Faith War battle known as Armageddon, the Lieutenant has chosen to withdraw from normal human interaction. Refusing all psychiatric treatment, he has instead employed gene-modification techniques to turn himself into a werewolf with "clawlike nails ... a prognathous snout and teeth like a dog's" (319). In this lycanthropic form the Lieutenant haunts Edinburgh's Greyfriars cemetery late at night. He appears only twice during the novel. At Skulk's request he frightens two neo-Gnostic "terrorists" at the local cemetery. Later at the novel's climax he appears in midtown to remind Adam Ferguson that: "There are no lies in religion. There are apparent facts that are illusions" (319). The Lieutenant's response to his changing world has been to flee it altogether, leaving him with a life at the boundaries only.

At the other extreme of the techno fix is the local "loli" journalist and secret policeman, Mikhail Aliyev, "all peaches and cream in a tiered knee-length white dress" (70). Aliyev, "a guy trapped in a woman's body" (73), has embraced "gender modification" techniques (140) to become comfortable with everything from shopping for an evening outfit with Dave Warsaw's girlfriend, Jessica, to engaging in sex with Jessica and Dave simultaneously. When Dave wakes up shocked following his tri-encounter: "Aliyev reached across the table and laid his hand on Dave's. 'It's all right,' he said. 'I understand. Many people find themselves feeling a little abashed after their first time with a secret policeman'" (142). Eventually Aliyev uses his ability to mingle with everyone to help Adam Ferguson identify and track down the robot Hardcastle. Significantly, it is another transgendered character, Arlene, who at novel's end helps Ferguson's counterpart, J.R. Campbell, to begin to mitigate his fundamentalist homophobic ethic.

But then MacLeod's novel is "merely" science fiction, which, as many critics whose chosen home is the Master Canon continually assure us, is about as relevant to the "real world" as are the posters of engineers like *Night Session's* Harold Ford: "depicting landscapes, ecologies and deep-sky images that might or might not have been imaginary" (248). Ken MacLeod would counter with the observation that:

> what distinguishes sf from previous ways of thinking about the future is precisely what distinguishes Marxism from other forms of socialism — it investigates the possibilities of the future by looking at the tendencies of the present [Butler 117].

In a similar manner, Homi Bhabha writes in *Locations of Culture*:

> Being in the "beyond," then, is to inhabit an intervening space, as any dictionary will tell you. But to dwell "in the beyond" is also, as I have shown, to be part of a revisionary time, a return to the present to redescribe our cultural contemporaneity; to reinscribe our human, historic commonality; *to touch the future on its hither side* [7].

"Imperialism and colonialism," as Edward Said has pointed out "are supported and perhaps even impelled by impressive ideological formations which include notions that certain territories and people *require* and beseech domination" (8). If the title of MacLeod's novel refers literally to the weekly "night sessions" of preaching that J. R. Campbell provides for both his Waimangu congregation of robots and Edinburgh's Third Covenant, it also refers to the "groping in the dark" that characterizes both Adam Ferguson's own nightmares, dating from his semi–Gestapo days as a boot man, and all of our own nightmares about how current technology seems to be dehumanizing us, its creators, and destroying the Earth. Inventions that ought to be "our servants" seem to be controlling us, driving us like Victor Frankenstein into the coldest of realms, far away from the safe and comfortable homes we thought we were building for ourselves. We have become J. R. Campbell's Piltdown Man, broken "in the house of Rimmon," with our heads stored in one place and our bodies apparently living in another.

But as Farah Mendlesohn has noted in her essay "Impermanent Revolution," "In MacLeod's novels technological change drives widespread social dislocation and intellectual reconfiguration: it creates cognitive dissonance out of which new possibilities emerge" (Butler 17). When J. R. finally finishes his repair and reintegrates Piltdown Man, MacLeod notes that "hair hid the join" (56). And as Homi Bhabha has noted for all of us who, like the Lieutenant, feel so disjointed by technological change that we want to flee the world altogether: "To live in the unhomely world, to find its ambivalences and ambiguities enacted in the house of fiction, or its sundering and splitting performed in the work of art, is also to affirm a profound desire for social solidarity: 'I am looking for the join ... I want to join ... I want to join'" (18). Perhaps MacLeod's novel begins to show our emerging post-national world ecotones where that join can lie, the only way for us to find our way home.

Works Cited

Ashcroft, Bill, Gareth Griffiths, and Helen Tiffin. "Cultural Studies: Postcolonialism, African-American Criticism, and Queer Theory." In *Literary Criticism: An Introduction to Theory and Practice*, edited by Charles E. Bressler, 4th ed. Upper Saddle River, NJ: Pearson/Prentice Hall, 2007.
Bhabha, Homi K. *Locations of Culture*. New York: Routledge, 1994.
Butler, Andrew M., and Farah Mendlesohn, eds. *The True Knowledge of Ken MacLeod*. Reading, UK: Science Fiction Foundation, 2003.
"ecotone." *Merriam-Webster Online Dictionary*, 2009. http://www.merriam-webster.com/dictionary/ecotone, 12 July 2009.
Gandhi, Leela. *Postcolonial Theory: A Critical Introduction*. New York: Columbia University Press, 1998.
Graves, Benjamin. "Homi K. Bhabha: The Liminal Negotiation of Cultural Difference." Political Discourse — Theories of Colonialism and Postcolonialism, *http://www.postcolonialweb.org/poldiscourse/bhabha/bhabha2.html*, 14 July 2009.
Heidegger, Martin. "Building, Dwelling, Thinking." In *Rethinking Architecture: A Reader in Cultural Theory*, edited by Neil Leach. New York: Routledge, 1997.
"Languages Spoken in Bonaire." Netherlands Antilles, 2003–2005. Bonaire.info, *http://www.bonaire.info/language/*, 14 July, 2009.
MacLeod, Ken. *Night Sessions*. London: Orbit, 2008.
Said, Edward W. *Culture and Imperialism*. New York: Knopf, 1993.
Spivak, Gayatri Chakravorty. *The Post-Colonial Critic*, ed. Sarah Harasym. New York: Routledge, 1990.

4

The Language of Postnationality
Cultural Identity via Science Fictional Trajectories

CHRIS PAK

Postcoloniality and the Language of SF

Postcolonial theory is a process of struggle against historic representation. It has

> begun to deal with the problems of transmuting time into space, with the present struggling out of the past [...] like much recent post-colonial literature, it attempts to construct a future [Ashcroft 35].

It is concerned with the problem of constructing identities in which cultural factors that are perceived in terms of a monolithic temporal linearity can be transformed into a space of plurality. History is often understood as a linear progression from a pre-technological state to one in which particular conceptions of both science and technology occupy the logical end point of a nation's development. This monolithic outlook indulges in imagining an interpretation of the future in which all nations are homogeneous. By transmuting this temporality into an understanding of history (in epistemological terms) as spaces populated by a multiplicity of perspectives, postcolonial literature and theory contribute to construct SF futures that can accommodate a plural, postnational conception of identity wherein alternatives to a nationalism that exclude minority voices can be imagined.

Michelle Reid connects postcolonialism and SF when she asserts that

> we need to examine what makes science fiction so strongly identified as a literature of empire and expansion, and how this might be resisted and subverted from within the genre itself [1].

The discourse of travel narratives, colonialism and fantasy, which was projected beyond the sphere of the familiar, provided conceptual spaces from which SF began to articulate itself. Edward Said notes another connection between SF and empire when he comments on Jules Verne's novels: by advocating the "scientific mind at a very high peak of ratiocination," Said claims that Verne's narratives among others were "channeled into support for colonial acquisition" (218). Reid identifies three strategies that postcolonial literature employs to examine and counter this dynamic (appropriation, writing back to the imperial centre, mimicry), along with three specifically SF ones that offer starting points to consider the unique contribution SF makes to postcolonial debates (the colonization of other worlds, the alien as Other and the imagining of postcolonial futures). These latter icons of SF offer writers a way to interrogate postcoloniality and move beyond this state toward a postnational awareness by mapping the structures underlying representations of the Other.

Damien Broderick carefully notes that the "iconic weight" of such tropes can be restructured by the discourse, or megatext, of SF:

> A vast range of connotations hang in generic phase space above or behind its manifestation in a given text, drawn together by association and practice into certain most-probable-use vectors, but the image or concept of the sf emblem remains parsable as a new noun or verb, a signifier which posts notice to us of an "absent signified," an empirically empty but imaginatively laden paradigm [61].

The "sf emblem" is therefore open to strategies of mimicry and appropriation that offer spaces for exploring postnational identities. By reconfiguring these coded icons via these strategies, statements are made that resonate with the connotations that can be derived from what Broderick calls "most-probable-use vectors": the thematic and linguistic expectations readers develop toward SF texts (the megatext). This paradigm is "empirically empty" as the referents are displaced to some future signaled by a specific subjunctivity that codes them as "blanketly defined by: *have not happened*." Subjunctivity is a way of reading SF which takes into account its temporal relationship to the reader's world. Such icons are also "imaginatively laden" because the indeterminateness of this future referentiality holds possibilities of actualization together in an imaginative space (Delany, *Jewel* 44). While the sentence itself indicates one possibility, the possible statement that it makes offer, for the initiated reader, a critical, polyphonic space in which particular formulations of SF emblems within and between texts can be used to explore postnationality.

Bhabha's notion of hybridity is centrally important to this understanding of SF and its potential as a genre to offer readers and writers spaces whereby we can attempt this struggle from out of the past, engage with our present and imagine postnational futures. The intersections of multiple discourses and the subjunctivity of SF allow us

> to dwell "in the beyond" [...] to be part of a revisionary time, a return to our present to redescribe our cultural contemporaneity; to reinscribe our human, historic commonality; *to touch the future* on its *hither side* [Bhabha 10].

SF is productive of spaces between discourse; combined with the exploration of interpenetrating cultural discourse SF becomes an ideal vehicle for examining our contemporary hybrid world. It allows us to re-imagine and reclaim the past but also to imagine possible futures where the potential to work towards constructing futurity becomes essential to a contemporary postnational identity. As Bhabha implies, the way in which these texts experiment with the megatext illustrate how appropriation of SF's language allow a re-examination of hybridity:

> The social articulation of difference, from the minority perspective, is a complex, ongoing negotiation that seeks to authorize cultural hybridities that emerge in moments of historical transformation [3].

I examine the SF icon of the colonization of other worlds in *Nova* and the imagining of postcolonial (and postnational) futures in "Delhi," and consider how these texts construct hybrid spaces that foster the exploration of issues of cultural identity from minority perspectives.

Postnationality from the SF Perspective

Delany's *Nova* explores the contours of far future galactic powers through the colonization of other worlds, considering questions of culture and the possibility of maintaining tradition in a civilization of societies fragmented by the spaces and economic tensions between planets. Jeanne Murray Walker identifies the text's appropriation of the grail-quest form, contending that "*Nova* articulates the need for and the difficulty of exchange between individuals and among groups" (221). Her observation that, "In the book's metaphor of the quest, illyrion [...] is the grail. It is the image and potential of the re-united land" is suggestive for examination of postnational identities. This borrowing allows Delany to comment on the possibility of a rapprochment between societies and of the individual's ability to construct their postnational future.

Nova employs the trope of the spaceship and crew to model the relationships between individuals of diverse cultural identities. The text's most salient linguistic feature is its experimentation with syntactic patterning, playing as it does with language to convey a sense of plurality, from the diversity of accents and therefore cultural backgrounds that it signifies, and futurity, from the changes time makes upon language. Several characters' reflection on such variations of language show a privileging of both adaptability and plurality. Lorq's crew respect his facility with dialects from different cultural and socio-economic groups, an ability that has allowed him to develop beneficial relationships that aid him on his quest.

In a revealing past episode Lorq (as a child) recognizes the boundaries between people signaled by dialect:

> "What language is he talking?" Prince demanded.
> Ruby giggled. "You understand *that*?"
> Another realization hit Lorq; he and his parents spoke to the people of Sao Orini with a completely different set of words than they spoke to each other and their guests. He had learned the slurred dialect of Portuguese under the blinking lights of a hypno-teacher sometime in the fog of early childhood [Delany, *Nova* 51].

Prince and Ruby's exclusion prompt different reactions: an urge to know founded upon the desire for control ("demanded") and disdainful humor, implied by the italicized deixis "that," which works to marginalize the language and by extension the group using it. Because Lorq learned this dialect through a "hypno-teacher" questions are raised regarding the implications this has for the formation of experiential relationships to the cultural group using that language. Mouse's language proficiency contrasts with this, who "at ten [...] spoke some half dozen of the languages bordering the Mediterranean much more facilely than people like Leo who had learned his tongues under a hypno-teacher" (13). Nevertheless, Lorq's free use of appropriate dialects throughout the text makes a statement that supports interaction and a blurring of cultural and socio-economic boundaries.

Mouse, a gypsy who grew up at the periphery of the technological societies of the far future Earth, is an appropriate symbol for the marginalized. His experiences resonate with the history of persecution and diaspora experienced by diverse minority groups and provide a historical background referenced by the symbolic aspects of the novum. Katin locates the focus for the earthbound gypsies's persecution as their rejection of plugs, sockets that allow an individual to connect themselves to and manipulate a range of technologies. Mouse explains that "We never had them. We never wanted them" and yet has them installed after separation from his group: "I took them because I was by myself, and — well, I guess it was easier" (Delany, *Nova* 120). Accepting plugs makes Mouse part of the industrial workforce to which the majority of the interplanetary population belong. The text shores up support for the relevance of cultural background to futurity by exploring the confluence of SF's subjunctivity on Mouse's ethnicity and by drawing parallels between historical diaspora and the interplanetary diaspora entailed by the colonization of space. It references a history of racism while refiguring these terms to address a future where the major difference between periphery and centre are technologies that signify a blurring of boundaries between the biological and the technological.

Humans have become cyborgs in response to the possibilities and demands placed upon an interplanetary industry made possible by illyrion. Lusuna, a student at a dinner party Lorq eavesdrops on, laments the dispersal of peoples throughout space and the erosion of a tradition based upon a coherent centre:

> There's no reservoir of national, or world solidarity, even on Earth, the center of Draco. The past half dozen generations have seen such movement of peoples from world to world, there can't be any. This pseudo-interplanetary society that has replaced any real tradition, while very attractive, is totally hollow and masks an incredible tangle of decadence, scheming, corruption —[Delany, *Nova* 48].

This view represents tradition as cohering in a centre metaphorized as a reservoir of solid substance possessing depth. It implies that any legitimate cultural identity must be based upon traditions that are structurally univocal and static. This contrasts with Katin's interpretation, for which he takes Mouse as a symbol for the continuity of tradition and the subject for his ongoing book. *Nova*'s opening chapter establishes a frame from which the text's present is contrasted with episodes of Mouse's past. The narrative relates his history as beginning with his acquiring a syrynx, a multi-sensory instrument and another boundary transgressing technology, and progresses through several objects that act as symbolic "landmarks": "he had his certificate as a cyborg stud for any inter- and intra-system ship. He still had his gold earring, his little fingernail, his puzzle ring — and the syrynx" (17). Each item functions as a sign of different cultural spheres of experience and are metonymies for a range of perspectives toward the multiple worlds that make up this "pseudo-interplanetary society," a gesture towards a postnationality made possible by the threat of a homogenizing industry that references aspects of contemporary globalization.

Mouse's experiences contribute to construct a coherent textual character whose identity is syncretic. As Katin explains

> You've collected the ornamentations a dozen societies have left us over the ages and made them inchoately yours. You're the product of those tensions that clashed in the time of Clark and you resolve them on your syrynx with patterns eminently of the present —[Delany, *Nova* 206].

It is this observation that allows Katin to refute the common stance toward tradition and assert that "There are cultural traditions that have matured over the centuries, yet culminate now in something vital and solely of today" (206). He sees tradition not as a metaphorical reservoir functioning as a repository of forms and content to be adhered to but as something that accumulates depth and texture dialectically. The individual is the site of this syncretism; in this world, cultural identity is established through competing discourses that allow individuals to retain continuity with the past while offering spaces to create new identities. Mouse can no longer deny the impact of his history and is "forced to accept that what had happened in his past affected present action." Katin connects this process of establishing an identity to Mouse's artistic creativity with the materials of his past. Mouse, on the other hand, also supplements his engagement with "long, private sessions of self-definition" (136). Through both methods Mouse is able to assuage the fear that his experiences as a marginalized subject have led him to expect.

Katin contrasts Mouse's creativity, which is centered in the present but "impelled by terror" of the past, with his methods for writing his long delayed novel, which is firmly centered in the past. Both look toward the future: Mouse's art attempts to construct futurity from fragments of the present and past whereas Katin's is focused upon identifying the structures underlying society, their links and the implications of their impact on the future. In one of his many notes he connects biological, political and physical discourses in a manner that models his view that "It's only when all one knows of life is abstracted and used as an underlining statement of significant patterning that you have what is both beautiful and permanent" (Delany, *Nova* 168). He juxtaposes the idea of severing a nerve cluster which "connects the sensory impressions originating outside the brain with the cerebral abstractions forming within," the action of "Cut[ing] through the loose tangle of [political] intrigues that net world to world [...] [and] ties star system to star system" and the characteristics of the formation of a star, foregrounding their volatile nature (29). The image of a sun going nova thus becomes the structuring symbol of the text and the repercussions of Lorq's success in ushering political and economic change into the universe relates the individual to the socio-political world. Walker has commented that Katin and Mouse "confirm that any ideal of absolute social unity is artificial and unattainable in a social system of economic exchange" as any change based upon power conferred through control of resources cannot realize the grail-quest theme of a reunification of the land "where the object of exchange is used to divide rather than to unite" (230, 227). What the text states, however, is that there is the possibility of exchange at the level of the individual, who is a strand in the web of interlinked communities of diverse cultural spaces, thus supporting a dialogic movement toward a postnational society.

Politics is metaphorized as a web whose interrelations form a matrix that balance cultural and individual pressures. While the political matrix can be used to adversely control social pressures this metaphor also implies a political and cultural alternative to the rigidity of a society grounded upon cultural identity defined by a centre:

> imagine, a great web that spreads across the galaxy [...]. Each individual is a junction in that net, and the strands between are the cultural, the economic, the psychological threads that hold individual to individual. Any historical event is like a ripple in the net [Delany, *Nova* 163].

In all these examples internal pressure causes each of these structures to implode. This metaphor is dramatized by the conflicts that arise as Lorq aims to disrupt these balances to reconfigure the distribution of economic power throughout the galaxy. He explains that his political motivations are based on a desire for change: "You're for stasis. I'm for movement. Things move. There's no ethic there" (191). While Lorq rejects an unchanging past's excessive influence on the present and attempts to make changes at the political level Katin sees his role as revealing the form and interrelations between the individual and group through his proposed biography of Mouse: "There's my social significance, my historical sweep, the spark among the links that illuminates the breadth of the net—" (206). In contrast to Lusuna's view of culture as "an incredible tangle of decadence, scheming, corruption—" both Lorq and Katin see possibilities for effective human action in constructing a future even if such action is limited by the societal structures individuals are embedded in (48).

Vandana Singh's "Delhi" in the "Future Earth" section of *So Long Been Dreaming* operates within a prototypically conventional SF paradigm but makes use of the megatext to examine postcolonial futures in unfamiliar ways. The megatextual trope is a form of time travel, the focalizer's ability to perceive time as space. The text gives a voice to the marginalized by orienting the narrative from Aseem's perspective; he is one whose "grammatical Hindi and his fair English labels him middle class and educated [...] but [whose] [...] appearance says otherwise" (Singh 84). This combination of linguistic and physical signs of identity, which is itself a colonial legacy, mark uncomfortable transgressions between socio-economic boundaries. There are other boundary crossings:

> he has a theory that his visions are tricks of time, tangles produced when one part of the timestream rubs up against another and the two cross for a moment. He has decided (after years of struggle) that he is not insane after all; his brain is wired differently from others, enabling him to discern these temporal coincidences [80].

His theory that "his brain is wired differently" is a further sign of radical difference. He imagines time as a tangle, a metaphorical thread that floats in a void and so is liable to fold over itself and intersect at various points in space-time. These intersections allow Aseem to observe Delhi's past and offer the text a strategy by which to recover a sense of the city's growth, tradition and history while gesturing toward the possibilities of a postnational future. By reflecting the narrative through his consciousness the text shows how these differences allow him a special insight into the city.

These visions inspire his own research into Delhi's history:

> There is plenty of history in Delhi, no doubt about that — the city's past goes back into myth, when the Pandava brothers of the epic Mahabharata first founded their fabled capital, Indraprastha, some 3,000 years ago [Singh 80].

This statement claims for Delhi an "objective" past and one infused with a long tradition of myth. The novum allows the text to play with the presuppositions a reader may have of a city in a country claimed in the author's introductory paragraph to be "*the planet known as the Third World*" (79). Before Aseem's explanation the narrator states that "once he saw a milkman going past him on Shahjahan road, complete with humped white cow and tinkling bell. Under the stately, ancient trees that partly shaded the street lamps, the milkman stopped to speak to his cow" (80). It is at this point that the text is coded to promote the reader's assumption that such differences (from "western" perspectives) in the distribution of milk are a consequence of a less developed economy proper to India. The rest of the sentence, "and faded into the dimness of twilight," countermands this statement. It could be read metaphorically to describe the way darkness obscures these figures as they retreat from Aseem's field of vision but in a SF text where the protagonist sees visions of the past appear and fade we must read it as it is coded. This is a vision of the past that literally fades and disappears, which Aseem thinks of as an apparition or ghost. Through their playful recognition of attitudes toward the "third world" these sentences form statements acknowledging that Delhi and India in general is viewed as economically deprived and that representations of its economic development remains trapped by stereotypes which, like ghosts, haunt perceptions of the city. The novum allows this image to be used to deconstruct notions of a culture trapped in the past.

Delhi has incorporated the architecture introduced by invading groups into its character. Aseem thinks that "In medieval times alone there were seven cities of Delhi [...] the eighth city was established by the British during the days of Raj" (Singh 80). In modern Delhi he "buys ice-cream from a vendor and eats it sitting by one of the fountains that Lutyens built." This illustrates the syncretic character of a city that absorbs elements from other cultures into its identity, changing and becoming changed by each new addition. The continuity of monuments to its history show Delhi to retain its identity even as each invasion, such as that of "the British invaders, who brought one of the richest and oldest civilizations on earth to abject poverty in only two hundred years," result in disaster. Delhi perseveres as "Kings came and went, the goras came and went, but the city lives on" with Aseem standing witness to the traces of this violent history (81). Singh explores a postnational future that subsumes the question of postcoloniality to that of national identity. It investigates the desirability and possibility of a postnational future that looks beyond an identity defined solely in opposition to the socio-economic impact of colonialism and moves toward postnationality by recognizing the multivocality of the cultural syncretism central to Delhi's identity.

These visions also allow Aseem to see a future radically split in two, which bring to mind Wells's *The Time Machine* and its vision of a future split between the decadent Eloi and savage Morlocks:

> a city of the poor, the outcast, the criminal, in the still-to-be-carved tunnels underneath the Delhi that he knows. He thinks of the Metro, fallen into disuse in that distant future, its tunnels abandoned to the dispossessed, and the city above a delight of gardens and gracious buildings, and tall spires reaching through the clouds [Singh 90].

As with Wells's text, the division of groups in terms of a privileged/marginalized binary is aligned with references to a pastoral space open to the sky on one hand and a subterranean space on the other. Unlike Wells's text the group aligned with subterranean space is marginalized; the "gracious buildings, and tall spires" are signs combining symbols of both power and grace through the respective metaphorical conceptions of height as power and spires with exoticism and artistry. Still more interesting is the way that "Delhi" juxtaposes this future binary with accounts of present Delhi and the way in which its hybrid spaces refuse assimilation:

> One of the things he likes about the city is how it breaks all rules. Delhi is a place of contradictions — it transcends thesis and antithesis. Here he has seen both the hovels of the poor and the opulent monstrosities of the rich. At major intersections, where the rich wait impatiently in their air-conditioned cars for the light to change, he's seen bone-thin waifs running from car to car, peddling glossy magazines like *Vogue* and *Cosmopolitan*. Amid the glitzy new high-rises are troupes of wandering cows and pariah dogs; rhesus monkeys mate with abandon in the trees around Parliament House [80].

The present Delhi is a space that fosters a division of society into rich/poor groups who are brought into proximity at the physical intersections of the city. These intersections are themselves symbols, like Aseem with his linguistic signs of affluence and physical signs of marginalization, of the intersections between two socio-economic cultures; intersections that appear to have disappeared from future Delhi. The novum of the text allows further juxtaposition of spaces through the superimposition of a future topology over the city's present space. The "tall spires" of the future have their analogue in the "high-rises" and it is clear that they are coded as extrapolations. This vision employs signs of a developed "westernized" city complete with American "glossy magazines" and establishes a new context for them that diverges from the schema of a busy downtown American city. The combination of "bone-thin waifs [...] peddling" these magazines and "cows and pariah dogs" amidst skyscrapers causes readers to contrast and re-evaluate their schemas of possible busy cities. However, it may be more likely that it prompts the formation of a new schema based upon a model of a western reader's concept of a busy city proper to their notion of a "third world" developed city.

Important throughout "Delhi" is the way in which affluence is connected to signifiers of western culture: the waifs peddle American magazines to the rich while in the quote discussed above, Aseem's fair English, and therefore his association with a cultural Other, marks him as middle class. The racialized Other is not congruent with an economic Other, but forms a postcolonial and socio-economic intersection that works to establish a hierarchy of privilege in which a colonial legacy remains inscribed. One may wonder how far the final binary between monkeys/Parliament is intended to be read as a contradiction or whether there is not some coded metaphorical correspondence between the frenzied sexual abandon of the monkeys and the operations of the political level referred to by the metonymy "Parliament House." The following sentences of the next paragraph imply as much as the narrator reports that "Some foreign VIP was expected in the morning so the riffraff on the roadsides were driven off by stick-wielding policemen" (Singh 88). The activities of the political sphere are conducted at the expense of the marginalized with various institutions and possessors of power, associated with the police and by extension with the hierarchical subordination of the discourse and operation of law to politics, working to enforce the rich/poor dichotomy. Aseem's visions of Delhi, informed by his historical research, imagines a nightmare vision of a postnational future as well as possibilities for averting it.

Aseem's visions are complemented by another novum, that of a computer that can predict the future. This signification brings in the discourse of the megatext by referring to those conceptions of previous narratives that involve computers with sophisticated statistical analytical abilities that enable them to consider the probability of certain events occurring (cf. Cordwainer Smith's "Alpha Ralpha Boulevard" or Stephen Baxter's *Time*). Such an idea is predicated upon a conception of a predictable universe of deterministic causality and implies that the computer has access to data with which it can accurately predict the future. Om Prakash explains that

> A computer is like a beehive. Many bits and parts, none is by itself intelligent. Combine together, and you have something that can think. This computer is not an ordinary one. Built by Pandit Vidyanath himself [Singh 86].

This explanation goes further to claim AI for the computer. Rather than explaining its operation it, and by extension consciousness and the human mind itself is likened by simile to a beehive whose interconnecting parts form a whole that allow intelligence to develop, resonating with a similar use of the image in *Neuromancer*. This is consistent with Aseem's theory that his mind, conceptualized as a machine, is wired differently.

As we never meet the inventor/wise man figure Vidyanath the reader is right to be as suspicious as Aseem. This inventor figure is represented under the title of "Pandit," which the online *OED* defines as "a learned or wise person; a person with knowledge of Sanskrit and Indian philosophy, religion, and law; (also) a Hindu priest or teacher," and thus aligns the SF trope of the inventor to a long history of knowledge transmitted by learned figures particular to Indian culture. Furthermore there is a playful contrast between the SF recognition of the technical and moral difficulties associated with AI and the unassuming office run by a man identified as a "BSC Physics (Failed)" (Singh 86). But this ambivalence toward the idea of a computer that knows and can supply printouts of the future for individuals to interpret allow the text to interrogate the meaning individuals apply to life and the capacity for those who feel marginalized to make an impact on the future. The narrator reports that "As the days pass it grows on him, and he comes to believe it, if for nothing else than to have something in which to believe" (87). Expectation gives Aseem an alternative to the suicide that he contemplates and that would have left his life forgotten for having left no record. Even after recording his and others' stories he is again prevented from considering suicide by a vision of his time traveling self that again orients him to the possibilities of the future.

Given the computer's prescience and Aseem's visions of a divided Delhi it seems inevitable that despite whatever actions he or anyone else takes there can be no question of having any effect on the future. Prakash takes on the role of disciple to the spiritual advisor and speaks for Vidyanath when he explains that "Each person has their own dharma, their own unique purpose" (Singh 86):

> Whatever you do affects the world in some small way. Sometimes the effect remains small, sometimes it grows and grows like a pipal tree. Causality as we call it is only a first-order effect. Second-order causal loops jump from time to

time, as in your visions, sir. The future, Panditji says, is neither determined nor undetermined [91].

Dharma is tied to a discourse of Indian religion and philosophy but is given a new paradigm of operation through the SF tropes of AI and time travel. They are characterized as distinct from the absent signified of other narratives and given a new context that is compatible with them. Like the reference to the trope of the spaceship as an "udan-khatola" the associations brought together in the SF sentence radically reconfigure the discourse of the text and create an imaginative space delineating a culture that has incorporated technology into the cultural growth of the city (89). The foreign terms of the text operate in a manner analogous to the neologisms of a SF text with the difference that while the sense of the term may differ very little to a reader unable to read it as either a neologism or a foreign term, its reference brings in a web of potential signifiers that delineate a cultural space. The application of an apparently foreign term to a SF trope (spaceship) operates as an appropriation in miniature by resituating the discourse of SF into this new discursive space. The very nature of technology and the cultural assumptions underlying their representation is interrogated by Singh's linguistic appropriation and forces the reader to reconfigure their image of a future Delhi.

It is within this imaginative conception of the city that Aseem reflects on his own purpose as an individual with the capacity to effect others. He imagines himself metaphorically as "a corpuscle in its [Delhi's] veins, blessed or cursed to live and die within it, seeing his purpose now and then, but never fully" (Singh 93). Delhi is conceptualized as a body with individuals as part of its necessary existence. This metaphor is modeled by the image of the beehive:

> the beehive fascinates him, how it is still and in motion all at once, and the way the bees seem to be in concert with one another, as though performing a complicated dance [86].

From Aseem's point of view it is the web of interaction between the bees and their relationship to the space of the hive that gives a coherent meaning to their existence. The similes "concert" and "complicated dance" associate harmony and complexity with their actions and implies a like existence between the individuals of Delhi. These similes highlight the modeling function of this image while linking the conception of the city to the computer AI and Aseem's mind and, by extension, consciousness itself. Aseem's speculations about the future, "whether complexity and vastness are sufficient conditions for a slow awakening, a coming-to-consciousness" ties these megatextual tropes to the trope of the city (93). It is an image of a city that itself develops a consciousness and oscillates between the metaphorical hive mind of the bees and a literal AI. The city is refigured according to the trope of the alien other as Aseem takes this idea to its logical conclusion and thinks that "The city's needs are alien, unfathomable. It is an entity in its own right, expanding every day" (94). What these speculations dramatize is the marginalization and subjection individuals face when brought up against inexplicable forces. But, like the contrast between the stillness and motion of the hive, because these individuals are an essential part of this entity with the capacity for influencing others around them there is also the possibility of having a real impact in constructing a plural, postnational future that is at once neither determined nor undetermined.

Conclusion: Opening Spaces

These texts exemplify the intersections and interaction between SF and cultural discourse, prompting questions regarding the relationship between metaphorical and SF language and its relationship to postnationality and empire. Paul Ricoeur considers scientific models and their relationship to metaphorical language when he explains that

> The mechanism of Descartes and that of Newton are cosmological hypotheses that are universal in character. The question is precisely whether poetic language does not break through to a pre-scientific, ante-predicative level, where the very notions of fact, object, reality and truth, as delimited by epistemology, are *called into question* by this very means of the vacillation of literal reference [299–300].

This vacillation between the literal and metaphorical readings of a text open up an interrogative space whereby poetic language is used to undercut and question the presupposed conditions and perspectives that scientific discourse is built upon and that inform the discourse of empire. Ricoeur splits the concept of model into three categories and identifies the theoretical model as "not things at all; rather, they introduce a new language, like a dialect or idiom, in which the original is described without being constructed" (284). This notion is congruent with Adam Roberts's claim that SF is a "*symbolist* genre, one where the novum acts as symbolic manifestation of something that connects it specifically with the world we live in" (14). It is this symbolism and the special language of the SF megatext that allows the form to so productively engage with postcoloniality and imagine futures where individuals struggle to negotiate the tension between a national identity and a postnationaliy that can accommodate a genuine plurality.

However, Roberts cautions that a reduction of SF texts to a reading as metonymy or metaphor along Aristotlean lines can prevent us from understanding how such texts exceed interpretation as single extended metaphors. With reference to Delany, Roberts discusses the concept of "the *surplus* of metaphor [...] the imaginative motor behind the genre" (139) and quotes Delany's claim that it is "the tension between the logical semantic structure and the psychological, poetic surplus [[...] that] produces the energy and vividness of metaphor" (145). He goes on to discuss Ricoeur's conception of living metaphor which he claims, like SF, possesses two "dialectical arms": poetic and speculative discourse. SF is a symbolic genre that operates according to a process of "'distanciation'" (similar to Suvin's cognitive estrangement) which is "the imaginative space that opens up" between our lives and the world of the text and that "SF *is* metaphorical, but in the strong sense of living metaphor that Ricoeur outlines" (146). It is this surplus that allows the language of SF to engage with the presupposed conditions underlying discourse.

In SF, time is indeed transformed into the space of multiple texts and multiple perspectives. Each text is a microcosm of the SF tradition itself. They are polyphonic and put into play a range of discourses and perspectives, filtering them through the lens of different linguistic strategies. They share a coded language of their own that offer another space for the re-interpretation of statements and thus open for the reader a multiplicity of worlds. In this way SF can be seen as modeling hybridity itself, thus demonstrating its capacity to creatively engage with our contemporary postcoloniality and to imagine the individual's role in constructing postnational identities.

Works Cited

Ashcroft, Bill, Gareth Griffiths and Helen Tiffin. *The Empire Writes Back: Theory and Practice in Post-Colonial Literatures*. London: Routledge, 2002.
Baxter, Stephen. *Time: Manifold I*. London: Voyager, 2000.
Bhabha, Homi K. *The Location of Culture*. London: Routledge, 2004.
Broderick, Damien. *Reading by Starlight: Postmodern Science Fiction*. London: Routledge, 1995.
Delany, Samuel R. *The Jewel Hinged Jaw: Notes on the Language of Science Fiction*. New York: Dragon, 1977.
_____. *Nova*. London: Milenium, 2001.
_____. "The Semiology of Silence." 1987. Science Fiction Foundation, *http://www.depauw.edu/SFs/interviews/delany42interview.htm*, 8 August 2008.
Gibson, William. *Neuromancer*. London: HarperCollins, 1984.
"Pandit." Online OED. 7 Sep 2008 *http://dictionary.oed.com/*.
Reid, Michelle. "Postcolonial Science Fiction." 2005. Science Fiction Foundation. *http://www.sf-foundation.org/publications/academictrack/reid.php*, 5 July 2009.

Ricoeur, Paul. *The Rule of Metaphor: The Creation of Meaning in Language.* Trans. Robert Czerny, Kathleen McLaughlin and John Costello. London: Routledge, 2007.
Roberts, Adam. *Science Fiction.* London: Routledge, 2000.
Said, Edward W. *Orientalism.* London: Penguin, 2003.
Singh, Vandana. "Delhi." *So Long Been Dreaming: Postcolonial Science Fiction and Fantasy.* Hopkinson, Nalo and Uppinder Mehan, eds. Vancouver: Arsenal Pulp, 2004.
Smith, Cordwainer. "Alpha Ralpha Boulevard." *The Norton Book of Science Fiction.* Ursula K. Le Guin and Brian Attebery, eds. London: Norton, 1993.
Walker, Jeanne Murray. "Reciprocity and Exchange in Samuel Delany's *Nova.*" *Extrapolation* 23 (1982): 221–234.
Wells, H.G. *The Time Machine.* London: Ernest Benn, 1999.

Part II

The Nation and Ethnicity in Science Fiction

5

The "Popular" Science
Bollywood's Take on Science Fiction and the Discourse of Nations
SWARALIPI NANDI

Science fiction movies, in the context of India, are an intriguing issue. The Indian theatres reap substantial revenue from the science fiction movies of Hollywood. Hindi dubbed Hollywood science fictions like *Jurassic Park* and *The Mummy* became two of the highest grossing American movies in India (Banker 9). Yet, when it comes to the homespun science fiction movies, instances are strikingly rare even in the otherwise thriving Hindi commercial film industry. There is, however, a long history of science fiction literature in the regional languages. Arshad Khan asserts that the modern genre of SF finds its earliest Indian counterpart in as early as 1879 in the Bengali story "Shukra Bhraman," or "Travels to Venus," written by Jagananda Roy. The dynamics of SF in popular film is nevertheless different from the literary scene. Being the dominant cultural institution, the Indian film industry, also known as Bollywood,[1] shapes and is itself shaped by specific themes and motifs aligned with the popular imagination. Consequently, the Bollywood SF films operate on a referential scale of the Hindi film industry, giving rise to an interesting genre of cinema that both conforms to the norms of Bollywood as well as subverts its popular motifs. I present a study of three popular Bollywood SF films—*Mr. India*, *Koi Mil Gaya* and *Krrish*—from different time periods of postcolonial India, to exemplify how these films apply the popular themes of commercial cinema to invoke a discourse of science in sync with the changing notions of nationhood in India.

Are Science Fiction Films Enough Science?

Commenting on the genre of science fiction films, Weingart states: "Science, it seems, is too esoteric a topic for a popular mass medium such as the movie" (280). Science fiction as a cinematic genre has been sharply criticized by several scholars for its lack of intellectual matter in comparison to its literary counterpart. As early as 1970 John Baxter vehemently attacks science fiction films as "anti science" (10) making a marked distinction between SF literature and films: "Science fiction supports logic and order, SF film illogic and chaos" (10). Andrew Gordon asserts that this has been the dominant critical attitude towards science fiction films, whereby the SF writer Frederick Pohl too perpetuates Baxter's ideas, stating that "Sci-fi pleases the senses and stimulates the glands. But it is not likely ever to stir the intellect" (267). The films, which undoubtedly reach a larger and more composite consumer base reflect the popular notion of science among its target audience than invoking a specialized discourse of scientific knowledge. "The popular market for science," as Gerbner notes, "is a mixture of great expectations, fears, utilitarian interests, curiosities, ancient prejudices, and superstitions," and "mass media appeal to all of these" (110). More often than not, the science fiction movies thus transgress the domains of scientific reasoning and enter into the realms of the wondrous fantasies — focusing more on the spectacles of science for mass consumption than the intellectual speculation behind them. The recurrently popular science fiction screen adaptations, most of which are based on the fantastic imaginings of space travel like the *Star Trek* and *Star Wars* series, attest to the fact that extraordinary spectacles "generate more onscreen excitement than strict science" as Anand Parthasarathy would put it. The rarity of Indian science fiction films can thus be attributed to the technological paucity of the indigenous filmmakers to generate these wondrous spectacles of science. Rakesh Roshan (the maker of both *Koi Mil Gaya* and *Krrish*) articulates the same concerns in *Hindustan Times*, "because we never have budgets of $100 million and $200 million for special effects like in *King Kong* and *Superman*. We can't play around with our visuals as much as them [Hollywood]." While special effects form the core attraction for the generic audience of SF films, since the audiences are also particular to the specific cinematic culture in question, the science fiction movies in commercial Hindi cinema need to be understood with reference to the specific cultural trends in Bollywood as well as its changing dynamics.

Nation, Morality and Mythology: the Dominant Themes of Bollywood

There is a unique dynamics of the cinematic imagination in popular films made in Hindi, which churns out approximately 800 films a year and reaches out to a pan–Indian audience in spite Hindi being a regional language. Immensely diverse in form and genre, the Hindi films nevertheless project some dominant motifs. Jyotika Virdi asserts that the idea of the nation and discourses of contemporary nationalism emerges as the most dominant idea in all films, past or recent, whereby several factors identify it as a national film industry, namely "inheriting and calculating notions of national identity, negotiating conflicts experienced by the imagined community, producing new representations of the nation, and constructing a collective consciousness of nationhood" (7). Sumita Chakravarty endorses a similar view in asserting that "cinematic culture, like other forms of widely disseminated communal discourse, can be seen as a mediated form of national consciousness" (8). While the trope of nation remains of utmost importance in the scheme of the film, the imagination of nationhood changes with the changing dominant political discourse of each decade. Virdi aptly sums up the changing trends of Bollywood villains that reflect the changing narratives of nation:

> The hero fights the nation's "enemies"— threats to the nation at the moment of film making. These enemies took the form of unprincipled profiteers in the 1950s, foreign aggressors in the 1960s, "smugglers" in the 1970s, separatist "terrorists" and politicians in the 1980s, and authoritarian patriarchs in the 1990s [87].

Though it will be an exaggeration to label Hindi cinema as a documentary of national history, it definitely takes the nation as a reference point for its plot.

However, though Virdi dismisses the critical practice of reading Hindi films as a repository of Indian myths, critiquing such moves as an "appeal of an anti-western, anti-imperialistic epistemology (3), the films do conform to a moral order that embodies tradition and *dharmik*[2] values. As Vijay Mishra notes, "In the realm of the popular, dharma is rarely if ever distorted" (5). Thus, there is a strict moral universe within which the film operates, as Carol Brekenridge asserts, that is "clearly divided between good morality and evil decadence" and the audience is likely to reject a film that "transgresses the moral code" (163). The moral question in these Indian science fiction films is raised through the ethical issues in science and the distinction between "good" and "bad" uses of scientific power.

Apart from the tropes of the nation and the moral order, Hindi films perennially derive elements from the "mythological."³ Mythological elements, as Linda Hemphill defines them, are mediated through both the epic and the myth (3) and are built on a *dharmik* parable as well as the trope of wondrous spectacle, including special effects (2). While "mythologicals" were regarded as belonging to a former era of cinema, Hemphill observes that motifs of the mythological continue in contemporary cinema, even in films that are set on realism. In the same strain Gregory Booth observes that even in "explicitly secular and non-ritual(istic) narrative" the religious content is used within "a worldly plot structure and performance context." He asserts that "modern commercial releases ... abound in miracles, such as interventions by the gods — or in some cases Allah" (175–76).⁴ Thus, while epic stereotypes and themes are replicated in the characterization and themes like the righting of *dharma*, the wondrous elements of the mythological get re-constructed in modern films in scenes of divine marvel (where the power of prayer prevails over modern medical science), miraculous turn of events, phenomenal good fortune or the super-human strength of the otherwise normal heroes. As mythological beliefs and notions of mystical prevail dominantly in the collective psyche of the Indian society,⁵ these cinematic motifs recurrent in Hindi films thus form the "cinematic institution"⁶ in the sense Metz uses it to denote the multidimensional, socio-cultural complex that exists outside the text of the film, governing the exchanges between the spectator and the film. The Indian science fiction films too invoke those very tropes of the religious-cultural fabric as familiar signifiers for the audience, however with a subversive effect.

Bollywood SF as Postcolonial Science Fiction

While SF as a genre often alludes to contemporary socio-political realities and issues about morality/ethics as well, the question remains as to how Hindi SF films negotiate the theme of science within the popular motifs of the religious and the mythological. Critics like Stableford strongly contend that "science fiction stands in a more problematic relationship to religion than any other literary genres" (36). However, the theme of the mystical is not always considered antithetical to scientific fiction. Though Farah Mendlesohn notes a dominantly secular tradition of Western SF after 1960s, when religion came to be seen as "essentially of the 'Other,' the backward and the primitive" (264), ironically, more and more science fiction narratives since then have been interpreted for their mythical and religious allusions. Wendy Doniger O'Flaherty's study of the survival of myths in science fiction reveals the numerous religious allusions in the space operas like *Star Trek* and *Star Wars* as well as in more recent SF literature of Ray Bradbury, Ursula K. LeGuin, and Madeline L'Engle.[7] The boundaries of SF thus often stretch to embrace the very tropes of the mystical that empirical science seems to reject, dissolving the binaries of rationality and mysticism.

However, the divide between the mystical and the rational becomes problematic when taken in the context of the colonial discourses. As Uppinder Mehan notes: "In the Orientalist scheme the West is rational and scientific; the East is mystical and fantastic. Technology is a cultural artifact: it is value laden as well as instrumental" (54). Discourses of colonial science are often based on the trope of technology. Daniel R. Headrick stresses that technological inventions were vital in the spread of nineteenth century European imperialism (11–12). Michael Adas forwards this, saying that not only did the Europeans justify their colonial dominance over others through the discourse of their own technological superiority (6–7), the driving force of imperialism through technology continues today in the spread of global capitalism (402–17). Consequently, the postcolonial counter-narratives of science, as Gyan Prakash points out especially in the context of India, that emerged with Indian nationalism and continue to shape the notions of modernization in India, were also based on a popularization of technological knowledge. Jawaharlal Nehru's vision of the newly independent India was also based on the very tenets of modern science as he proclaimed: "It is science alone that can solve the problems of hunger and poverty, of insanitation and illiteracy, of superstition and deadening custom and tradition ... I do not see any way out of our vicious circle of poverty except by utilizing the new sources of power which science has placed at our disposal" (176). Technology thus forms the central issue in postcolonial science fictions. As Michelle Reid asserts "I think representations of technology are the key to an idea of postcolonial science fiction; it is the genre's fascination with technology that identifies it as a literature of empire" (par. 12). Simultaneously, she argues for the resistive potential that the trope of technology offers in science fiction: "In science fiction, technology provides both the means of writing back to the power base of empire, and writing forwards towards new paradigms" (par. 28).

The SF films that I have chosen for this essay are the ones that particularly deal with this issue of technology from a postcolonial perspective in the context of India. Using realistic contemporary contexts, the films project several technological fantasies achieved by a scientifically advanced, postcolonial India that can both challenge and surpass the scientific sophistication of the Western world. Simultaneously, the films also subvert the popular tropes of miracles and myths, so recurrent in Bollywood, by invoking them and rationalizing them with a scientific logic. However, these films are not unmitigated celebration of technological fantasies and postcolonial empowerment through empirical science — the postcolonial tenor of these films also lies in their questioning of the existing power structures. Set against a realistic socio-political backdrop, the films question the social pertinence of technology as the nation evolves from its postcolonial tropes towards globalization.

Mr. India and the Early Nation

Shekhar Kapoor directed *Mr. India* in 1987 and hailed it as the first science fiction film of the mainstream Hindi movies. The story is quite derivative, echoing various elements from the major Western science fiction stories. However, the film is thoroughly contextualized as a Bollywood product as it re-creates motifs of the popular myths with the technological fantasy of an invisibility gadget.

The film opens with the Indian home minister summoning all the defense personnel to warn them of the enemies lurking outside the nation that are threatening the integrity of India. The scene shifts to highlight the enemy — the ruthless and eccentric Mogambo (played by the Hindi cinema's popular villain Amrish Puri), who plans to colonize India. Mogambo resembles the archetypal extravagant villain who maintains a private island equipped with a personal security force, various awe-inspiring technologies and modern weapons of mass destruction. On the other side is the hero Arun (played by Anil Kapoor), a poor man who brings up a group of orphans as his family and bears the brunt of poverty till he comes across his father's unique invention, the gadget of invisibility. Arun's life changes with this gadget that can render anyone invisible with a click of a button. Renaming himself as Mr. India for his invisible avatar, he uses his new found power to fight the injustices in society — all of which are someway controlled by Mogambo. His final confrontation is predictably with Mogambo, who wants the gadget for himself and is on the verge of releasing devastating missiles on India. Like a true hero, Arun as Mr. India manages to overpower Mogambo and succeeds to stop the missiles which on the contrary kill Mogambo himself.

This is one of the early and rare films that present the fantastical as technological rather than with mythological undertones. Mogambo's island is a technological wonder, quite awe-inspiring in its imagining, considering the 1980s Indian scene. However, what sets the "scientific" tenor of the film is the gadget of invisibility — conceptually an imitation of Huxley's *Invisible Man*— but claimed as an Indian invention. There is no exotic wonder about the gadget; rather it exemplifies a postcolonial appropriation of the Western scientific knowledge brought in with colonization. The scientificity of the gadget is emphasized by scenes of the inventor as an archetypal scientist working in a conventional lab, a science classroom with a blackboard scribbled with familiar mathematical formulae and the gadget rationalized by the existing theories of light refraction.

While it showcases a technological dream for modern India, the film is also significant in the way it invokes the mythical and religious aspects of Indian popular culture and subverts them to a comic effect. There are two basic emotions that Mr. India evokes in his onlookers: one of bedazzlement that is associated with magic and the other of fear associated with the supernatural, both of which replicate the familiar emotional responses to the spectacles of miracle common in Bollywood cinema. However, here, since the audience already knows about the secret of Mr. India's invisibility, the bewilderment of the onscreen characters gives rise to comic situations. The film thus subtly mocks the popular tropes of supernatural wonder that moviegoers often take seriously. A particular scene in point is the one with the Hanuman statue. Mogambo's aides steal a golden statue of "Bajrangbali," a Hindu warrior god, and sell it to a white smuggler. Mr. India arrives in time and makes it appear as if the god has come alive. As the statue (actually moved by the invisible Mr. India) flies in the air and strikes the astounded evildoers, the scene creates a comic situation for the audience who laughs at the befooled goons who think it is a divine intervention. There are numerous other scenes with similar effects, whereby the popular Bollywood tropes of divine miracle, supernatural presence, and magical powers, evoked due to Mr. India's invisibility are not only debunked (with a scientific logic) but also rendered ludicrous. It is interesting to note that a recent Bollywood film, *Gayab*, also narrates a similar story of an invisible man, but departs from *Mr. India* in showcasing invisibility as an evil supernatural curse. *Mr. India* is a bold attempt to challenge the common perceptions about the supernatural and its mythological plausibility in Indian films.

The film is an important narrative of nation against the contemporary socio-political backdrop of India in the 1980s, a period which, as Ashutosh Varshney describes, witnessed the worst case of "secessionary politics" since independence (73). More often than not, nationalistic discourses termed the separatist movements as conspiracies by the foreign enemy and the film too center's on the hero's mission to save the nation from a foreign power. Mogambo is definitely "foreign" in his non–Indian name, semi–Caucasian looks and accented Hindi. Interestingly, his main aide is a Chinese scientist Fu Manchu,[8] whose character adds another meaning to the theme of colonization in the historical context of China's aggressive military policies against

India in the 1970s. By vanquishing these colonial powers, the film projects an anti-colonial fantasy where technology plays an ameliorating role for the indigenous society.

The moral question of the film centers on the distinction between Eurocentric science which Dhruv Raina conceptualizes as "transcendental and disengaged from social context" in contrast to postcolonial science that is more "context bound" (177). The *dharmik* battle between good and evil, in this film, thus centers on the social utility of science for common good. Mogambo symbolizes colonial science, which is sophisticated and advanced but is directed towards the purpose of colonization and exploitation. Arun's invisibility gadget, on the other hand, is a postcolonial tool of resistance — it is crafted by an Indian scientist but using the tools of Western science. *Mr. India* is thus the dream of the technologically enabled nation that can resist the other technological superpowers and work towards the welfare of its people.

Koi Mil Gaya and the Modern Nation State

A decade and a half after *Mr. India*, after Bollywood entered its post-globalization phase, there was a revival of the SF theme again through the success of *Koi Mil Gaya* (2003) and its sequel *Krrish* (2006).[9] While the film industry underwent a major stylistic transformation for the global audience, it also saw, as Meheli Sen asserts, a "meteoric rise of Hindu nationalism" (145). Consequently, there was a resurgence of traditionalism and a religio-mythic narrative in the films, resonances of which are prominently present in both *Koi Mil Gaya* and *Krrish,* which, however continue to be subversive in their interpretation and treatment of the mystical. However, while the scientific tenor remains the same, the films show a radical departure from each other in the changing idea of the nation. As Aswin Punathambekar and Anandam Kavoori remind us that the earlier categories of Indian cinema, nation, public, culture and politics become problematic in the context of now global Bollywood (1), the two contemporary SF films project new questions about the Indian nation state that is radically different from the nation of *Mr. India*. Consequently, the ethical questions of science and the moral order shift their foci as the nation goes through steady transformations in its power dynamics.

Koi Mil Gaya (I will use the abbreviation *KMG*) begins with an Indian scientist pitted against the Western center of knowledge, the space research center in Canada. The Indian space scientist Sanjay Mehra, played by Rakesh Roshan himself (the director and script writer), invents a computer to send signals to outer space and succeeds in receiving extra-terrestrial responses.

His technique is inspired from indigenous Vedic science which meets with ridicule and distrust from his fellow scientists. The technique however works successfully as a UFO comes down, the sighting of which distracts him into fatal accident. His pregnant wife, Sonia, travels back to India, hiding his invention in obscurity. The story takes a leap to a present-day Indian hill station, where Sanjay's wife stays with their son Rohit, physically grown up as an adult but mentally stunted due to the accident. He rediscovers his father's invention to repeat the experiment of contacting the aliens. The story hereafter imitates Spielberg's *E.T.* very closely, with a spaceship landing on earth, a similar amicable alien left behind, its friendship with the childlike adult Rohit and Rohit's final journey to return the alien to his spaceship. However, the plot of *KMG* shows a further complication of the question of science in the context of a nation state.

As a science fiction movie, *KMG* introduces images of spaceship and aliens for the first time on a Bollywood screen, aligning the plot with the present post-liberalization technology where India has made significant progress in the fields of space research and computers, both of which capture the scientificity of the film. However, the film echoes several motifs of the mythological, including the figure of a non-human, god-like, magical being that changes the fate of the hero. Dominic Alessio and Jessica Langer strongly criticize the film for its overt religious allusions which, they argue, project the fantasy of a Hindu nation in face of technological progress in India. They draw their argument from the mythological references particularly substantiated by Coleman's (the special effect designer) comments on the making of the alien, Jadoo, which he claimed to be designed on the Hindu gods Ganesh (for his features) and Krishna (for his blue skin). However, while they are prompt to identify the mythological references in the film, they miss the subversive undertones. The film undoubtedly alludes to Jadoo as a god descending from heaven and his powers — telekinesis, magic healing, levitation — are more mystical than technological. However, the film also rationalizes the mystical powers as otherworldly (instead of divine) and thereby echoes a Daniken like argument that gods of folklore are actually aliens with superior skills.[10] *KMG* thus attempts to rationalize the divine and the magical through the fantasy of aliens that empirical science has not completely dismissed, if not established. Like *Mr. India*, *KMG* invokes the tropes of the mythological only to subvert them to a non-mystical interpretation.

The *dharmik* battle in the film continues to revolve around function of science, which has now changed its role with the evolution of the Indian nation state. Unlike *Mr. India*, the enemy is no longer a larger than life foreign force out to colonize the whole nation. Rather, the power discrimination lies within the boundaries of the nation. *KMG* touches upon the crucial theme of general social insensitivity towards the mentally retarded, exemplified in the exploitation and active cruelty meted out to Rohit by the other "normal" boys. Consequently, the social role of Sanjay's technology lies in the ultimate empowerment of Rohit, who is rendered "normal" by Jadoo's powers. However, though technology still plays an ameliorating role in the scope of the narrative, the film raises important questions about the state's use of empirical science. While *Mr. India* was a dream of the scientific self-reliance of postcolonial India, *KMG* reveals the repressive role of the technologically adept modern Indian state. The discriminating gesture of the computer teacher, who excludes Rohit from his class because he is mentally disabled, questions the very equitability of state sponsored technology. Again, Rohit fights a different oppressive order for saving Jadoo, who being the "other" is vulnerable to state exploitation for the purpose of scientific experimentation. The trope echoes the colonial projects of scientific enquiry where the "other" was scrutinized as a curious subject of study. The postcolonial Indian nation state thus adopts the same tenor of its colonial predecessors, having adopted the same models of state power and scientific research from its Western colonizers. As the battle between the powerful armed personnel of the Indian state against the pitiable Jadoo and unarmed Rohit constitutes the central conflict of the film, the Indian nation emerges as the repressive state machinery of insidious intent. From the vulnerable postcolonial nation of *Mr. India*, which was tottering against powerful foreign forces and helplessly witnessing the chaos within its borders, *KMG* shows a technologically enabled and powerful postcolonial state which has however replaced the colonial order and authoritatively controls its people to the point of violent repression.

Krrish and the Post-Nation

A sequel to *Koi Mi Gaya*, *Krrish* is about Rohit's son, Krishna (again played by Hritick Roshan), who possesses superhuman powers as a legacy of Jadoo's effects on his father. Both his parents being dead, he stays with his grandmother (Rohit's mom from *KMG*) who virtually hides him in a remote mountain village, fearing his special powers might be found and exploited. A super-human by birth, Krishna is both weird and a loner, till he meets Priya — a girl camping in the jungles — and saves her from a paragliding accident. They grow closer and Krishna develops romantic feelings for her, realizing which Priya asks him to come over to her house in Singapore. Priya's actual intention is however to showcase Krishna's powers for the TV channel she works with. Krishna comes over to Singapore but refuses to reveal his supernatural powers till he gets into situations where he needs to save people. To hide his identity, he becomes the archetypal superhero and wears a mask and renames himself as Krrish. During this time he learns that his father is actually alive and is held a captive by the evil technology moghul Dr. Arya, who has exploited Rohit's super-human intelligence to build a machine that can forecast the future. A final conflict ensues between Krishna, who is on a mission to save his father, and Dr. Arya, who has foreseen Krishna to be his killer, though finally Krishna succeeds to overcome the villain and save his father.

Krrish projects more overt mythological connections in the figure of the superhero, as Hemphill asserts that his "name suggests his god-like powers" (6). Krishna is born with supernatural powers that defy natural laws; however the film rationalizes the element of mythological wonder by referencing to Jadoo as the source of his powers. Again, though Krishna's feats bear strong mythic resonances, the effect to which the film uses them is interestingly subversive of the mythological traditions. Unlike in the mythological, where miracles evoke awe and devotion, *Krrish*'s supernatural feats evoke comic effects. Priya thinks Krishna is a ghost and is terrorized to the point of being comical, while the audience (who knows the secret) revels in Priya's ignorance. The supernatural being rationalized from the very beginning, Krishna's extraordinary feats subvert the emotional import of an onscreen miracle — usually fear, awe, amazement etc — to one of humor. The subversive effects continue as Priya finally realizes that Krishna is not a ghost but a super-human, only to exploit his powers for commercial purposes! The seeming neutrality with which Priya and others accept Krishna's super-humanness, taking it either as a common exception or a commercial prospect, subverts the trope of wonder and devotion of religious-mythical allusions. Again, as Krishna conceals his powers, feigning normalcy in situations that are designed to expose his extraordinariness for commercial showbiz, the film completely turns the traditions of the cinematic supernatural upside down, where ordinary situations usually reveal the miraculous.

Though the primary premise of the film is based on the marvels, *Krrish* projects a technological dream that blends the empirical with mystical knowledge: a future-foretelling machine explained in the film as a spectacular "combination of astrology, astronomy and technology." Inspired by the Hollywood version of Philip K. Dick's novel *Paycheck*, the machine has been projected as a unique piece of technology that operates only with a sophisticated technical password of Rohit's retina and heartbeat scan. The film is strewn with other technological wonders in a modern urban space — the wondrous cityscape of Singapore, the technological empire and private island of Dr. Arya, and the sophisticated life support machine that keeps Rohit physically suspended and in a state of half-life. *Krrish* brings in the spectacle of technology on a much grander scale than its predecessors, and consequently raises more pertinent questions about the power dynamics of technology on a global scale.

While Krishna plays the archetypal superhero in his rescue of the common people in distress, his mission as the embodiment of "good" lies in his final battle with the technology moghul Dr. Arya. *Krrish* shows a revolutionary transformation in the identity of the villain, who is neither a foreign dictator like Mogambo nor an oppressive official of the state like in *KMG*— rather Dr. Arya is the embodiment of new-age global corporation. On a simpler level, Arya owns the largest technological company named as Technotronics but on a symbolic level, he himself personifies the cunningly exploitative nature of a corporation. His villainy draws from his exploitative capitalistic tendencies which manipulate Rohit's intellectual labor. Dr. Arya thus signifies the corporatization of technology in a globalized world, whereby the earlier dynamics of power are restructured to a new order of domination. Accordingly, the focus shifts from the issues of the nation state to a transnational scale where the categories of the oppressor and the oppressed can no longer be defined with the nation as the reference point. Dr. Arya is Indian by ethnicity but operates on an international scale while Rohit too is an Indian by ethnicity and nationality but represents the transnational flow of labor in the global market. On the other hand, Krishna is an Indian superhero rescuing the troubled people of Singapore, a place outside the geographical borders of the Indian nation state. Again, what Dr. Arya does on a larger scale is what Priya (and her friend Honey) wanted to do on a smaller scale — to exploit Krishna's powers for commercial showbiz. Thus, the categories of the oppressor and the oppressed get restructured according to the new order of global capitalism, whereby it is the corporate giants who control power and take up the role of the neocolonizers. Similarly, *Krrish* represents a transnational resistance operating beyond the boundaries of the nation state that is no longer static.

The Bollywood science fiction films thus project a trajectory of scientific fantasy in a postcolonial nation that evolves from its early stages of nation building to a transnational global identity. As the nation moves towards more technological modernization, the films disseminate a scientific discourse by appropriating the non-rational tropes of mysticism in popular culture. Yet, these films are not unadulterated tributes to technology; rather they question the ethics of science in the contemporary context. The films thus echo the eternal question of the science fiction genre that has complete faith in the powers and potentials of science, and yet is apprehensive about its results (Bleiler x), reminding us that science has the potential to both empower and oppress.

Notes

1. The term Bollywood, though used widely, has been often criticized for its imitative undertones.
2. The term "dharma" in this context refers to a Hindu code of conduct.
3. Hemphill defines the mythological as the genre that "stand apart from other film genres in their subject matter and characterization, their extensive use of special effects to produce screen miracles. As in other genres, melodrama is the preferred form in which to express an individuals' social and familial relationships, good fights evil.... Where mythological differs is in their use of known epic and mythological plots and their habitual use of special effects" (29).
4. For a detailed study on the religious imagination of Indian films see Rachel Dwyer's *Filming the Gods: Religion and Film in India.*
5. Talking about the state of science fiction in India, Jayant Narlikar, one of the leading scientists and science fiction writer regretfully says: "Although there is more awareness of science in the society, the superstitions continue to dominate. And even in the modern generation there is no discernible improvement towards a more scientific temperament.... Although astrological columns appear in the western newspapers also, I have not come across marriages there being fixed by horoscope-matching!"
6. Christian Metz explains "cinematic institution'" as "not just the cinema industry that works to fill the cinema, it is also the mental machinery — the mental machinery which spectators accustomed to the cinema have internalized historically and which has adapted them to the consumption of films" (7).
7. Also see Benjamin Plotinsky, who asserts how, though being overtly political, the genre increasingly employs Christian allegory mostly in its cinematic adaptations.
8. This Indian adaptation of the Chinese villain is perhaps inspired by the famous Fu Manchu, originally featuring in Sax Rohmer's novels, who came to signify the archetypal Chinese villain in Western popular imagination.
9. The post-globalization turn in Bollywood is marked by the significant diffusion of Hindi film industry in the global market with the diasporic Indians forming an increasing consumer base (Mishra 2002; Virdi 2003).
10. Though Eric von Daniken has been criticized by many scholars, it is his claims about certain architectural wonders that have been challenged. His basic premise of the existence of more advanced aliens has not been disproved as empirical science continues to search for aliens in space research projects.

Works Cited

Adas, Michael. *Machines as the Measure of Men: Science, Technology, and Ideologies of Dominance.* Ithaca, NY: Cornell University Press, 1989.
Alessio, D. a. "Nationalism and Postcolonialism in Indian Science Fiction: Bollywood's Koi ... Mil Gaya (2003)." *New Cinema: Journal of Contemporary Film*, 5 (2007, 3), 217–229.
Baxter, J. *Science Fiction in the Cinema.* New York: Paperback Library, 1970.
Bleiler, E. F. *Science Fiction: The Early Years.* Kent, OH: Kent State University Press, 1991.
Breckenridge, C.A. *Consuming Modernity: Public Culture in a South Asian World.* Minneapolis: University of Minnesota Press, 1995.

Chakravarty, S. *National Identity in Indian Popular Cinema, 1947–1987.* Austin: University of Texas Press, 1993.
Daniken, E. v. *Chariots of the Gods.* Trans. M. Heron. New York: Berkley, 1984.
Dwyer, R. *Filming the Gods: Religion and Indian Cinema.* Abingdon, Oxon and New York: Routledge, 2006.
Gokulsing, K. M. *Indian Popular Cinema.* Staffordshire, England: Trentham, 1998.
Gordon, A. (1982). Review: Science Fiction Film Criticism. *Science Fiction Studies,* 9 (1), 93–95.
Hemphill, L. *The Bollywood Mythological : Rise and Decline.* Koln: LAP Lambert Academic, 2009.
Jha, S. K. "Krrish Will Wow Audiences." Hindustan Times, 19 June 2006, http://www.hindustantimes.com/News-Feed/nm12/Krrish-will-wow-audiences/Article1-111072.aspx, retrieved 7 May 2010.
Kapoor, S., director. *Mr. India,* 1987 [motion picture].
Kavoori, A. a. (2008). *Global Bollywod.* New York and London: New York University Press.
Khan, A. S. "Udankhatola Redux." *Tehelka Magazine,* December 2008, http://www.tehelka.com/story_main36.asp?filename=hub081207udankhatola.asp, retrieved May 10, 2010.
Mendlesohn, F. "Religion and Science Fiction." In *The Cambridge Companion to Science Fiction,* edited by E. a. James. New York: Cambridge University Press, 2003.
Mishra, V. *Bollywood Cinema: Temples of Desire.* New York: Routledge, 2002.
Narlikar, J. "Scientific Temper Yet to Take Root." *The Hindu,* 17 May 2005.
Nehru, J. *The Unity of India: Collected Writings, 1937–1940.* London: Drummond, 1941.
O'Flaherty, W. D. "The Survival of Myth in Science Fiction." In *Mindscapes: The Geographies of Imagined Worlds,* G. E. Slusser, ed. Carbondale: Southern Illinois University Press, 1989.
Parthasarathy, A. "Across Time and Space." *The Hindu,* 21 November 2003, http://www.thehindu.com/thehindu/fr/2003/11/21/stories/2003112101020100.htm, retrieved May 2, 2010.
Plotinsky, B. A. "How Science Fiction Found Religion." *City Journal* vol. 19 (1) (Winter 2009), retrieved April 25, 2010, from http://www.city-journal.org/2009/19_1_urb-science-fiction.html.
Prakash, G. *Another Reason: Science and the Imagination of Modern India.* Princeton, NJ: Princeton University Press, 1999.
Raina, D. "Multicultural and Postcolonial Theories in Science and Society." *Science, Technology, Imperialism and War* XV (1), J.B. Gupta, ed , and D. Chattopadhyaya, comp. Delhi: Center for Studies In Civilization, 2007.
Raman, P., director. *Gayab,* 2004 [motion picture].
Reid, M. "Postcolonial Science Fiction," n.d. Retrieved 30 May 2010 from Science Fiction Foundation, http://www.sf-foundation.org/publications/essays/reid.html.
Roshan, R., director. *Koi Mil Gaya,* 2003 [motion picture].
_____ . *Krrish,* 2006 [motion picture].
Sen, M. "'It's All About Loving Your Parents': Bollywood, Hindutva and Bollywood's New Fathers." In *Bollywood and Globalization: Indian Popular Cinema, Nation and Diaspora,* edited by R. B. Mehta. London, New York, New Delhi: Anthem, 2010.
Stableford, B. *Space Time and Infinity: Essays on Fantastic Literature.* San Bernardino, CA: Borgo, 2006.

Varshney, A. *Ethnic Conflict and Civic Life: Hindus and Muslims in India.* New Haven, CT: Yale University Press, 2002.
Virdi, J. *The Cinematic Imagination: Indian Popular Films as Social History.* New Brunswick, NJ: Rutgers University Press, 2003.
Weingart, P. "Of Power Maniacs and Unethical Geniuses: Science and Scientists in Science Fiction Films." *Public Understanding of Science, 12:3* (2003), 279–287.

6

Postcolonial Ethics and Identity in *Kirinyaga*

JENN BRANDT

Mike Resnick's *Kirinyaga: A Fable of Utopia* (1998) is a collection of related stories set in a utopian space colony, Kirinyaga, and features the character Koriba, a Cambridge and Yale educated *mundumugu* (witch doctor). Set in a future where Africa has been entirely colonized and modernized, complete with cities in the European tradition, *Kirinyaga* uses the science fiction technique of extrapolation to explore and challenge ethical values within postcolonial societies and structures of power. Within the artificial community of Kirinyaga, Koriba and his tribe have isolated themselves from the modern world in order to live by the adapted traditions of the Kikuyu tribe, which hails from the former Kenya. Imagined as a futuristic space, Kirinyaga becomes a site for the exploration of what one considers a utopia, shedding light on the understanding of the legacy of colonization. Through Koriba's first-person narration, Resnick explores the ambiguities and dualities of social change and the (mis)uses of power that are common themes in both science fiction and postcolonial literature. The reader becomes complicit through his/her identification with Koriba, who embodies the position of both the colonizer and the colonized. While *Kirinyaga* examines the multifaceted debate between ethnocentrism and cultural relativism, specifically through the character of Koriba, Resnick is careful to avoid final judgment in his exploration of cultural motivations for individual and collective actions that relate to both the colonizer and the colonized. Consequently, he presents an exercise in ethical and philosophical rhetoric that highlights the nuances in both science fiction and postcolonial literature.

Both science fiction and postcolonial literature are complicated genres that often elude attempts at concrete definition. As with most genres, there are a series of conventions and themes that tend to reappear, but the scope and variety of topics, especially under the umbrella of "science fiction," are quite varied. Similarly, just as there is no unified definition for what constitutes a postcolonial culture, postcolonial literature also escapes a precise mode of classification. Therefore, the elusive nature of these literary domains provides an ongoing conversation not only within their respective frameworks, but also result in interesting dialogues when brought together. Conquest and the resulting clash of cultures are obvious themes in both genres. They each question the intrinsic value of certain customs and bodies of knowledge, as well as the discourses that arise and shape resulting power structures. While science fiction, particularly during the Campbell era, or the "Golden Age,"[1] is more often than not concerned with the narrative of the conquest, postcolonial literature attempts to bring visibility and give a voice to the historically marginalized. Both, however, reveal the violent and disruptive nature of colonization, and the paradoxes that surround its fallout.

Resnick's *Kirinyaga: A Fable of Utopia* addresses these complexities in a unique way, using the literary tradition of science fiction to explore not only the effects of colonization on a specific group of people, but also to show what happens when the said group attempts to return to their pre-colonized mode of life. Resnick began the project by writing the short story "Kirinyaga" for a proposed collection by Orson Scott Card. Card asked contributors to create a story about a utopian society, but with the catch that any member was free to leave the society at any time without question and that the protagonist of the story needed to believe in the created utopia. Working on the story, Resnick quickly realized that his vision for this utopia expanded beyond the one tale. He decided to publish *Kirinyaga* one chapter at a time, each one a standalone story in its own right, but also contributing to a larger narrative of the complex utopia first described in "Kirinyaga."

Kirinyaga begins on Earth in the year 2123 with the novel's protagonist, Koriba, preparing to leave Earth to settle the space colony of Kirinyaga. Named after the Kikuyu word for Mt. Kenya, Kirinyaga is created as an ancestral, utopian vision of Africa (specifically Kenya) before colonization and European modernization. Koriba, educated in Western schools, has worked with government officials in setting up the charter for Kirinyaga and has appointed himself its *mundumugu*, or the spiritual leader. While the charter allows for Kirinyaga's sovereignty, the colony is monitored from Earth by a subset of the Eutopian Council known as "Maintenance." Using a personal computer kept in his home, or *boma*, Koriba has sole contact with Maintenance and outside civilization. Science fiction allows for the plausibility of this premise, and it is through technology such as Koriba's computer that the conflict of the story is conceived and established. In direct opposition to this technology are the ancient customs of the Kikuyu. The role of tradition is paramount to Koriba, and he rejects modernization as staunchly as he strictly enforces his Kiyuku customs.

While tradition is the backbone of Kirinyaga and the guiding force in Koriba's work as *mundumugu*, the traditions that he values are his own constructed ideas of the past. The utopia of the Kikuyu is based on Koriba's personal vision of an idealized past, and is based upon a way he never actually experienced. Instead, it is interpreted and reconstructed through the lens of his experiences living in modernized Kenya and his education in European and American schools. Given his circumstances, Koriba embodies the unusual experience of being both the colonized and the colonizer. In Kenya, he resists the culture and influences that he sees being imposed upon Africa at the expense of traditional tribal customs. He complains to his son, "I have seen our people forget what it means to be a Kikuyu, and speak proudly about being Kenyans, as if Kenya was anything more than an arbitrary set of lines drawn on a European map" (5). Thus, Koriba resents the loss of tribal identities at the hands of European onslaught, and critiques the destructive and dismissive randomness of the process. Once on Kirinyaga, however, it is Koriba who becomes the one to impose a strict way of life on his people. While this is accepted with little opposition at first, it becomes increasingly difficult for Koriba to maintain order and *his* vision of utopia. The resulting struggle he faces becomes the overarching narrative of the stories.

Although Koriba is not the chief, as *mundumugu* he wields even greater power. The Kikuyu consider their god, Ngai, as the highest authority, and it is Koriba who acts as the direct link to Ngai. Accordingly, Koriba has convinced his people that his relationship with Ngai affords him magical abilities, such as casting spells, controlling the weather, and curing illness. Religion defines both the politics and the culture of the Kikuyu, and while the chief may enforce the law, Koriba wisely asserts that it is "a *mundumugu* who interprets it" (23). Since all of the stories in *Kirinyaga* are told through the first-person narration of Koriba, readers are presented with only Koriba's interpretation of the facts. To a certain extent, like the rest of the Kikuyu, the reader is dependent on Koriba's understanding of characters and events. Resnick, however, includes details such as the background information on Koriba's education and the use of his computer, which complicates the situation and calls into question some of Koriba's motives and actions. Through this process the text interrogates the legitimacy of values and tradition within both colonized and emergent, "utopian" cultures.

As Koriba explains, the "*mundumugu*, while he occasionally casts spells and interprets omens, is more a repository of the collected wisdom and traditions of his race" (20). Tradition is the key to Koriba as it serves as the unifying force of Kirinyaga. As the keeper of this force, it is up to Koriba to decide how tradition should be used in controlling the Kikuyu. While it seems odd to Koriba's son and others that a man educated at Cambridge and Yale would choose to spend his days "settling disputes over the ownership of chickens and goats, and supplying charms against the demons, and instructing [his] people in the ancient ways," (14) Koriba is actually quite shrewd in his decisions. While the rest of the Kikuyu struggle with their crops and hard labor, Koriba acknowledges, "I, alone of my people, planted no crops, for the Kikuyu feed their *mundumugu*, just as they tend his herds and weave his blankets and keep his *boma* clean" (17). Koriba's only job is to maintain the integrity of his utopia; everything else is provided for him. Therefore, Koriba's insistence on tradition is as much as a safeguard for ensuring his own comfort and way of life as it is his desire to maintain the integrity of the Kikuyu. In this sense, Koriba quite evidently dons the role of a colonizer.

What is unclear is whether Koriba realizes the hypocrisy of some of his beliefs. When a representative from Maintenance comes to Kirinyaga to question one of the Kikuyu's practices, Koriba refuses to back down. He argues that, "The first time we betray our traditions this world will cease to be Kirinyaga, and will become merely another Kenya, a nation of men awkwardly pretending to be something they are not" (23). Koriba insists on not changing any of the customs of the Kikuyu, fearing that one small change will cause the inevitable downfall that will start the process of modernization all over again. In this aspect he is correct, as European and technological intervention eventually cause his personal defeat and abandonment of Kirinyaga. What Koriba fails to understand, though, is that his enforcement of the Kikuyu traditions is no more natural to his people living hundreds of years in the future than those of the Europeans. In many ways, Koriba's own utopia is nothing but a nation of people awkwardly pretending to be something they are not.

Through this utopian experiment, *Kirinyaga* is a meditation on the intrinsic nature of values that shape a culture. Further, it asks readers to consider what is at stake in the dialectics between the individual versus the community in terms of these values. As the *mundumugu*, Koriba argues the need to enforce traditional customs for the sake of the whole community, but the irony is if the traditions of the Kikuyu are altered, then accordingly, their power structures could be altered as well. Therefore Koriba's steadfast beliefs not only maintain the order of the community, but more important, they also ensure his role as supreme authority. Ultimately, his insistence on tradition ensures his power on Kirinyaga. This brings into question whether Koriba's allegiance is to the values of his community or to his own power over his people.

Further complicating Koriba's position as leader is his use of technology in safeguarding his utopian vision. This is most readily visible through Koriba's attitude toward his computer. As he explains:

> There are only four computers on all of Kirinyaga. The others belong to Koinnage, the paramount chief of our village, and two chiefs of distant clans, but their computers can do nothing but send and receive messages. Only mine is tied to the data banks of the Eutopian Council, the ruling body that had given Kirinyaga its charter, for only the *mundumugu* has the strength and the vision to be exposed to European culture without becoming corrupted by it [199].

Here Koriba blatantly reveals an arrogance that is only implicit in other parts of the text. As the *mundumugu* he feels that he is the only one capable of interpreting Kikuyu traditions and is exclusively immune to the influences of outside cultures. That does not stop him, nevertheless, from using the technology from the outside world to achieve his own means.

Instances of Koriba's exploitative actions abound. From time to time Maintenance provides minor orbital adjustments to Kirinyaga to approximate the seasonal climate changes that would have naturally occurred on Earth. Koriba, however, does not let his people know that their weather is controlled in such a manner. Instead, he invokes ancient customs as an explanation: "Lowering myself gently to the ground, I spread my pouchful of bones and charms out before me and invoked Ngai to cool Kirinyaga with a mild rain, which Maintenance had agreed to supply later in the afternoon" (44). Not only does he purposefully deceive the Kikuyu, but in doing so, he manipulates the traditions that he proposes to hold so dearly.

When Koriba is questioned by a representative from Maintenance about his use of the computer he replies, "As long as the facts are correct, what difference does it make whether I read them from the bones or the computer?" (18). Likening technology to soothsaying is not an entirely unrealistic comparison. What is problematic with Koriba's rationale, however, is his use of the word "fact." Throughout the text this concept is debated and open to interpretation. While Koriba never wavers in his unflinching faith in his capabilities that all that he says and does are true and factual, the merits of these "facts" are questioned throughout the text. This questioning occurs first by outside sources such as Maintenance, and later, more critically, by Koriba's people.

The collection's second chapter, "For I Have Touched the Sky," begins to challenge the validity of Koriba's assumptions in a tragic way. The most anthologized of all the stories in the collection, it also brings into question

6. Postcolonial Ethics and Identity in Kirinyaga (Brandt) 93

the role of gender on Kirinyaga, and how this might influence one's idea of utopia. The story narrates Koriba's fateful interactions with Kamari, a brilliant young Kikuyu girl. While assisting Koriba at his *boma*, Kamari discovers a book and convinces Koriba to read to her from it. Enthralled Kamari asks to be taught to read, but Koriba forbids it, explaining, "No woman is permitted to read [...]. It is a woman's duty to till the fields and pound the grain and make the fires and weave the fabrics and bear her husband's children" (41–2). Although disappointed, Kamari is not defeated, and eventually she figures out how to use Koriba's computer to not only teach herself how to read, but to also create her own alphabet and language. When Koriba discovers this he forbids her from reading and prevents her from using his computer again. The two argue and, after it is apparent that Kamari will not be able to change Koriba's mind, she kills herself. Next to her body, on a strip of leather inscribed with the symbols of her created language, is the couplet: "I know why the caged birds die — For, like them, I have touched the sky" (61).

Kamari's innocent desire to learn is heartbreaking, and Koriba is not immune to the complexity of this situation. He reasons to himself, "Did I have the right to stand aside and hope that her influence upon our society would be benign when all history suggested that the opposite was more likely to be true? My decision was painful, but it was not a difficult one" (54–5). Despite acknowledging Kamari's brilliance to himself, Koriba remains firm in his belief that no Kikuyu woman be allowed to read. As it is, other than Koriba and a few of the elder men, none of the members of the tribe have this ability. Koriba dismisses reading as a European convention and warns Kamari that, "Reading will make you aware of other ways of thinking and living, and then you will be discontented with your life on Kirinyaga" (43). When she questions the fact that Koriba reads, he explains to Kamari that it is because he is the *mundumugu* and he can distinguish facts from lies. The issue here is the debate over the right to knowledge. In preventing his people from learning to read, Koriba limits their intellect and potential for advancement. This is reminiscent of colonizing tactics used as a means of control. Koriba fears education may make the Kiyuku more critical about their life on Kirinyaga, posing a potential threat to his utopia. Therefore, while Koriba's decision might be painful, since it is ultimately in his own best interest, it is not difficult for him to forbid Kamari and the other Kikuyu from reading.

This incident does not fail to leave an impression on Koriba, though, as it causes him to wonder what his people think about and discuss, considering that they are isolated from ideas and outside influence. The life of the Kikuyu is simple, with clearly defined rules, practices, and divisions of work. As "For I Have Touched the Sky" describes, women bear a large brunt of this labor.

They must tend to the crops as well as maintain the homes and take care of their families. The men are responsible for far less physical labor and have fewer responsibilities overall, but hold a great deal more authority and influence. This gendered discrimination once again questions the idea of a universal utopia on Kirinyaga.

This becomes more obvious when a Kenyan couple immigrates to Kirinyaga. As eager as they are to assimilate, they can never completely become one with the Kikuyu. It is especially difficult for the wife, Wanda, to fit in, as the other women are both jealous of, as well as inspired by, her modern sensibilities. Koriba, threatened by the potential power of this couple to disrupt the stability of Kirinyaga, finds it increasingly difficult to tolerate their presence. Eventually, knowing that Wanda will not agree, he invokes the Kikuyu law that all married women must be circumcised. Unwilling to have this performed, Wanda and her husband return to Earth, but not before she warns, "We are talking about human beings, not animals, and no matter how many rules you make and no matter how many traditions you invoke, you cannot make all human beings think and feel and act alike" (149).

Essentially, Wanda summarizes the greatest problem Koriba faces on Kirinyaga.

In maintaining his vision of utopia it becomes increasingly difficult to control his people to think and feel in exactly the same way as him. Koriba fears that change will corrupt the Kikuyu way of life, but he fails to recognize how subjective the concept of utopia truly is. Discussing "utopia" with his apprentice, Ndemi, Koriba explains,

> To the true Kikuyu, it means to live as one with the land, to respect the ancient laws and rituals, and to please Ngai [...]. You cannot begin to imagine how many millions of men have died because their definition of Utopia differed from their neighbor's [94].

Here Koriba acknowledges that there is no one singular definition of utopia, and that as a result, many wars have been waged because of this. What Koriba fails to recognize, however, is that the Kikuyu is not a single person, but rather a growing population. In idealizing his own vision of utopia, Koriba falls victim to the common mistake of the colonizer by failing to recognize the individuality of his people.

While this was easy for Koriba to suppress an "uprising" from Kamari, a single Kikuyu girl, it becomes more difficult for him to ignore the growing dissent of some of the Kikuyu in the later story "The Lotus and the Spear." In this tale, the sixth chapter in the collection, Koriba is faced with the suicides of a number of young men in the village. Aside from concern over their deaths, this raises an even larger problem for Koriba. He is again forced to question his understanding of utopia, reasoning, "We had built a Utopia here, and to admit that suicides would occur from time to time meant that it was not a Utopia for all our people, which in turn meant that it was not a Utopia at all" (189). This is the dilemma that will plague Koriba throughout *Kirinyaga*. If everyone must be happy for there to be a utopia, then it is a near impossible dream. This brings into question if a collective utopia can ever truly exist, or if perhaps "utopia" is a subjective, singular entity.

In the case of the suicides, the young men killed themselves because their lives lacked meaning. As one young man explains to Koriba,

> Most of them are content, as I said. And why shouldn't they be? The hardest work they were ever forced to do was to nurse at their mothers' breasts? [...]. You have offered them a dream, and they have accepted it [...] I was trained to be a warrior. Therefore, give me a reason to carry my spear, to walk unfettered ahead of my wife when her back is bent under her burden [186–7].

As addressed in earlier stories, the division of labor between the sexes is quite unbalanced on Kirinyaga. Having previously discussed the implications of this on some of the women in the village, in this story Resnick examines the potential effect of this on the men. While most of them are content to spend their days without much of a care, a growing number of young men are driven to suicide by boredom and the realization that on Kirinyaga there is no potential for their lives to ever change. The Kikuyu men were traditionally trained to be warriors, but on Kirinyaga they face no threats. Those that are not married and have no families spend their days in an idleness that becomes increasingly intolerable. Evidently, Kirinyaga is not a utopia for them.

The solution that Koriba devises for this problem is to turn these men into outcasts. Removed from the comforts of the village they must fend for themselves against nature and the elements, finding their own food and shelter. While not a perfect solution, it gives these young men the challenge they seek. It also removes their influence from the rest of the tribe, preventing the possibility of any of them starting an uprising in the village. Although this is a satisfactory compromise, Koriba "cannot help wondering what must become of a society, even a Utopia such as Kirinyaga, where our best and our brightest are turned into outcasts, and all that remains are those who are content to eat the fruit of the lotus" (195). Here even Koriba recognizes the inherent flaw in a utopia that excludes its most promising youth, while those who are content with little knowledge or curiosities flourish. Stagnation is the only means of preserving the utopia he envisions.

The stability that Koriba reinstates after the suicides does not last long. Not unlike the outcasts, Koriba's protégé, Ndemi, too has a growing, inquisitive mind. Koriba had selected the boy to be his apprentice based on Ndemi's intellect and potential, and the boy assists Koriba at his *boma* for many years. After six years of training, Koriba trains Ndemi to use the computer to communicate with Maintenance to adjust the orbital settings of Kirniyaga. In doing so, he exposes Ndemi to technology that introduces him to the outside world, and more specifically the history of Kenya and the Kikuyu. Tensions arise when Ndemi finds that much of this information contradicts what Koriba preaches, and he begins to spread his newfound knowledge throughout the village. Koriba learns of this when he goes to teach the children of the village a lesson about the Kikuyu by telling them a story. Things do not go as Koriba plans when the children challenge what they have been told all their lives. As the children begin to argue with Koriba, one questions him, "He [Ndemi] tells us dates and places, and you [Koriba] speak of wise elephants and foolish lions. It is very hard to decide who is telling the truth" (206). Exposed to differing sources of information for the first time, the children are naturally inquisitive. They are also unsure how to evaluate and process what has been brought into question. Koriba is able to regain control of the situation in this specific instance, but he is unable to prevent Ndemi from continuing to spread what he has learned from the computer.

One of Ndemi's main points of contention is Koriba's storytelling, which is Koriba's primary rhetorical tool for imparting knowledge and ensuring the strength of Kikuyu traditions. As part of his daily duties as *mundumugu*, Koriba often makes time to sit with the children of the village to tell the stories of Ngai and the ancient Kikuyu. Using fables, Koriba both amuses the children but also takes the opportunity to teach them a lesson and explain the reasons behind particular Kikuyu customs. After researching Kenyan and Kikuyu history on the computer, Ndemi finds it difficult to accept Koriba's fables and calls them lies. He further presses Koriba asking:

> "If we do not know how it [history] happened," continued Ndemi, "how can we prevent it from happening again? You tell us stories of our wars against the Maasi, and they are wonderful tales of courage and victory — but according to the computer, we lost every war we ever fought against them. Shouldn't we know that, so if the Maasi ever come to Kirinyaga, we are not deluded into fighting them because of the fables we have heard?" [209].

While it is unlikely that the Maasi, or any other rival tribe of the Kikuyu, would come to Kirinyaga, Ndemi brings up a valid point. Without history or education, what is there to ensure that the same actions and mistakes will not be repeated again? For Koriba, the answer is simple. As long as the Kikuyu hold onto their traditions and customs, ignoring any outside influence, the integrity of the utopia and Kirinyaga will remain intact. What Koriba fails to recognize is the possibility that his version of history might also be false, and could be a misrepresentation that could have equally dire consequences to the Kikuyu.

As was the case before, Koriba runs into a debate over philosophical questions of "truth." Attempting to make Ndemi understand his position he explains, "History is a compilation of facts and events, which is subject to constant reinterpretation. It begins with truth and evolves into fable. My stories begin with fable and evolve into truth" (211). Koriba's wisdom is evident here in his discussion of history, especially when one considers the history of colonization. Facts and events are perpetually reinterpreted, with those in power granted the right to "truth." As such, history itself becomes a fable. Koriba's argument is that by beginning his stories as fable, he is actually removing the "facts" in order to end up with the "truth." The details are not important, but rather the lesson one carries away in the end matters. Koriba hopes that through his storytelling the children will not only learn about the Kikuyu, but also the actual lesson that Koriba intends to impart.

Despite his best efforts, Koriba is unable to convince Ndemi to conform to his way of thinking. Ultimately, Ndemi chooses to leave Kirinyaga, but not before leaving an impression on some of the elders of the community. Koriba finally admits:

> I came to the realization that a Utopia does not lend itself to such tellers of tales. Kirinyaga seemed divided into two totally separate groups: those who were content with their lives and had no need to think, and those whose every thought led them further and further from the society we had labored to build [226–227].

Upon this realization, it is only a matter of time before Koriba's utopia begins to alter before his eyes. Villagers begin to question his ways and disobey his directives without fear. Slowly they begin to make adjustments to their practices and daily routines. Koriba tries to reason with the tribal council and elders, but they no longer are quick to agree with him. In attempting to remind them of the vision of utopia they created, they counter, "If the Kikuyu have not word for it [utopia] and the Europeans do, perhaps it is a European idea [...]. And if we have built our world upon a European idea, perhaps there are other European ideas that we can also use" (217). It is at this time a spacecraft crashes on Kirinyaga necessitating the need for Western medicine and a doctor sent by Maintenance. Once the Kikuyu see the power of this "magic," Koriba loses credibility and eventually decides to abandon Kirinyaga.

Koriba's decision to leave Kirinyaga is not an easy one. The question over what constitutes a utopia becomes central in the time leading up to his departure. He questions, "Was it possible that a true Utopia could not outlast the generation that founded it, that it was the nature of man to reject the values of the society into which he is born, even when those values are sacred?" (227). These questions reveal a theme of the overarching narrative of *Kirinyaga*, where the development of the settlement eventually becomes an experiment in the possibility of an existence of utopia. For a time, Koriba believes he had achieved a utopia, however, as the stories progress, he continually faces resistance and has to defend himself and his beliefs. Further, while Koriba may for a time experience his own utopia, it is doubtful if this vision is experienced and shared by all on Kirinyaga. Ultimately it is Koinnage, paramount chief of Kirinyaga, who explains to Koriba, "Your day — and mine — has passed. Perhaps, for a fleeting second, we did achieve Utopia — but that second is gone, and the new moments and hours require new Utopias" (253). The one that came before it will influence each subsequent generation, and it is inevitable that changes will occur. Their needs will be different and, therefore, society and culture will need to adapt and change even in a utopia.

In the epilogue of *Kirinyaga*, "The Land of Nod," Koriba's return to Kenya results in an epiphany. He muses, "The thing that I had not realized is that a society can be a Utopia for only an instant — once it reaches a state of perfection it cannot change and still be a Utopia, and it is the nature of societies to grow and evolve" (284). He finally understands that a *society* cannot be a utopia and that a utopia is not something that can be achieved on a grand scale. With this insight, he heads off alone to Mt. Kirinyaga, and the tale ends with Koriba embarking on a search for utopia again. The difference is this time he sets off with the realization that it must be a personal utopia, and that for him this can only be achieved on the individual level by staying true to one's own convictions without compromise.

The fate of Koriba is left ambiguous, and as with the rest of the text, it is up to the reader to decide whether he will achieve his goal. Just like the fables of Ngai and the Kikuyu that Koriba tells, *Kirinyaga* is, as Resnick calls it, a "fable of utopia." The tradition of science fiction becomes a device for exploring the legacy of postcolonialism by extrapolating recent and current events to a distant time and place. This removal allows for an examination of the consequences of colonization on both the oppressor and the oppressed. And through the character of Koriba, the complexities of cultural relativism and ethnocentrism are revealed. Further, *Kirinyaga* forces readers to reevaluate the notion of utopia, asking not only if a utopia can exist, but also should we even want one to? Whether Resnick answers these questions through the fates of Koriba and Kirinyaga is open to debate. More than anything, *Kirinyaga* demonstrates the complexities of science fiction and postcolonialism and the rhetorical and ethical dialogue that can result when the two are put into conversation.

Notes

1. Associated with SF editor and publisher John W. Campbell, the "Golden Age of Science Fiction" is the period from the late 1930s to the mid-1950s where science fiction gained increased popularity and prominence in popular culture. Many "classic" science fiction narratives were created in this period, which put an emphasis on technological advances and space exploration.

Work Cited

Resnick, Mike. *Kirinyaga: A Fable of Utopia.* New York: Ballantine, 1998.

7

The Frontier Myth and Racial Politics

Ángel Mateos-Aparicio Martín-Albo

> Mars was the challenge we needed.... No easy challenge, but its difficulties might have united the race. We needed union, needed a common goal, needed a total devotion to something greater than ourselves.
>
> We might have found our future on Mars. A new frontier, demanding new technologies, it could have created the genius to invent them. Demanding greatness, it would have made common man heroic. Demanding sacrifice, it could have revealed the splendor of the human spirit.
>
> Jack Williamson, Beachhead

> Others may need new frontiers, but Mars is still a frontier in itself. Mars is young but strong. We can grow, and will grow, to our own maturity in our own time.
>
> Greg Bear, Moving Mars

> Millions on Earth wanted to come to Mars, to the "new frontier," where life was an adventure again: waiting lists for emigration both real and fake were massively oversubscribed.
>
> Kim Stanley Robinson, Red Mars

> Conquest? Jamie's mind flashed pictures of the white man's conquest of America. That's not what we're here for. Nobody's going to conquer Mars.
>
> Ben Bova, Mars

Federations of Planets and Other Post-National Fantasies

As the place for speculation about the future and for the expression of utopian ideas, science fiction (SF) has often envisioned imaginary scenarios where all the countries, nations and races of the world coexist peacefully under one unified global government. In these fictional future universes, individual states have been superseded by supra- or post-national political entities that bring an end to competition and conflicts among different human groups, in order to establish a new era of global cooperation and a new "Enlightenment." These imaginary world states already appear in early examples of science fiction and are the genre's response to what it perceived as a cultural preoccupation with the world's political division in different nations that are often in open conflict. The goal of achieving planetary political unity already appears in pioneering SF writers like H.G. Wells, who used his stories to promote the creation of the League of Nations, of which he was a strong supporter. Although many SF works coincide with the belief that humans invariable advance towards global political unity as a consequence of the evolution towards a higher degree of civilization, other SF pieces have envisioned supranational political entities in negative terms, because far from being the result of cooperation, these imaginary planetary states reenact the dreams of global dominance that pushes imperialism. So H.G. Wells's hope for the world's political unity finds its counterpart in famous dystopian novels like George Orwell's *1984* (1948) and Philip K. Dick's *The Man in the High Castle* (1962), where the planet is divided into two or three political blocks that wage continuous war against each other. In these cases, supranational alliances have merely substituted existent nations but not the mentality on which national states are based, and they become the higher expression of the old policy of joining efforts against other human beings. Nevertheless, SF rarely accepts it own speculations unquestioningly. Another version of this interpretation of supranational political organization as oppressive and hegemonic has appeared in more recent SF: the multi- or transnational company. These global economic conglomerates are typical of cyberpunk, and account for the concentration of all economic and political power by international firms which are often beyond the control of national states and can therefore dominate and exploit the planet at will in cyberpunk's gloomy visions of the future.[1]

Nevertheless, the fabled models of global political organization have not been set exclusively on our planet. SF often assumes that planetary unity is the logical result of civilization and progress, and consequently believes that the creation of a global state on Earth will only be a matter of time. The fictional universe therefore offers many examples of (inter)planetary political structures. Intergalactic space travelers frequently find global political entities in control of planets and even whole galaxies. These planetary or interplanetary states replicate the relationships among nations to be found in human history, and tend to draw a clear line between political entities created by violence and those attained by voluntary (or democratic) alliance. The former are the epitome of repressive and totalitarian expansionist states, and are very often represented by galactic empires (perhaps with the exception of Asimov's empire in the *Foundation* novels). The latter owe their popularity to film and television series like *Star Wars* and *Star Trek*, where federations of planets appear as models of democratic and inclusive political entities. According to this model of coexistence, civilization and progress will bring about the peaceful coexistence among all the peoples, races and species not only to Earth, but to the whole universe.

It is quite obvious, though, that notions like "federations of planets" and "melting pots" as imagined, for instance, in the *Star Trek* series, are not free from a very specific cultural bias. As a representative of American SF, the *Star Trek* films and TV series clearly suggest that the idea of an intergalactic melting pot is regarded as a continuation of the United States' own defining elements. In fact, the imagery surrounding space travel is often inspired by the American national mythology of exploration and conquest of the unknown territories of the West. After all, as the well-known voice-over introduction to the *Star Trek* films and television series argues, space is the "final frontier."

In this sense, planet federations seem to endlessly reenact the myth of the Conquest of the West and the incorporation of new territories and peoples into the U.S. federal political structure. Similarly, it would be possible to argue that these intergalactic melting pots (re)produce the racial policies applied in the Western frontier: The multiracial crew of starship *Enterprise* may serve as an example of Earth's (and the United States') mixed population that confronts different extraterrestrial beings (warlike Klingons, expansionist Borgs) which fill the position of complete otherness/alienness previously occupied by Native Americans in stories about the Conquest of the West. Furthermore, it is also quite significant that although interplanetary federations are said to be willing to include all races and species at a general or abstract level, there are virtually no references to how this mixture of cultures and races generates cultural and/or ethnic hybridization. In fact, this lack of mixed-race (or mixed-species) characters affects SF in general, and is more relevant if we take into account that the human-computer consciousness, artificially created humans and human-machine hybrids like the cyborg are common in the genre. The cyborg, for instance, has been read as a creature that could bring an end to the opposition between genders (Haraway).

It is reasonable to presume that the typical citizen of a post-national, multicultural and multiracial global (or even intergalactic) political organization is likely to be of mixed race and culture, and the reason why these hybrids do not appear more often in SF stories dealing with encounters with aliens is precisely what this article will try to discuss by using theoretical notions like the "mestiza consciousness," proposed by postcolonial Chicana writer Gloria Anzaldúa (1999), and a series of SF novels about the colonization of Mars that speculate about the cultural, sociological, ideological and political implications of the human settlement on Mars and show evident signs of the influence of the myth of the American West. The fictional colonization of Mars is permeated by Western frontier imagery, since Edgar Rice Burroughs created a whole Martian mythology based on his experience in the Indian wars at beginning of the twentieth century. The first section of this essay is therefore dedicated to the analysis of the symbolic relationship between the Martian landscape and the deserts of the U.S. Southwest, the same harsh conditions historian Frederic Jackson Turner considered the origin of the American democratic and egalitarian (meaning free of social, cultural and national prejudices) ideal. Then the discussion will focus on the representation of Martians in Ray Bradbury's novel *The Martian Chronicles* (1951), published at a time when the vision of Indians in American culture was also changing. This discussion will create the background for the central topic of this paper, that is, the analysis of a Red Man in the red planet: Jamie Waterman, the protagonist of Ben Bova's Mars trilogy, who is half–Indian. His "Indianness" (or rather, his mixed racial heritage) is a continuous issue in the novels that make up Bova's trilogy about the colonization of Mars: *Mars* (1992), *Return to Mars* (1999) and *Mars Life* (2008). Waterman could stand as the hybrid that reconciles the Indians in American history and the "mestizo" that anticipates the future of humans in a post-national, multicultural and multiracial society. The comparison of Bova's trilogy with virtually contemporary novels which describe the colonization of Mars as a multinational effort, like Kim Stanley Robinson's Mars trilogy and Greg Bear's *Moving Mars* (1993), will also prove useful to better understand the quality of Bova's main character. Finally, the final part of the paper will evaluate Bova's mixed-race protagonist in the light of Anzaldúa's notion of "mestiza." Born and raised in the U.S. territory (the Southwest) where the confrontation with the alien is nowadays more significant, this Chicana writer and critic has substituted the image of the frontier as a limit or horizon (which implies separation and expansion) with an idea of "borderlands," a space for cultural and racial hybridization and transgression. In Anzaldúa's melting pot, races and cultures do not merely coexist; they actually mix to create something new. For this writer and critic that the future of the U.S. society and of humanity in general lies in cultural and racial hybridization, and the "New Mestiza" is precisely the mythical figure that assimilates and adapts different cultural and racial origins to create a new general human consciousness.

Immense Canyons and Vast Plains: Mars as the Space of the Final Frontier

When in 1961 President J.F. Kennedy identified space as the new American frontier, he was merely certifying what was already apparent in American culture: that the conquest of space, actually a by-product of the Cold War, had been progressively assimilated in the imagery and ideological implications of one of the most persistent myths of American culture. After Kennedy's famous speech, the American space program became a unifying objective that pushed the country towards a spectacular victory when the American astronauts first landed on the Moon. As a recycled symbol of national destiny, the exploration of space became thus a successful substitute of the old frontier myth probably because it had a double expression that reinforced its mythical qualities. On the one hand, space travel was a reality thanks to American technology; on the other, SF literature, films and television series contributed to the cultural presence of this reality by adding exciting — and stylish — stories, characters, and adventures to the limited dramatic possibilities of actual space travel, like westerns had done before. The connections between the real and the fictional exploration of space in American culture are quite evident: one NASA shuttle was re-named *Enterprise* after *Star Trek*'s renowned starship due to a public write-in campaign.[2] The frontier myth has therefore permeated SF to the point of becoming virtually inescapable, as many critics have already pointed out.[3]

As articulated by historian Frederick Jackson Turner in his well-known essay "The Frontier in American History" (1893), the frontier myth was based on a symbolic reading of the landscape of the U.S. West which presumably had a decisive impact on the formation of American character. Turner suggested that the rugged individualism, strong democratic convictions and radical egalitarian thinking that distinguished Americans had been the result of the confrontation with the harsh conditions of the wilderness during the colonization of the Western territories of the U.S. (Turner 1–39). The frontier stories will therefore always be associated with the most striking geological elements of the West: the empty wilderness, vast plains, high mountain ridges, deep canyons and scorched deserts. In this sense, no other extraterrestrial setting has proved as convenient for the reproduction of the geological elements normally associated with the frontier myth as the red planet. The Martian landscape is also one of vast empty plains, profound canyons and dry, rocky deserts, which continuously evoke the American West. Furthermore, unlike the cold blackness and empty immensity of deep space, Martian geology offers recognizable landmarks easily associated with the typical western scenery.

7. The Frontier Myth and Racial Politics (Martín-Albo)   105

The novels about the colonization of the red planet have been well aware of this similarity between the Martian landscape and the scenery of the American West. In fact, it was Edgar Rice Burroughs who first established this connection in fiction, when he made his hero John Carter travel from a cave in Arizona to the red planet in his novel *A Princess of Mars* (1912). The transition comes right after a detailed description of the Arizona scenery which focuses on some of the typical elements of western landscapes:

> Few western wonders are more inspiring than the beauties of an Arizona moonlit landscape; the silvered mountains in the distance, the strange lights and shadows upon hog back and arroyo, and the grotesque details of the stiff, yet beautiful cacti from a picture at once enchanting and inspiring; as though one were catching for the first time a glimpse of some dead and forgotten world, so different is it from the aspect of any other spot upon our earth [12].

Later novels about the red planet would continue this tendency to treat the Martian and Western landscapes as equivalent. In Ray Bradbury's *The Martian Chronicles* (1951), Lewis Shiner's *Frontera* (1984), Jack Williamson's *Beachhead* (1992), Kim Stanley Robinson's *Red Mars* (1993) and Ben Bova's *Mars* (1993) it is easy to find examples of this equivalence. In Shiner's and Robinson's novels, the association between the Martian and the typical American Western scenery are obvious and focus on the inspiring feelings of the contemplation of desert land. When describing the main character's impression after landing on Mars, Shiner writes: "The land was more subtly alien than the cold white dust of Deimos, warmer, more like the deserts of northern New Mexico or Arizona" (90). Similarly, Robinson's first explorers have the same reaction when contemplating the loneliness of the Martian landscape:

> Boone said, "When I was there before, I got the impression that it was already Earthlike."
> "Except two hundred degrees Kelvin," Russell said.
> "Sure, but it *looked* like the Mojave, or the Dry Valleys. The first time I looked around Mars I found myself keeping an eye out for one of those mummified seals we saw in the Dry Valleys" [*Red Mars* 40].

Robinson's Mars trilogy (*Red Mars* [1993], *Green Mars* [1994], and *Blue Mars* [1996]) is a long narrative of the arrival, settlement and transformation of the Mars for a period of over two hundred years. The enterprise begins as a Russian/American project, but it soon becomes a multinational effort. The American frontier is the symbolic and ideological framework in which the colonization of Mars develops. At the end of the trilogy, the "new" Martians become independent from Earth after a revolution and give themselves a radically democratic and egalitarian constitution that allows them to construct a mosaic of complex political systems coexisting with each other and a multicultural social structure. Robinson's novels explicitly recognize the connection between these Martian geographical features and the American cultural imagery. Seen through the eyes of one of the Russian members of the expedition, "[t]he outflow of canyons and the high land between them reminded Nadia of the landscape of American cowboy movies, with its washes and mesas and isolated ship rocks" (*Red Mars* 183). Furthermore, Robinson also acknowledges the similarity between his epic and the frontier myth also in symbolic and ideological terms, as this quotation shows: "That was Mars as the twenty-second century began; with the elevator returned they were back to the old gold rush mentality, it seemed, as if it really were a manifest destiny, out on the frontier with great tools wielded left and right" (*Green Mars* 218).

By contrast, in Bradbury's and Williamson's novels, the similarity between Mars and the American West does not rely so much on the description of the physical features of the landscape, but on the mental connection established by the characters, who clearly experience the colonization of Mars as a reenactment of the U.S. expansion to the West. In *The Martian Chronicles*, the similarity between Earth and Mars is treated ironically, with the intention of making the reader realize and be shocked in their own naive expectations. Bradbury's explorers find in Mars a town so similar to one real American municipality that is indistinguishable from it: "This town out here looks very peaceful and cool, and so much like Green Bluff, Illinois, that it frightens me. It's too *much* like Green Bluff" (52). The situation becomes comical when the astronauts try to establish contact with the natives, who claim: "This [...] is Green Bluff, Illinois, on the continent of America [...] on a place called the world, or, sometimes, the Earth. Go away now. Goodbye" (56). Likewise, the main character of Williamson's *Beachhead* is a Texan named Sam Houston Kelligan who carries his frontier spirit and ideology to the red planet. While training for the journey to Mars he has to remind himself of the fact that he is coming to a new land which requires a different mentality: "His spirits lifted when he began to glimpse the brown-and-green checkerboard plains of West Texas giving way to the naked gray New Mexico mountains and the promise of space. *All that's past and gone*, he urged himself. *Think Mars!*" (76). In the same way, Ben Bova's novel *Mars* uses both the direct reference to the similarity between Martian and Western geography and the characters' reaction to the Martian landscape. The description of the red planet immediately recalls one of the most famous sites in the U.S. West: "Mars. Picture Death Valley at its worst. Barren desert. Nothing but rock and sand" (21). This affinity between the two landscapes and the two colonizing experiences (Bova's explorers will find an extinct cliff-dwelling civilization) is reinforced by the fact that the protagonist, Jamie Waterman, is a half–Navaho Indian, familiar with the scenery of the Navaho reservations in New Mexico and northern Arizona. Through the eyes of this character, the association between Mars and the typical western landscape is evident and ever-present: "Standing out in the open, Jamie realized once more how much Mars reminded him of the rocky, mountainous desert of northwestern New Mexico" (77).

What this dual referential background implies, then, is that the arid deserts, enormous canyons and vast dry plains of the Martian landscape do not merely recall the landscape of the U.S. West, but also the symbolic framework of the imagery of the American frontier. The fictional colonization of the red planet creates an extraterrestrial setting in order to test the ideological implications of the new frontier by revisiting and evaluating the previous assumptions of the frontier myth, which include Turner's ideological and political reading. In most novels about Martian settlements, the tough conditions of the Martian landscape are expected to raise a number of issues related to individual freedom, the social and political structure and the question of utopia. The exploration and conquest of the red planet repeats the political implications of the American expansion towards the West: the Earth becomes the decadent, aristocratic location for freedom-restricting political systems, like those of the old European colonial empires, whereas Mars turns into the planet of liberty and individual fulfillment, like the American Western territories. This outline of the "Old World" as the place for oppressive regimes and "New World" as the land of freedom also happens, for instance, in Williamson's novel when the Martian settlers declare independence from Earth, creating the "Mars Republic" (363), but also in Robinson's trilogy, where the radical democratic and independent nature of the first settlers causes a revolution against domination from Earth. Other novels follow the same pattern: Robert L. Forward's *The Martian Rainbow* (1991) narrates an independence war between Mars and the Earth, a planet led by an egomaniac religious dictator, and Greg Bear's *Moving Mars*, where the conflict between the Martians' desire for independence and the Earth's traditional policy of domination of the Solar System is resolved by the Martians' cutting all contact with the "mother" planet and moving to a new, completely unknown and alien location.

The novels about the exploration and conquest of Mars thus become the perfect fictional setting for the reenactment, analysis and revision of the cultural and ideological implications of the frontier myth in American culture. Following Turner's interpretation of the myth, the Martian landscape, the new wilderness, and the difficulties for settling on Mars should be the basis for the creation of a new society based on the principles of individual freedom and democracy. Martian settlers would therefore develop a new egalitarian society, a new cultural composite, and a new post-national identity that could on its turn function as a model for Earth's global consciousness. Mars could thus turn into a new "melting pot," that is, a new location for the utopian creation of a human society where the questions of race, class, gender and nationality were substituted by one common goal: the colonization of new territories (a planet, the galaxies).[4] In order to achieve this, the Martian settlers would have to forget their nations and cultures of origin, and produce and follow their own version of "destiny." As Jamie Waterman, the protagonist of Ben Bova's trilogy, states: "Mars has tested us. Each and every one of us. None of us is the same person we were when we arrived here" (*Mars* 545).

Nevertheless, the identification of the Martian landscape with the symbolic, cultural and ideological coordinates of the American frontier myth implies that the novels about the colonization of Mars also incorporate issues left unresolved by the classical view of the Conquest of the West: the exploitation of natural resources in the name of progress and the question of the rights of the native inhabitants of this "wilderness." The vast deserts and monumental canyons of the red planet become the natural spaces in their pristine origin to be protected from human exploitation, and the diverse living organisms imagined by the writers stand for the Indians adapted to survive in this environment. Not all novels about the colonization of Mars envision the existence of biological life on the red planet, but when they do, these creatures, whether intelligent or not, tend to find themselves in a position of otherness similar to the one occupied by Indians in the traditional version of the American West. Moreover, they also repeat the stereotype of the "good" or "bad" Indian. In this sense, it is possible to trace the characteristics of the Martians in relation to the evolution of the representation of the Indian in American culture.

Red Men in the Red Planet

Ben Bova's trilogy about the colonization of Mars consists of three novels, *Mars* (1992), *Return to Mars* (1999) and *Mars Life* (2008),[5] which recount the initial steps of the human settlement on the red planet. The main connection between the three novels is the half–Indian protagonist. James Waterman is a half–Navaho, half–Anglo geologist sent in the first expedition who becomes the leader of the exploration of the red planet. "Indianness" is often a racial and political issue, and it is his Indian intuition that presses him to the greatest discovery of Bova's trilogy: the remains of an extinct Martian civilization. Although other characters make fun of this kind of Indian sixth sense (in the second novel, Dex Trumball, a companion in the second expedition, mocks him: "Injun scout know-um territory, uh?" [*Return* 77]), Jamie follows his instinct to discover Martian cliff-dwellings similar to those existent in the New Mexico territory of his ancestors. Waterman is not only the pride of the Navaho nation, but also a strong defender of the frontier spirit, as these words show: "The frontier is where new knowledge comes from, whether it's the intellectual frontier of a laboratory or the physical frontier of an unexplored territory" (*Life* 113). In this sense, Bova's protagonist is designed to signify the reconciliation of the Anglo pioneering spirit and the achievements of Western civilization with the spiritual qualities and the close relationship with nature attributed to Native Americans. The description of his ancestry is revealing in this sense: his Navaho father is an expert in the history of Native American tribes, who lived in "the insulated life of academia" (*Mars* 103), while his mother's family history can be traced back to the first American colonists:

> Lucille Monroe Waterman was a small woman, pert and beautiful, who had been born to the considerable wealth of an old New England family that had dated itself back to the *Mayflower*. The first time her family had allowed her to venture west of the Hudson River was the summer she had spent on a dude ranch in the mountains of northern New Mexico. There she had met Jerome Waterman, a young Navaho fiercely intent on becoming a teacher of history [*Mars* 103].

As this quotation shows, Jamie Waterman's identity stands midway between the East Coast and the West, between the wealthy and the virtually dispossessed social classes, and between a pragmatic view of reality and the intellectual world of academics. With these antecedents, Waterman can be described as the perfect citizen in the American "melting pot" and seems destined to become the first human to adapt to the Martian environment. His mixed origin therefore plays an essential role in his inclination for new frontiers and challenges.

Nevertheless, the positive connotations of Jamie Waterman's Indian ancestry in Bova's trilogy are the result of a constant re-writing of the clear identification of Martians with Indians to be found in several earlier novels about the exploration of Mars, the most evident and the best known of which is probably Edgar Rice Burroughs' Barsoom novels, as Abbot has pointed out (19–20). Burroughs published the first of his ten Martian novels, *A Princess of Mars*, in 1912, where he created the adventure formula he repeated in later books. His hero, Captain John Carter, "a gentleman of Virginia," travels from Arizona, where he was prospecting and fighting with the Apache, to the red planet, where he finds a whole new compendium of enemies which resemble the variety of Indian tribes in the West. The similarity between Martian and Indian tribes is manifest for John Carter:

> All were mounted upon the small domestic bull thoats of the red Martians, and their trappings and ornamentation bore such a quantity of gorgeously colored

feathers that I could not but be struck with the startling resemblance the concourse bore to a band of the red Indians of my own Earth [Burroughs 148].

Burroughs used his experience with the Apache in the Arizona Territory, where he had been sent as a soldier in 1896,[6] as a basis for the beginning of John Carter's adventures on Mars, and the identification of his fabled Martians with Indians reveals his conception of Native Americans and uncivilized warlike tribes. John Carter's violent dealings with green, yellow and red Martians uncovers Burroughs' attitude towards the Indians: the superiority of the white race (and Anglo civilization) is well established even in an imaginary Martian environment where violence and cruelty are common. When discussing their cultural differences with a group of Martians, John Carter states: "As you know I am not of Barsoom; your ways are not my ways, and I can only act in the future as I have in the past, in accordance with the dictates of my conscience and guided by the standards of my own people" (Burroughs 66).[7]

Burroughs's Barsoom novels illustrate the beliefs and values that had spread throughout the young republic during the Conquest of the West, and that became national symbols, as Turner showed in his articulation of the frontier myth. Nevertheless, even at the time Turner launched his idea, the myth of the American frontier was ceasing to exist in reality as the expansion to the West and the incorporation of new states into the Union was progressively shutting down the idea of "wilderness," as Gary Westfahl explains (1). According to Westfahl, the definitive end of the American frontier in the 1940s and 50s coincided with a period where cultural productions like films were inclined to represent the frontier in its prime, as if the mythical qualities of the frontier in American culture were reinforced by the nostalgia for its absence (2). This classical vision of the western, however, coincided with the first voices that began to criticize what had happened on the frontier from the perspective of the non–white population. As Westfahl suggests, "[t]he problem is that the frontier myth itself has become increasingly unappealing.... As we now realize, the American Conquest of the frontier looks like a quite different story from the viewpoint of Native Americans" (3).

The irruption of the Indian perspective on the vision of the frontier myth also had its consequences on cultural productions. The novels about the colonization of Mars written in the forties and fifties show the marks of both the insistence on the classical version of the myth as well as of the first attacks against the stereotypical representation of the Indians as "savages." Thus while novels like Cyril Judd's *Outpost Mars* (1951) and Lester Del Rey's *Police Your Planet* (1956) still depicted Martian colonies exactly as typical American frontier towns where all the settlers were losing their old identities to become "Martian" (and therefore become good frontier citizens in Turner's terms) and where there was not the slightest mention of native inhabitants (which recalls the invisibility of the American Indians in the West), other writers like Robert Heinlein imagined Mars in one of his early novels (*Red Planet* [1949]) as a place for frontier communities that coexisted with a mild version of native Martians. Heinlein's vision of the Martians in this novel resembles the idea of the "noble savage" and attributes them the patience, peacefulness, loyalty and spirituality of positive stereotypical representations of Indians. With an extremely generous attitude, the benevolent Martians of the story finally allow Earth's colonists to remain on the red planet, although they have the power to destroy them all. At the end of the story, there is a recognition of the difficulties to overcome racial and cultural difference, but at the same time an understanding that the natives to Mars had their rights even if they did not use the planet in the same way:

> "I can't," said Marlowe. "I'm satisfied that you managed to negotiate an agreement that permits us to stay on Mars. I suppose it will be years before we understand the Martians."
> "You are putting it mildly, Jamie. The white man was still studying the American Indian, trying to find out what makes him tick, five hundred years after Columbus — and the Indian and the European are both *men*, like as two peas. These are *Martians*" [Heinlein 227].

It is interesting to see in this quotation how the racial prejudices that separated Indians and Europeans are finally overcome when the presence of a third alien, the Martian, produces the realization that the racial and cultural differences between Europeans and Indians are minimal in comparison. What racial theorists had denied for a long time is here finally accepted: both Indians and European are "men" (recognition of the Indians' humanity) and similar as "two peas," that is, equal.

The change of perspective is complete in *The Martian Chronicles*, where some of Ray Bradbury's stories[8] envisage Mars from the perspective of its native inhabitants just before the first explorers from Earth came. Seeing Mars from this point of view allows Bradbury to create a poetic and utopian vision of the Martians and of the Martian landscape which increases the sense of loss when that civilization is destroyed by the human colonists. Crystal houses which produce golden fruit, dreamlike landscapes, metal books with hieroglyphs that play music when touched with the fingers, blue-topped hills and canals full of wine are just some examples of Bradbury's imaginary vision of Martians. This idyllic setting is suddenly disturbed by the arrival of the men from Earth, which accelerates the extinction of an already dying race. Bradbury's novel is full of similar examples of the devastation of a Native Martian culture which can be identified with the destruction of the Indian tribes by pioneers and settlers in the American West, although we do not have time to discuss them at length here.[9]

The possibility of seeing the frontier through the eyes of Native Americans, and the recognition of the great value, and even of the superiority of Indian culture constitute an alternative vision of the frontier myth which Slotkin calls "the Cult of the Indian" (629). The Indian began to symbolize a more spiritual bond to nature that served as a contrast to the exploitation by Western civilization, while the image of the stoic and peaceful Indian was a counterpart to the aggressive behavior of cowboys and gunfighters. In this sense, Ben Bova's half–Navaho protagonist may be considered as the epitome of this alternative representation of the Indian. In fact, the novel makes it quite clear that his affinity with the red planet and the intuition that thrusts him forward to discover the city of an extinct Martian civilization are qualities coming to be found in his Indianness, and not in the rationalistic mentality inherited from his Anglo ancestry:

> How like the desert homeland of the People, he thought. Rusty sand and red rocks, steep-walled mesas off by the horizon. He almost expected to see footprints out there, the trail of his ancestors.
> Nonsense! his Anglo mind scoffed [*Return* 68].

Intuitive knowledge, spirituality, proverbial patience, all these qualities are attributed to his Indian half, and in several occasions Waterman often plays the role of the stoical Indian, as his grandfather advised him when dealing with Anglos:

> Jamie took a deep breath and felt a calm warmth flow through him. He heard his grandfather's gentle laughter. "Never lose your temper with a customer," his grandfather had told him years ago.... "Let 'em whoop and holler, it don't matter. Once they calm down, they're so ashamed of themselves that they buy twice what they started out to buy, just to show they're sorry" [*Return* 320].

The most evident example of Waterman's conformity with the alternative image of the Indian is surely his commitment with the protection of the Martian environment against the attempts of white businessmen to begin the economic exploitation of the planet. In an ironic reversal of the strategies used by Anglos to appropriate land occupied by Indians, Waterman convinces the Navaho nation to claim utilization rights to the red planet, with the intention of keeping the planet in its original, natural condition. Dex Trumball, another of the expedition members, considers this move by Waterman as a payback to the white man, which he thinks is very funny: "The Indians pull a land steal on the white men! Wow!" (*Return* 499).

In terms of symbolic stance and ideological connotations, Jamie Waterman's "Indianness" is therefore a calculated move by Ben Bova, as the previous discussion shows. The continuous references to his racial ancestry have to be understood in the wider context of the traditional identification of the colonization of Mars with the American Conquest of the West. As the protagonist of the exploration of the red planet, Waterman stands for the retrieval of Native Americans and of their role in the frontier in the formation of the United States of America. His spirituality and his defense of the Martian environment are studied character traits designed to counter Anglo individualism, materialism and disrespect for nature. At the same time, Waterman's achievements indicate the recognition of minority groups in the United States, as well as a support for affirmative action in minority rights. Initial criticism by colleagues in the first expedition ("you can get on the first team because you're an Indian.... But being a red man hasn't hurt you with NASA" [*Mars* 8]) proves unjustified when compared with Waterman's prowess and success as explorer.

This concentration of positive qualities in Waterman, however, may result in a simplistic reduction leading also to the stereotypical representation of Indians as "noble savages." As Homi Bhabha explains (82), Western culture had oscillated between the representation of other people as savages and loyal servants. According to Bhabha, it is this thinking in dual terms that has to be superseded. The stereotype, as a means of domination of the Other, may also create what seems to be a positive image of the Other but is in fact a summary of the things considered corrupt by western standards. As Montaigne did in his famous essay "On Cannibals," the alternative vision of American Indians promoted by the criticism of the classic frontier myth could also be subverting reality. In this sense, the description of Jamie Waterman as intuitive, spiritual, and patient may well be a vision of the Indian idealized by Anglo culture, and therefore another stereotypical representation, that is, another version of the "noble savage." Spirituality and intuition could be qualities that respond to a set of values programmed by a western culture that has put too much emphasis on rationality and practicality. Similarly, his own identification with the frontier attitude could be a sign not of rebellion but of assimilation to western ideology. In a conversation with Vosnesensky, a Russian member of the first expedition to Mars, Waterman has to admit his adaptation to the notion of the American "melting pot":

"I'm not much of an Indian," Jamie replied. "I was brought up to be a white man."
"But you are not white."
"No, not entirely.... In the States we have people from every part of the world — all the nationalities of Europe, Asians, Africans" [*Mars* 235].

Furthermore, in the second novel Waterman has to compete for leadership with Dex Trumball, a character that conforms to the American pioneer/cowboy type, an aggressively individualistic and enterprising young man, son of Darryl C. Trumball, the typical "self-made" businessman so celebrated in American culture. In order to respond to Dex's pushing manners, Waterman acquires the personal traits usually associated with the frontiersman: initiative and individualism. He tells Dex: "Here on Mars it doesn't count who your father is or what happened back on Earth. Here on Mars the only thing that counts is what you can accomplish" (*Return* 51). He also warns Dex: "I'm part Navaho.... I'm rugged" (*Return* 64), using the very word often connected with pioneers and cowboys.[10] The second expedition psychologist, V.J. Shektar, explains the similarity between Dexs and Jamie in terms suspiciously influenced by social darwinism: "I told you [Dex] was an alpha male.... Same as you are" (*Return* 227).

Waterman's character therefore moves inside this duality between the good Indian and the determined frontiersman, probably symbolized by his double lineage, as explained above. This multiple inheritance, in addition to his love for (and adaptation to) Mars, understood as a new frontier for humanity, qualifies him as the perfect citizen of the multinational "melting pot" colonization is expected to create the red planet. All the novels about the human settlement on Mars share the idea that the project is too big for one nation, and therefore requires international collaboration, and, as a consequence, the improvement of international relations. Whether it is just a Soviet-American enterprise, as it happens in Lewis Shiner's *Frontera*, a kind of first world alliance, as it is the case in Williamson's *Beachhead* and in Forward's *Martian Rainbow*, or a truly multinational adventure, as in Bear's *Moving Mars* and Bova's and Robinson's trilogies, the result is often a multicultural society, forged in the melting pot of the red wilderness. Members of the new Martian society should hence forget their national, racial and cultural differences, and work together to overcome the difficult conditions of the red planet. In this sense, the figure of Jamie Waterman can be interpreted as an example of a willing adaptation to the new environment. Already a product of the American melting pot, Waterman could stand as the model of the assimilation of a double inheritance and creation of a new, multiple, post-racial and post-national identity. In short, his mixed origin could be read as the epitome of the future of the human race in a progressively globalized society. Waterman would be the perfect citizen of the red melting pot.

Citizens of the Red Melting Pot

The whole notion of "melting pot" can be safely applied to the Martian societies imagined in Greg Bear's *Moving Mars*, as well as in Robinson's and

Bova's Martian trilogies. As it has already been said, the exploration of space in general, and the project of the colonization of Mars in particular cannot help presenting alternative versions of the American myth of origin in the American mind, because the new frontier continuously evokes an idealized self-image. In this sense, the novels mentioned above might imagine the frontier scenarios on Mars differently, but they all establish a connection with the American past. Greg Bear is perhaps the most radical and pessimistic, because he assumes Martians will never be free from the influence of a decadent Earth. This writer envisions Martian political structure as something similar to a controlled anarchy, a mosaic of independent communities of settlers organized in "Binding Multiples" (extended families). The idea of a central Martian government is considered only as an option to counter Earth's domination with the strength provided by unity. However, once the threat of Earth's invasion is over, Mars would return to its original minimal political organization, as Casseia Najumdar, the novel's narrator and protagonist, explains: "With Many Hills [the Martian capital] gone, and Ti Sandra and much of the legislature dead, there was no government, no Republic.... Martians talked vaguely of returning to normal, but the instinctive pattern of society was the family, the station, the Binding Multiple; nothing else had yet had chance to take root" (Bear 440). So Mars remains a kind of idyllic frontier utopia in which the centers of political power were simply small communities of settlers united by family ties, free from the complexities of Earth's politics.

Robinson also imagines an anarchic mosaic of isolated communities as the result of multinational immigration from Earth. Arab nomads and Swiss enclosed cities coexist with a myriad of political and social structures throughout his trilogy. As it happens in Bear's *Moving Mars*, this decentralized political structure is possible because Mars remains a frontier territory, still not densely populated, distant and barely accessible from Earth, which means that the exploitation of its natural resources is slow. Both Bear's and Robinson's frontier melting pots are populated by new human (or even posthuman) types, which vary from religious fanatics to artificial intelligences, treated like free human beings. These postnational utopias, however, show a significant lack: Martians constitute a mixture of nationalities, cultures, professions, etc., but there are no evident references to racial questions in Bear's or Robinson's novels. Either they assume the question of race has already been overcome in their future societies, or they are not thinking in racial terms at all.[11]

Nevertheless, it is logical to expect that a multicultural, post-national society would consist of a wide variety of people of mixed ancestry. But only in Bova's Mars trilogy can we find an explicit reference to the mixture of races, represented not only by the protagonist, Jamie Waterman, but also by his two wives. Jamie's first wife is Joanna Brumado, a Brazilian woman who talks proudly and freely about her mixed-race heritage. In a conversation with Jamie, she states:

> Joanna said, "I understand that you are an Indian."
> "Half Navaho."
> "In Brazil you would be called a mestizo. I am a mestizo myself. My father and mother, both mestizos. There are millions of us in Brazil. Tens of millions in Latin America, from Mexico southward" [*Mars* 63].

Waterman's second wife, V.J. Shektar, is also a "dark-skinned" (*Return* 233) woman. She is the Australian physician and psychologist of the second expedition, but of Hindu descent, that is, she is another product of a frontier melting pot, in this case the Australian outback. The two characters explicitly recognize their condition, as one can read in *Mars Life*. When commenting about their U.S. citizenship, they suggest: "It was a joke between them: typical Americans, he a half–Navaho and she a Hindu from Australia" (*Life* 50). Jamie and V.J. are not only completely integrated in the American melting pot; their connection with Mars goes far beyond that, because they stand for the perfect inhabitants of the Martian frontier, the mix-race models of the Martian settlers:

> She and Jamie had ... traveled to Mars together, and slowly but irrevocably fallen in love. The two of them stayed alone on the red planet for four months after the rest of the team had left for Earth and before the replacement team had arrived, Adam and Eve in a barren, frigid new world that was to them like the Garden of Eden" [*Life* 52].

The Martian Adam and Eve, the first of a whole multiracial line of descent, the promise of a new beginning for humanity, new humans in a happy utopia.

Perhaps unknowingly, Jamie and V.J. could well actualize the figure of the "mestiza" suggested by Chicana critic Gloria Anzaldúa. Departing from the idea that the borderlands/frontier is not a division line, but an undetermined, ambiguous space ideal for the mixing of languages, cultures, races, etc., Anzaldúa predicts that the future posthuman, the further evolution of humankind in a postcolonial world would be one human model that has finally overcome all gender, cultural and racial differences. If progress consists of the generation of new ideas to substitute the old ones, then the mestizas will lead this development. She suggests:

> *En unas pocas centurias* [in some centuries], the future will belong to the *mestiza*. Because the future depends on the breaking down of paradigms, it depends on the straddling of two or more cultures. By creating a new mythos — that is, a change in the way we perceive reality, the way we see ourselves, and the ways we behave — la mestiza creates a new consciousness [Anzaldúa 102].

In its essence, the mestiza consciousness is a determined move towards the construction of a human identity free from all the constraints of race, nation, culture, language, gender, etc. Although perhaps rooted in the notion of the American melting pot, the mestiza goes far beyond that because, unlike the frontier myth, it does not assimilate individuals to one dominant culture, but defends undirected hybridization as the force of human evolution. Mestizos would then be the perfect citizens of the societies developing in the colonization of Mars, and mixed-race (or even mixed-species) protagonists could then be mythical figures in space exploration stories, and in science fiction in general.[12] In this sense, Jamie and V.J.'s mixed ancestries could well represent these future human beings, the new protagonists of science fiction stories that represent not just a collection of races, as it happens for instance in *Star Trek*, but real mestizo, hybrid characters.

Nevertheless, the representation of these mixed characters also needs to be taken into account. In the same way the ideology of the melting pot may overcome Anzaldúa's notion of the mestiza consciousness (with strategies like that of *Star Trek*, where society is actually multinational and multiracial, but still clearly *American*), the strength and persistence of the frontier myth in American culture may try to assimilate mestizo characters, substituting a real post-national society with a society in which the idea of nation is no longer valid because everyone feels absorbed by the dominant American culture. Although Jamie and V.J. are fictional characters of mixed descent, some of their personal qualities reveal the strong pull of the American frontier myth. On the one hand, Jamie's dual behavior, both as a stoical Indian and as a fearless and aggressive cowboy, already commented here, does not constitute a break with the stereotypical representation of the Indians and cowboys in the traditional version of the frontier myth. On the other hand, some details of Jamie's physical appearance would raise doubts about his hybrid (mestizo) condition.

Although Jamie Waterman is the main character of Bova's Martian trilogy, it is not until the beginning of the third novel that a detailed physical description is available. Looking at himself in the mirror in the first pages of *Mars Life*, Jamie reflects: "His unhappy face stared back at him: broad cheeks, coppery skin, dark brooding eyes. Strands of gray flecked his close-cropped jet black hair.... He saw his father's Navaho face; his mother's golden hair skin were inside of him, didn't show" (*Life* 22). As this description demonstrates, Jamie's appearance is too obviously that of an Indian, which means people would not recognize his Anglo half at first sight. In spite of all the references to his Indianness in the novels, Jamie is treated more like a Navaho than as an Anglo character. In addition, when his white side appears (to compete with

Dex Trumball), it is to reveal the stereotypical attitude of the white frontiersman, as we have already said. His Indian half is also stereotypical: as an Indian, Jamie is stoical, intuitive and patient. Besides, his sexual behavior hides deep racial fears. Jamie abandons his first Anglo girlfriend when he travels to Mars. After that, his relationships are restricted to women of color: Joanna Brumado and V.J. (an Australian of Hindu ancestry). His marriage with these two dark-skinned women produces no viable offspring. Although Jamie and V.J. have a son, he dies in an accident before he can continue his mixed lineage himself. If this couple considered themselves as the Adam and Eve of Mars, their line of descent is suddenly and tragically cut short. Finally, Jamie's acceptance of the frontier spirit, and his final surrender to the pressures of the economic powers that aspire to exploit Mars implies an eventual capitulation to the "inevitability of progress," as if he were some idealistic Indian finally defeated by civilization.

Similarly, in most of the novels about the colonization of Mars analyzed here, the American frontier myth lurks behind the fictional horizon, trying to penetrate space exploration with its iconography and ideology. Although science fiction tends towards the abstract when using imaginary territories, it cannot easily escape from its cultural bias, which intends to turn this American national goal into a global, human aspiration in its own terms.

Conclusion: Globalizing the Melting Pot

In her essay "Aliens 'R' U.S.: American Science Fiction Viewed from Down Under" (1993), Zoe Sofia reflects on how American films are perceived and interpreted from a non–American perspective. She points out that American audiences can easily identify themselves with the "good guys" in American SF, whereas the rest of the world cannot really distinguish between the aliens who deploy advanced technologies as tools for planetary domination from earthlings (Americans or others) using their technological power to maintain control over Earth's countries and regions. According to this critic, then, the fictional exploration of space in SF has provided an unlimited unknown territory where the national values implicit in the American frontier myth can be endlessly (re)produced and exported to the rest of the world. It follows that space "federations" do not actually offer a model for a new, inclusive and egalitarian global political unity, but a re-conception of the world as one global United States. Sofia's reminder of the danger of globalizing myths and ideas serves well to illustrate what the conclusion to this paper will suggest, because, although the novels about the colonization of Mars intend to construct a post-national, multicultural, and multiracial (utopian) society, very often they are unable to escape completely from the ideological coordinates of the American frontier myth and from the melting pot ideal, or even fail to represent the future by simply showing an alternative version of the American past. Frontier myth imagery infiltrates subtly into the fictional exploration of Mars (and other space travel stories), and the line that divides the revision and the reenactment of the American frontier myth is thin, as Robinson suggests in this conversation between the first American explorers and the representatives of Muslim settlers in *Red Mars*:

> "John Boone is the same as ever," the old Zeyk replied. "When he says he will make an indigenous Martian culture, he only means some of the Terran cultures will be promoted, and others attacked...
> "He thinks everyone on Mars should *become* American," said a man named Nejm.
> "Why not?" Zeyk said. Smiling. "It's already happened on Earth" [10].

In general, the novels analyzed here are aware that they may be recreating the American frontier myth and transforming it into a global unifying myth of origin and destiny (as it did in the formation of the United States), and they make explicit references to it. In *Return to Mars*, for instance, V.J. compares the Martian wilderness with the Australian desert: "God, it's even bleaker than the outback" (168). Similarly, in Robinson's *Red Mars*, Nadia, one of the Russian first explorers, identifies the red planet with Siberia, the Russian equivalent of the American frontier: "Nadia had never seen [Mars] properly before, or never really felt it, she realized now; she had been enjoying her life as if it were a Siberia made right" (141). Nevertheless, not all the novels react to this "globalization" of the frontier myth in the same way. The positions vary from novels like Williamson's *Beachhead*, which defends the notion of the frontier as a symbol valid for all humanity,[13] to novels that reject the possibility of peaceful coexistence between cultures, like Bear's *Moving Mars*, whose final solution — moving the red planet to another galaxy — to the conflict between Earth (the imperialistic old world) and Mars (the free new world) is extremely pessimistic. Robinson's and Bova's trilogies are somewhere in the middle, divided between the need to revise the historical version of the frontier myth and the desire to revitalize and expand some of the ideals implicit in it: the idea of challenge, the concept of progress and the notion of the "melting pot." In this sense, Robinson's trilogy seems more concerned with economic, social and political issues, whereas Bova's novels are the only story analyzed here that deals with the question of race and racial mixing explicitly, thanks to his main mestizo character, Jamie Waterman. Although Waterman may at times be a too typical American character, enterprising, individualistic and with an independent spirit, he is unique in the fiction about the exploration of Mars in the sense that he represents an advanced version of the melting pot, and not just the "collection of races" so typical of SF stories like the *Star Trek* series. Waterman may thus represent Anzaldúa's mestizo in a promising if incomplete manner. The lack of viable mestizo offspring is, as already suggested, the most evident impediment in this transformation of the existent idea of the melting pot into a real, global, mixed-race society.

The question of race is therefore the most obvious absence from the novels analyzed here and their revision of the frontier myth. This is perhaps the reason why the Martian frontier myth is still too similar to the experience of the American West and may appear as an attempt to "globalize" a culturally specific myth. Bear's pessimistic view of the coexistence between races and cultures, Robinson's expectation that the creation of a utopian society will eventually make the question of race meaningless, and Bova's lack of determination to pursue his promising layout of a mestizo family would have progressed with a resolute defense of cultural *and* racial fusion (*mestizaje*), as Anzaldúa proposes. In my opinion, Anzaldúa's notion of the "borderlands" is both a logical consequence and an improvement of the very idea of the American melting pot, and so decidedly American. In what we could call the symbol (or even myth) of the borderlands, the substitution of the concept of the frontier understood as a limit or horizon for the idea of a space available for exchange and mixture is essential. Being no longer a horizon, the borderlands no longer imply expansion and progress (mainly understood in economic and technological terms respectively), or any other cultural specific ideal that supposedly represents a unifying goal for humanity; being no longer a limit but a wide space, the borderlands do not symbolize a space "out there" (and therefore alien), nor do they offer the promise of a faraway — different — place where a change of values is possible. The borderlands signify an inclusive space where all human groups have their place, and represent the numerous places where actual cultural and racial exchange can happen. In this sense, the Earth and Mars are borderlands in themselves, just like the U.S. Southwest is a borderland as a whole.

The "globalized" version of the frontier myth cannot escape from its specific cultural bias for the same reason that the very notion of globalization fails to attract attention as a worldwide unifying ideal. In fact, the idea of globalization was not used without intention here. In its most conventional sense, globalization accounts for the reflection about a post-national world, a world where contact between cultures and races is increasingly fluent, and which should, theoretically, lead the progressive elimination of national borders and eventually generate a sense of identity where the issues of nation, race, and culture have been overcome. Nevertheless, the discourse of globalization, which promises to improve communication and understanding across cultures by creating a king of global melting pot, lacks an apparent political (as well as social and racial) agenda. Globalization is a term primarily applied to economics, and this is where it intends to remain. Unlike other international projects such as the European Union, whose construction is as least theoretically based on the belief that economic integration is a means to the political and cultural union of countries previously confronted, globalization does not propose any kind supra- or post-national political entity that would comprise all the countries in the world in equal terms and therefore guarantee that no country disrupts global cooperation. If the principle that economic integration can achieve political amalgamation is correct, then globalization could hypothetically carry out the myth of a human planetary unity where all nationalities, races, classes, ethnic groups, etc. could coexist peacefully and prosper. But this scenario of a unified world government, however, is suspiciously absent from the discourse on globalization.

Just like globalization, the possibility of a planetary government has been envisioned as an imaginary possibility mainly in cultural productions that reach a worldwide audience but originate mainly in the West. Furthermore, like in the novels about the colonization of Mars analyzed here, the attempts of SF to imagine a future society where the questions of race, class, gender, nationality and culture have been eventually overcome is laudable, but often unable to escape from its cultural bias. One of the explanations for this inability to rise above cultural specificity could be the lack of interest in the question of race in the genre. If, as it is often suggested, SF's role as a genre is to create a multiple, complex, collective vision of the future in a "communal act of discovery" (Slusser 21), this future appears to be full of societies where alternative humanities and human-machine hybrids are common, but devoid of all-human hybrids living in post-national planetary states that respect all races and cultures. As it has done with other human models, the genre could and should explore the ideological and sentimental implications of belonging to one common human race (the "mestiza consciousness"). In this sense, the novels about the colonization of Mars assume too easily that one global project like the exploration of the read planet could be the common goal that will unify all the countries in the world and create a democratic federation that guarantees freedom and prosperity for everyone, as the frontier myth presumably did in the United States. Besides, the fictional representation of Mars could also be the place to finally atone for the mistakes of the historical frontier experience so that it could continue to be used as a symbolic referent for America and for the rest of the world. Yet by depicting the colonization of

Mars in relation to the Conquest of the West, the novels recreate, perhaps unwillingly, the ideological framework of the frontier mainly from an American perspective, and this becomes too evident for non–American audiences. The main characters and events are dangerously similar, even if the authors' intention is to revise them, to the attitudes and episodes associated with the typical western. Their versions of the Martian melting pot avoid dealing with racial politics, because they take for granted that the new global frontier ideal will make up for any differences among cultures and races. Only Ben Bova's trilogy brings the question of race to the foreground. Being half Anglo and half Navaho, Jamie Waterman as a character is all about the question of race. Contrarily to what the other explores and in Bova's story assume, he is not an Indian but a mestizo. With his mestiza wives, he was in a perfect position to establish a mixed-race family on Mars, the hybrid "Adam and Eve" (*Life* 52) of a new planet, the first of—and perhaps the model for—a definition of humanity where the concept of race has finally ceased to be a dividing mark. Even as an incomplete project, Jamie Waterman's hybridity is an example of how persistent cultural myths may limit literary creativity and of the thematic possibilities that the question of race could generate in science fiction.

Notes

1. Cyberpunk is a term used by criticism to describe a tendency in SF writing dating from the 1980s. Cyberpunk writers share SF elements like virtual reality, hardware or software implants, a dystopian stance and the overall presence of big companies. One of the best known cyberpunk writers, William Gibson, coined a term for these transnational companies: the *zaibatsu*.

2. Gary Westfahl relates this and other similar anecdotes as examples of the influence of science-fictional productions on real space exploration (62–63).

3. The recurrent presence of the frontier in SF literature and film could not be overlooked in the analysis of the genre, and is a well established issue of SF criticism nowadays. Several studies have discussed this connection, from the already classical book by David Mogen *Wilderness Visions: The Western Theme in Science Fiction Literature* (1993), to more recent works like Gary Westfahl's essay compilation *Space and Beyond: The Frontier Theme in Science Fiction* (2000), Carl Abbot's *Frontiers Past and Future: Science Fiction and the American West* (2006) and William H. Katerberg's *Future West: Utopia and Apocalypse in Frontier Science Fiction* (2008). See also Slotkin (635–636).

4. Williams Katerberg emphasizes the connection between the frontier myth and utopian thinking in *Future West: Utopia and Apocalypse in Frontier Science Fiction* (2008). In the first chapter of his book, Katerberg discusses how the American West, described as a "New World" or a "promised land," did become a location for utopian expectations. Although this critic does not mention Bova's trilogy, which is the main focus of this paper, he does analyze Robinson's trilogy (and other novels) in relation to the idea of utopia. For Katerberg, Robinson uses the myth of the frontier as a

metaphor for utopia, and he even states that in Robinson's novels, "[t]he colonization of Mars ... parallels the history of the Americas as a New World frontier" (151). My argument here is that the utopian connotations of the frontier myth can be applied not only to Robinson's trilogy, but to many other novels about the colonization of Mars.

    5. From now on, quotations from these novels will be identified by "*Mars*" for the first novel, "*Return*" for the second and "*Life*" for the third, plus the page number.

    6. See Holtsmark (3).

    7. For a more profound discussion of E.R. Burroughs' use of Frontier Myth racist ideology in his Martian novels, see Slotkin (195–211).

    8. *The Martian Chronicles* is not a conventional novel, but a series of short stories which share the same theme: the human colonization of Mars.

    9. For a deeper analysis of the similarities between Bradbury's Martians and American Indians and of the similarities between the Martian colonization and the conquest of the West, see Ángel Mateos-Aparicio (165–173). Gary K. Wolfe was the first critic to suggest the presence of the American frontier myth in *The Martian Chronicles* (33–54). See also Mogen (82–93) Pfitzer (59–61) and Johnson (35).

    10. "Rugged" is in fact the word used by Frederick Jackson Turner to define the qualities of the frontiersman.

    11. An explanation for the marginality of racial issues in Bear's and Robinson's novels could be that their narratives are mainly focused on political and utopian questions, or even that they believe that the implementation of a more egalitarian and inclusive political structure would necessarily imply the end of racial, class and gender discrimination. Some attempts have been made to develop a postcolonial reading of Robinson's Mars trilogy (Franko), although it is mainly deduced from a more general analysis of the criticism of a notion of subjectivity based on the opposition of self and other. However, neither Bear nor Robinson deal with the question of race directly and evidently and noticeably.

    12. While this article was being written, a new science fiction film has raised racial issues but did not produce this mixed-species specimen: *District 9*, written and directed by Neill Blomkamp.

    13. The most evident example of this attitude is the quotation from Williamson's *Beachhead* that appears at the beginning of this essay.

Works Cited

Abbot, Carl. "Falling into History: The Imagined Wests of Kim Stanley Robinson in the Three California and Mars Trilogies." *Western Historical Quarterly* 34.1 (2003): 27–48.

_____. *Frontiers Past and Future: Science Fiction and the American West*. Lawrence: University Press of Kansas, 2006.

Anzaldúa, Gloria. *Borderlands/La Frontera*. 2d ed. San Francisco: Aunt Lute, 1999.

Bear, Greg. *Moving Mars*. 1993. New York: ORB, 2007.

Bhabha, Homi K. *The Location of Culture*. London: Routledge, 1994.

Bova, Ben. *Mars*. 1992. New York: Bantam Books, 1993.

_____. *Mars Life*. New York: Tom Doherty Associates, 2008.

_____. *Return to Mars*. New York: HarperCollins, 1999.

Bradbury, Ray. *The Martian Chronicles*. 1951. London: Flamingo, 1995.

Burroughs, Edgar Rice. *A Princess of Mars*. 1912. New York: Ballantine, 1979.

Forward, Robert L. *Martian Rainbow.* 1991. Lincoln, NE: Authors Guild, 2000.
Franko, Carol. "Working the 'In-Between': *Kim* Stanley *Robinson's* Utopian Fiction." *Science Fiction Studies* 21. 2 (1994): 191–211.
Haraway, Donna. "'A Manifesto for Cyborgs': Science, Technology, and Socialist-Feminism in the Late Twentieth Century." (1985) Rpt. in *The Uncanny: Experiments in Cyborg Culture*, Bruce Grenville, ed. Vancouver: Vancouver Art Gallery/Arsenal Pulp, 2001. 65–99.
Heinlein, Robert. *Red Planet.* 1949. New York: Ballantine, 2006.
Holtsmark, Erling B. *Edgar Rice Burrroughs.* Boston: Twayne, 1986.
Johnson, Wayne L. "The Martian Chronicles and Other Mars Stories." *Ray Bradbury.* Harold Bloom, ed. Philadelphia: Chelsea House, 2001. 29–38.
Katerberg, William H. *Future West: Utopia and Apocalypse in Frontier Science Fiction.* Laurence: University Press of Kansas, 2008.
Mateos-Aparicio, Ángel. *Visiones sombrías de un país inexplorado: Ciencia-ficci"n y humanismo en la narrativa norteamericana y británica de posguerra: W. Golding, K. Vonnegut, R. Bradbury y J.G. Ballard.* Saarbrücken: VDM Verlag, 2008.
Mogen, David. *Ray Bradbury.* Boston: Twayne, 1986.
_____. *Wilderness Visions: The Western Theme in Science Fiction Literature.* San Bernardino, CA: Borgo, 1993.
Pfitzer, Gregory M. "The Only Good Alien is a Dead Alien: Science Fiction and the Metaphysics of Indian-Hating on the High Frontier" *Journal of American Culture* 18.1 (Spring 1995): 51–67.
Robinson, Kim Stanley. *Blue Mars.* 1996. New York: Bantam, 1997.
_____. *Green Mars.* 1994. New York: Bantam, 1995.
_____. *Red Mars.* New York: Bantam, 1993.
Shiner, Lewis. *Frontera.* London: Sphere, 1984.
Slotkin, Richard. *Gunfighter Nation: The Myth of the Frontier in Twentieth-Century America.* 1992. Norman: University of Oklahoma Press, 1998.
Slusser, George. "Reflections on Style in Science Fiction." In *Styles of Creation*, edited by George Slusser and Eric S. Rabkin, 3–23. Athens: University of Georgia Press, 1992.
Sofia, Zoe. "Aliens 'R' U.S.: American Science Fiction Viewed from Down Under." In *Aliens: The Anthropology of Science Fiction*, edited by George Slusser and Eric S. Rabkin, 128–141. Carbondale: Southern Illinois University Press, 1993.
Turner, Frederick Jackson. "The Significance of the Frontier in American History." *The Frontier in American History.* New York: Henry Holt, 1921. 1–39. Project Gutenberg eBooks, http://www.gutenberg.org/files/22994/22994–8.txt, retrieved 16 July 2009.
Westfahl, Gary, ed. "Frontiers Old and New." Intro. to *Space and Beyond: The Frontier Theme in Science Fiction.* Westport, CT: Greenwood, 2000.
Williamson, Jack. *Beachhead.* New York: Tom Doherty Associates, 1992.
Wolfe, Gary K. "The Frontier Myth in Ray Bradbury." In *Ray Bradbury*, edited by Martin H. Greenberg and Joseph Olander, 33–54. New York: Twayne, 1980.

8

Dystopia and the Postcolonial Nation

SUPARNO BANERJEE

Ruchir Joshi's *The Last Jet-Engine Laugh* (2001), published half a century after national independence, expresses disillusionment towards the idea of India as a unified nation. This novel invokes the classic science fictional elements, especially of the future — dystopia tales — space warfare, cybernetics, environmental degradation, roving street gangs, etc.— to bring out the unsettling and violent trends of post-independence India, in both personal and public spheres. The novel examines the past, the present, and the future of the nation: from its struggle with the British colonists and the political upheavals of the 1970s to the future war against foreign enemies through the eyes of the protagonist, Paresh Bhatt. In the process of telling this story Joshi highlights the intrinsically hybrid nature of the Indian nation. On the one hand this hybridity reflects the dystopic fragmentariness of the country, but on the other, it also shows a way of debunking unidirectional ideologies.

The fragmentary yet intertwined narrative of *The Last Jet-Engine Laugh* tracks the life of Paresh (once a famous photographer) in a nightmarish future Kolkata. The present setting of the novel finds him as an old man, whose daughter Para (Paramita Bhatt) is a high ranking air force officer at an Indian space station. The book opens in Kolkata of the 2030s, but then continuously jumps back and forth between the colonial India of the 1930s and '40s, the India under emergency rule in the 1970s, and then to 2030, stopping and turning at different points in between. Although Paresh is the primary first person narrator of the novel, the narrative perspective often shifts to several other characters' points of view. These fragmentary narratives come together to highlight the sinister aspects of the future that India is treading towards, and locates the origin of this baleful tomorrow in acts committed in the past. The novel also intrinsically connects the idea of techno-scientific progress with the shadow of a menacing social outcome; but it never for once suggests that the world can go on without such progress.

Placing *The Last Jet-Engine Laugh* in the context of Indian science fiction, Anna Guttman comments that this novel follows the popular techno-centrism, yet simultaneously posits technology itself as the source of trouble and indeterminacy. In *The Nation of India in Contemporary Indian Literature* (139) she compares *The Last Jet-Engine Laugh* with Amitav Ghosh's *The Calcutta Chromosome* positioning them at two opposite poles. While Ghosh's book challenges Western knowledge and Western epistemology, Joshi's novel takes such knowledge for granted. Moreover, *The Last Jet-Engine Laugh* shows a marked ambivalence to West and Western knowledge and technology compared to most other postcolonial, especially Indian, science fiction. Rather, the book calls the reader's attention to the ubiquity of technology (Western or non–Western) in the future: in countering environmental pollution, or causing it, in the theater of war and in the interchangeability of cyber and real worlds.

Technology in Joshi's book belongs both to the imperial powers of the West and to the non–Western authorities. The water capsules that hydrate the inhabitants of the future Kolkata are Japanese; the spy station in space, and the highly advanced fighter jets that Para flies are Indian; and the artificial storm blanket that the Saudi-Pakistani-U.S. alliance uses against India are Western. The book still refuses to pass judgment on these ever intruding technological presences. This over commitment to technology marks *The Last Jet-Engine Laugh* as a perfect specimen of what Tom Shippey calls "fabril" literature. In the "Introduction" to *The Oxford Book of Science Fiction* Shippey writes:

> "Fabril" is the opposite of "pastoral." But while "the pastoral" is an established and much-discussed literary mode, recognized as such since early antiquity, its dark opposite has not yet been accepted, or even named, by the law-givers of literature. Yet the opposition is a clear one. Pastoral literature is rural, nostalgic, conservative. It idealizes the past and tends to convert complexities into simplicity; its central image is the shepherd. Fabril literature (of which science fiction is now by far the most prominent genre) is overwhelmingly urban, disruptive, future-oriented, eager for novelty; its central image is the "faber," the smith or blacksmith in older usage, but now extended in science fiction to mean the creator of artifacts in general — metallic, crystalline, genetic, or even social [ix].

Joshi's novel is essentially an urban tale marked by all the possible technological connotations. It flows to and fro between a number of metropolitan centers in India and abroad: Kolkata, Ahmadabad, Mumbai, Delhi, Paris, New York. Although events outside the cities always lurk on the periphery, the urban centers pump the life blood of this book. The Naxalite violence in the rural Bengal affects the life style in Kolkata, so do the ravages of the India-Pakistan wars that devastated the countryside of Bengal; and the poisoning of the water sources outside the cities leads to the various contraptions that clutter the city life.[1] The novel takes off from this "fabril" universe into Paresh's mental world; this is a world that materializes before the reader simultaneously through Paresh's narrative flashbacks and Para's reconstruction of past incidents while playing the computer game *Megalopolis 3000*. Such predominantly urban locale and techno-centric life-style of the novel underpin the atmosphere of dystopia.

In fact, the world of *The Last Jet-Engine Laugh* is molded in the classic dystopian tradition. The socio-economic matrix in which Joshi locates the future India is marked by a scarcity of clean water that has lead to violent internal riots and has sparked a war between India and the Pakistani-Saudi alliance. This bleak future is also dominated by Japanese corporate houses that not only control the economic sectors — in this case the management of water resources — but also intrude into the Indian cultural sphere. Durga Puja, the most popular festival in Bengal, which has always been a community affair, is transformed into a commercial event sponsored by the "Japs." Furthermore, the age old problem of Indian national life, communal unrest, lurks at the corners, while Mumbai and Karachi (in Pakistan) are now dead zones as a result of reciprocal nuclear strikes. Even Paresh's life in Europe hints at constant anxiety of systematic racial profiling and fear of terrorist strikes. A French policeman tells him, "Zees is a war. You are luucki we don't shoot you" (375). The streets of urban India though, are depicted as far more dangerous. The novel describes a water riot in Delhi, where fashion savvy armed gangs, wearing American Ivy league school tee-shirts, engage in merciless violence. Kolkata is also divided into territories of various gangs who have the jurisdiction to extort "Puja subscription" from the residents. Even the sky of Kolkata is overcrowded and highly hazardous with unmaintained helicopter shuttles dangerously ferrying people around.

These images of environmental degradation, dependence on technology (cause and effect of the first) and violence aligns this novel with the classic Western dystopias, like Orwell's *1984*, but specifically to the feminist science fictions such as Joanna Russ's *The Female Man* (1975), Merge Piercy's *He, She and It* (1990) and Pat Cadigan's *Tea from an Empty Cup* (1999), which focus on oppression in different forms and find a corollary in the degradation of environment. In the matter of water riots and creation of simulacra of life through cybernetic manipulations, the novel closely anticipates Ian McDonald's *River of Gods* (2004) which unfolds in the backdrop of a severe drought and an imminent war between the northern and southern states of India in

2047. Joshi's book also echoes Ghosh's *The Calcutta Chromosome* and its International Water Council, which controls water affairs of the world. All three, Joshi, Ghosh and McDonald, seem to find the issue of water a major cause of worry in the near future; and all of them project the corporate entities as the real exploiters, rather than any political organization.

Evidently, these dystopic elements are rooted deeply in the present realities of the Indian nation. The main environmental concern in the book — water pollution — is a matter not far from national concern in the real world. Water bodies around the major urban centers are often highly polluted from Industrial refuses. Cleaning up the rivers Ganges and Yamuna has become one of the major projects for civic authorities. Clamping down on industries for their contamination of ground water sources is also seen as a primary imperative by many environmentalists and political parties. The novel, however, assigns the cause of this degradation to chemical warfare. But, Joshi is equally scathing in his indictment of hazardous industries and castigates the upper stratum of Indian society for its stark disregard of environmental issues and human dignity, referring to the gas leak in the Union Carbide plant on the night of 2–3 December 1984 that killed thousands of people from its immediate and sustained effects.[2]

The gloom of this future further deepens when we come to the awareness of a pervading sense of terror and communal hatred, and realize that the country is at war with its neighbors. These terrorist acts and the war with Pakistan presented in the book arise from historical territorial disputes and, more importantly, from a deep communal enmity between Hindus and Muslims.[3] *The Last Jet-Engine Laugh* does not, however, specifically allude to the Hindu fundamentalist discourse, which defines India on the basis of Muslim exclusion; yet, through oblique references the novel leaves unmistakable hints of the stirring communal tensions rocking the country. The uneasy calm in Ahmadabad anticipating a riot in the street, which Paresh and his family sense from their home, and the late night war cry in Kolkata definitely indicate communal clashes. This same religious anger becomes national hatred against Pakistan, through Viral's (a friend of Paresh) emotional public celebration at the news of a successful Indian airstrike inside Pakistani territory; but, most of all, in the derogatory way in which Para uses the word Pakistan as a substitute for latrine, even after much discouragement from Paresh and his German wife Anna.

To be fair to the novel's subtlety, *The Last Jet-Engine Laugh* does not employ only these obvious references to the specters of communalism and xenophobia. The novel goes much deeper into the psyche of violence and nationalism in an indirect manner — through the personal fantasies and uncorroborated anecdotes about the Indian nationalist leader Subhas Chandra Bose. The legacy of Bose's armed rebellion against the British, and his mysterious disappearance at the end of World War II, provide the context of the book's other violent trends, though not in any direct historical sense. Rather, Bose's ideology, which in many respects was dictatorial and the exact opposite of Mahatma Gandhi's non-violence, provides a mythical subtext that continuously informs all the other violence depicted in the book.[4] He actively sought help from Hitler's Germany and also visited the Soviet Union and Italy for support before finally joining forces with the Japanese Imperial army. His militant version of nationalism was much criticized as a form of Fascism from various political camps.[5] What is important here, however, is to realize that though not always recognized, violence played as crucial a role in India's independence as Gandhi's non-violence. It is also important to acknowledge that this violent nationalism was often marked by overarching religious or communal identity. From Bankimchandra Chatterjee's fiercely nationalist novel *Anandamath* (1882) to the armed movements in the 1930s and Bose's militarism, all try to imagine the country as an embodiment of purity, as a mother and a goddess — a typical Hindu view of the nation that discounts any other imaginary constructions. Although Hindu Nationalism during colonial times did not seek to promote communal violence between Hindus and Muslims, it still shared the tendency of exclusivity with the ideology of Hindutva (militant Hindu Nationalism) promoted by the Hindu Nationalists of today.[6]

Joshi links these aspects of past violence with the future India by associating references to Bose in Paresh's mind with acts of violence and convoluted logic. Two images that recur are the images of Bose's last flight — two Japanese fighters destroying his plane in midair and Bose's sense of incredulity at the suddenness of this violent ending — and Bose's passing of the civil service interview by tricking his interviewer with a logical trap.[7] These images, in a roundabout manner, suggest Bose's adoption of the same strategies of violence and false reasoning that were used by the colonizers he was fighting against. To put it differently, this book places Bose and the British in the same boat of domination tactics.

Bose's legacy is also brought in through Kalidas's anecdotes that hint towards the purposelessness of authoritarianism. Kalidas, Paresh Bhatt's family friend, claims to have met Bose in a Soviet gulag in the 1960s. Kalidas's account, which is as much apocryphal as the claim of Bose's death in an air crash in 1945, takes apart Bose's larger than life image. Not only is he shown as a broken old man on the verge of losing his mind, half of the time he is craving for small material comforts than reflecting upon issues of larger import. Even his death is portrayed as miserable rather than tragic. Kalidas's narrative is interspersed with Bose's own mental images — mostly about his journey from Germany to Japan in a German U-boat and a Japanese submarine. However, these images provide an oblique association in his mind of violence and his own act of joining the Axis power in an effort to free India. Most vivid of these is the imagery of dead dolphins in the Indian Ocean, the ocean with the name of his own country. Kalidas explains to the Russian army-man, "He is saying, 'Blood on my water. Innocent blood on my sea'" (134) — an obvious association between violence and the Indian struggle, but more importantly a sense of underlying guilt for his role in abetting this violence.

The association of violence and nationalism is further reinforced through the references to Durga, the mother goddess, whom the militant nationalists, including Bose, prayed to. Durga is the warrior goddess in Hindu mythology, who vanquished Mahishasur, the buffalo-demon, and freed heaven and earth of evil. In fact, the Vedic and Puranic texts assign Durga's origin specifically for the purpose of destroying Mahishasur. She is a purely military deity, almost a cyborg warrior, emerging from the collective powers of different gods. Not surprisingly, the image of Durga is painted on the fighter jets that the all female squadron flies into Pakistan to subdue the modern day "demons." Even the use of women for the purpose of war, with their bodies almost fused to the bodies of the multi armed war machines (thus creating a cyborg entity), refers back to the violent aspect of Durga. This is a lucid association of violence, nationalism and the Mother Goddess. All these connections ultimately assert the tradition of violence and domination that underlies Indian nationalism and Indian society in general.

Joshi not only employs the images of indigenous tradition of violence to the broader national contexts, but also to the smaller quotidian matters as well, most of the time with crushing irony. He refers to the sinister aspects of Durga Puja — collection of money through intimidation, wastage of resources, and the complete chaos that the city plunges into during the time of the celebration. Mahadev (Paresh's father) points out this indigenous tradition of wastage to Paresh's wife Anna during her visit to Kolkata. Paresh also mentions the intimidation techniques employed by the local goons to raise subscription money. Even in 2030, when the "puja" has become a corporate sponsored affair, the essential intimidating aspect remains the same. Instead of the local thugs, the coercers now belong to the multinational companies that run the economy of the country. The most important points here are the connections among the different types of violence — divine or mortal — and the unmasked assertion that this violence belongs purely to India; it is not imported by the foreign entities that has influenced the nation at different times.

Joshi further emphasizes the importance of these indigenous violent traits by drawing a relationship between the Hindutva movement and the dictatorial rule of Indira Gandhi during the imposition of emergency from 1975 to '77 and the Naxalite rebellion of the late sixties and the early seventies. In his article "Looking over the Shoulder" Joshi claims, "India's sectarianism predates the nationalist government of the BJP and has yet to work out of the system" (164).[8] In this article he connects the ideologies of violence and domination evident in Hindu fundamentalism since the late 1990s with the emergency days, and argues that if this tendency continues India would not be much different from Pakistan under military dictatorship. In the novel, the days of emergency are marked by a claustrophobic atmosphere of tension.[9] Mahadev, who is an old Gandhian and an anti–Indira writer, is constantly under the threat of arrest. Kalidas and many of Mahadev's friends are arrested for political dissent. Mahadev is even physically assaulted after a meeting for expressing anti-government sentiments. This state sponsored oppression which was perpetrated by the same Indian National Congress (INC) party that followed Gandhi's doctrine of nonviolence, and rejected Bose for his dictatorial tendencies, underlines a major theme in the book — a stark lack of faith in any form of political ideology.

The reality of the Indian political scene only supports this opinion. Indira Gandhi, who made sweeping changes to the Indian constitution during the emergency to strengthen her power, lost the election in 1977 due to a political miscalculation. This defeat is depicted in Joshi's novel as giving rise to euphoria and regaining of faith in democracy. Yet the Janata Party, the replacement for INC, proved to be an ineffectual substitute resulting in a re-election within three years and victory for Indira Gandhi. Political events of such magnitude only buttress Joshi's doubt over any type of political "isms" and the sustainability of democracy in such a scenario.

The Naxalite rebellion serves a similar purpose in the novel. *The Last Jet-Engine Laugh* incorporates in its narrative both the violence and lack of any sustained purpose of this era. The references to police atrocities against the Naxalites and reciprocal violence is incorporated through a police officer's visit to Paresh's home, especially when the officer lets Paresh hold a handgun and reminds that killing people should be the last recourse, especially for the police. Mahadev's comment, however, best sums up the book's underlying sentiment for any type of political violence, "the Naxalites are busy electrocuting themselves in other ways, political ways. They think they are revolutionaries. They don't waste time trying to commit suicide by stealing live electricity wires on a rainy night" (303).

In Joshi's novel the violence that has marred India in the past and that troubles India today, is what will haunt India in the future. He finds no solace in any political approach. In a way, Joshi is unfolding the concept of Kali Yug (the age of Kali), or the last era of human civilization in the Hindu mythology.[10] Kali Yug is marked by degeneration of environment and of human nature, and anarchy in the society, which is to be set right by Kalki, the tenth and the last avatar of Lord Vishnu. The chaotic future in the novel definitely implies these dystopic connotations, but the book denies this world an avatar. The only dynamic and charismatic character, Para, turns out to be another quick-witted trickster; but nothing more. The novel, thus, refuses to fit into any holistic metanarrative such as religion or mythology that presumes narratability of the real events through their metanarrative structures. Rather, it highlights the contingent nature of history. The book suggests history is as much embedded in material reality as it is gleaned from flow of information — at some point the barrier collapses between tangible materiality and intangible (sometimes unverifiable) data stream.

The computer game *Megalopolis 3000* is the central, though not the only, device that insists on this point. This game is what Jean Baudrillard would describe as "simulacra of simulation" or the simulacra of the third order, "founded on information, the model, the cybernetic game" (121). Megalopolis is conceived as a cross between role playing games (like *The Sims*) and municipal strategy games (such as *Caesar* or *Pharaoh*), only on a much advanced level. In *Megalopolis* the characters and locations are real persons and places from each player's individual life. Unlike the current games, the environment does not depend totally on the AI, but on individual player inputs. When Para wants to replay the scenario of her grand parents' first meeting, she has to provide the program with all the minute details of the incident. The living world that the game creates is a "simulacra" based entirely on information — information that the program received from Para, who procures it from her father, who again in his turn learnt it from his parents. Paresh in fact confesses that he made up a lot of the elements when he narrated the story to Para; there are also hints that the story that he heard from his mother may as well have been emotionally enhanced. However, the distance between the event and its simulacra does not create a clear boundary between the real and unreal; instead, the computer generated simulacra becomes the only real event that Para and Paresh can directly access — the original event dissolves into the plethora of information — information which are either empirical or imagined, information that are in themselves simulations. The further down the chain the reconstruction moves, the further it loses its affinity with the original. *Megalopolis* thus becomes the generator of simulacra of simulation.

Yet the totalitarian element of the game, the player's total control over the course of the events being played out, comes under some ironic treatment;

especially in the matter that the first encounter between Mahadev and Suman (Para's grandparents) can only be seen from a horse's point of view despite Para's efforts to do otherwise. This element establishes the game's own logic that controls even the player. The suggestion is very clear — people don't control technology anymore; technology controls people. This point is further reinforced by frequent overlapping of game scenarios and narratives of real events. During their meeting in a restaurant Paresh tries to re-dress Para in his mind from her air-force uniform to the attire of a regular girl, and realizes that he is not in the virtual world. The opposite happens when he replays an uncomfortable encounter with his mother regarding Anna's nude photography in *Megalopolis* — he exits the game when the situation gets out of control and reflects on the unavailability of such an escape key in real life. Although the novel suggests the existence of a boundary between real and unreal, at various moments it deliberately dissolves this boundary to indicate the propensity of the future.

In the matter of real and unreal Baudrillard remarks: "There is no real, there is no imaginary except at a certain distance. What happens when this distance, including that between the real and the imaginary, tends to abolish itself, to be reabsorbed on behalf of the model?" (121). He answers that the tendency is always towards disappearance of this distance which leaves no space for an "ideal or critical projection" (122), but that varies according to different orders of simulacra. Baudrillard continues that in the era of total information this gap disappears entirely:

> The models no longer constitute either transcendence or projection, they no longer constitute the imaginary in relation to the real, they are themselves an anticipation of the real [...] and thus leave no room for any kind of imaginary transcendence. The field opened is that of simulation in the cybernetic sense, that is, of the manipulation of these models at every level (scenarios, the setting up of simulated situations, etc.) but then *nothing distinguishes this operation from the operation itself and the gestation of the real: there is no more fiction* [122].

In certain ways, *The Last Jet-Engine Laugh* is a product of the "implosive era of models" (122) not only because it uses *Megalopolis* as a simulacra of history — which renders history and fiction the same. In this book, the very act of telling, the "operation," cannot be distinguished from the story itself. The projection of the idea of nation in this novel is not utopian where a "transcendent universe takes form" (122), neither is it exactly an "unbounded projection of the real world of production" (122); it is rather a work where the differences between past, present and future are carefully abolished; it is a work where story creates history, the future is already present in the past, and the present only acts as a point of narration. This book in a way reiterates

Baudrillard's claim that science fiction cannot exist anymore — we are living science fiction.

Nevertheless, the world today is far from reaching this perfect state of simulacra, especially the postcolonial world, where reality is too much dependent on day to day physical survival, not on flow of information — as Baudrillard would have it. Political strife and violence are all too real for people living in that world; they are neither hyperreal nor models; and people sometime do need transcendental imagination to dream of a promised millennium. However, Ralph Pordzik mentions that the postcolonial utopias or dystopias offer a "fictional strategy to disrupt the hierarchized relation between reality and fiction which dominates traditional utopian writing with its ideological bias towards social realism and the systemic closure it ministers to" (133). He also mentions that these writings rather than depending fully on pre-colonial models for future development express a penchant for a hybridized future. Likewise, *The Last Jet-Engine Laugh* employs its postmodern narrative techniques in a science fictional context in disrupting the hierarchy of real and fictional and also by stressing the intrinsically hybridized nature of future India.

The book highlights the discourse of purity/hybridity through Para's concealing of her Indo-German origin to fit in with the doctrine of purity practiced by the Indian armed forces. Yet, in all its cultural aspects the novel is nothing but a profusion of hybridity — the Westernized urban culture, Indianized English language, and the interaction between Indian and European arts. In a way, this text is a perfect embodiment of the Bakhtinian "heteroglossia." Not only does the novel exploit the socio-cultural assumptions of class language, but it also uses a "chautney" English consisting of English, French, German, Hindi, Bengali and Guajarati words, in the Rushdian manner to imply the essential hybridity of the postcolonial Indian culture. Although the creation of this heteroglossia and hybridity is a marked feature of most postcolonial literature, the science fictional element adds another futuristic dimension to it. Not only does the novel engage into the discourse of the past and the present but also about the imminent future. The novel does not foreground the Western/Indian dialectic; neither does it make the purity/hybridity question central to its concerns. Rather, this book takes those oppositions as pre-existing conditions, and works towards constructing a world pivoted on those unuttered assumptions.

The protagonist Paresh and his daughter Para act as the axes on which the wheels of the story turn. In his nationalist parents and his Westernized life style, in his Brahminical origin, in his love for Kolkata and his penchant for Italian coffee, Paresh is the quintessential high class postcolonial subject — turning and churning at center of all the dialectical forces. And Para is the future of such subjecthood — mixed in her origin, highly influenced by her nationalist grandparents, acceding to the doctrine of purity, unflinching in killing the national enemy, yet ready to bend the rules to achieve her goals. Such amalgamation complements the hybrid structure of the novel and its non-commitment to any form of ideology. The novel in the end suggests the futility or superficiality of the "ideology" of a pure India and plainly presents the "fact" of a mongrel nation. *The Last Jet-Engine Laugh* ultimately narrates a fiction which is the reality of the disillusioned postcolonial nation.

Notes

1. The Naxalite movement started as a peasant uprising backed by the Maoist faction of the Communist Party of India (started since the Sino-Soviet split in Indian Communism) against the landlords in Naxalbari in northern part of West Bengal in 1967. The movement soon turned into a mass revolution that resorted to excessive violence and murder and was ultimately put down by authorities in the early seventies. At present, the Maoist unrest has resurfaced and is being considered as the worst threat to India's internal security.

2. Estimates put the total death toll from this incident in Bhopal in central India near 15,000, which makes this the world's biggest industrial accident. The stark disregard for human dignity in this disaster is attested by the two-decade-long public litigation and the minimal punishment meted out to the guilty party.

3. The novel mentions that the reciprocal nuclear strikes by India and Pakistan prompted an enforced nuclear disarmament of both countries. Although such disarmament does not have any present bearing, the terrorist nuclear attack on Bombay (Mumbai) that the book refers to has real echoes in the 1993 Bombay Stock Exchange bombing (which left hundreds dead) and the increasing number of terror attacks in various parts of the country. The future war in 2030 also has its resonances in the past; the novel itself recounts the past wars between the two countries — the Bangladesh war in 1971 and the two previous wars over Kashmir in 1947 and 1965. Published in 2001, the novel itself comes at the heels of a fourth conflict in 1999, again over Kashmir. *The Last Jet-Engine Laugh* also brings up India's uneasy relationship with its other nuclear armed neighbor, China, in predicting a three-way conflict between India, China and Pakistan in 2007.

4. Bose's own account of India's freedom struggle in *The Indian Struggle 1920–1942* (1964) as well as most of his biographers mention his propensity towards authoritarianism, rule of discipline, and lack of faith in the weakness of democracy. Anton Pelinka's *Democracy Indian Style: Subhas Chandra Bose and the Creation of India's Political Culture* (2003) and Leonard A. Gordon's *Brothers Against the Raj: A Biography of Indian Nationalists Sarat and Subhas Chandra Bose* (1990) provide accounts of Bose's life and career. *The Indian Struggle, 1920–1942* (1964), compiled by the Netaji Research Bureau, includes a collection of letters, speeches and other documents covering the years 1935 to 1940 as well as the original manuscript of *The Indian Struggle, 1920–1934*.

5. Peter Heehs mentions the name "India's Fuhrer" assigned to him in an effort to mark him out as an Indian version of the German original. Alfred Tyraneur, a British journalist, portrays Bose as a bloodthirsty leader looking for "human sacrifice" for the

deliverance of the motherland. Still, in spite of its failure in its military efforts the Indian National Army raised by Bose had a tremendous symbolic and psychological effect, giving rise to the subsequent naval mutiny in the Royal Indian Navy in 1946, which undoubtedly played a role in making up the mind of the British to finally withdraw from India.

6. In "Encountering *Hindutva*, Interrogating Religious Nationalism and (En)gendering a Hindu Patriarchy in India's Nuclear Policies" (2006) Runa Das argues:

> Savarkar defined the boundaries of Hindutva in a rather communal manner and further circumscribed its usage in defining the parameters of a modern India. Pitrabhoomi (Fatherland), jati (bloodline) and sanskriti (culture) were identified as the three principles of Hindutva, of which jati became the most critical in establishing the basis of communalism in modern India [...]. This is because the concept implied that only those whose sacred land (sacred to their religion) lay within their fatherland (India) actually had the moral basis for claiming citizenship of India, thereby privileging a cultural/religious rather than a territorial concept of Indian citizenship, which consequently for the Hindu nationalists became the basis of cultural nationalism in India [374].

Under this rubric any one whose sacred land existed outside the geographical boundaries of India were considered foreigners. This ideology was primarily geared towards excluding the Muslims but also other faiths (Jews, Christians etc.) that came to India from abroad. Thus, as Das puts it, "Savarkar's definition of a Hindu community was a purely political entity based on race and the joining of religious dogma so as to mobilize the majority of the Hindus, while streamlining differences, to face an immoral Other" (375).

7. When asked to pass himself through a small ring to get the government job Bose wrote his name on a piece of paper and passed it through the ring.

8. BJP, or Bharatiya Janata Party (Indian People's Party), founded in 1980, is a major political party in India with inclination towards right wing conservative ideologies and links with Hindu fundamentalists. BJP was in power at the time the book was published.

9. India was under emergency rule from June 25, 1975, to March 21, 1977, which bestowed exceptional political and authoritarian power to the then Prime Minister, Indira Gandhi. Under the pretext of protecting national interests, this period witnessed massive crackdowns on political opposition to Indira Gandhi and severe flouting of human rights. The emergency period is seen as the biggest threat to democracy in the history of independent India.

10. Not to be confused with the goddess Kali.

Works Cited

Bakhtin, Mikhail. "Discourse in the Novel." *The Norton Anthology of Theory and Criticism*. Vincent B. Leitch, ed. New York: Norton, 2001. 1190–220.
Baudrillard, Jean. *Simulacra and Simulation*. Ann Arbor: University of Michigan Press, 1994.
Bose, Subhas Chandra, and Netaji Research Bureau. *The Indian Struggle, 1920–1942*. Bombay: Asia, 1964.
Ghosh, Amitav. *The Calcutta Chromosome: A Novel of Fevers, Delirium and Discovery*. New York: Avon, 1995.

Gordon, Leonard A. *Brothers Against the Raj: A Biography of Indian Nationalists Sarat and Subhas Chandra Bose*. New York: Columbia University Press, 1990.
Guttman, Anna. *The Nation of India in Contemporary Indian Literature*. Basingstoke: Palgrave Macmillan, 2007.
Heehs, Peter. "India's Divided Loyalties?" *History Today* 45.7 (1995): 16. *Academic Search Complete*, retrieved 8 December 2008.
Joshi, Ruchir. *The Last Jet-Engine Laugh*. New Delhi: HarperCollins India, 2001.
_____. "Looking Over the Shoulder." *Index on Censorship* 33.4 (2004): 164–71. *Communication and Mass Media Complete*, retrieved 8 December 2008.
McDonald, Ian. *River of Gods*. Amherst: Pyr, 2007.
Pelinka, Anton, and Renée Schell. *Democracy Indian Style: Subhas Chandra Bose and the Creation of India's Political Culture*. New Brunswick, NJ: Transaction, 2003.
Pordzik, Ralph. *The Quest for Postcolonial Utopia: A Comparative Introduction to the Utopian Novel in the New English Literatures*. Studies of World Literature in English. New York: P. Lang, 2001.
Seth, Sanjay. "From Maoism to Postcolonialism? The Indian 'Sixties,' and Beyond." *Inter-Asia Cultural Studies* 7.4 (2006): 589–605. *Academic Search Complete*, retrieved 1 April 2010.
Shippey, T. A. "Introduction." *The Oxford Book of Science Fiction Stories*. T.A. Shippey, ed. Oxford: Oxford University Press, 1993. ix–xxvi.
Tyranauer, Alfred. "India's Would-Be Fuhrer." *Saturday Evening Post* 216.37 (1944): 22–110. *Academic Search Complete*, retrieved 13 November 2009.

PART III

Towards a Postnational Discourse

9

Body Speaks

Communication and the Limits of Nationalism in Octavia Butler's Xenogenesis Trilogy

KATHERINE R. BROAD

Octavia Butler's *Xenogenesis* trilogy suggests an optimistic outlook for society: disease is eliminated or recast as change, the mind and body merge to harmonize both self and society, and future survival seems assured. The catalyst for these transformations comes when an alien species called the Oankali rescues the last survivors of a nuclear apocalypse on Earth. Much of the scholarship on *Xenogenesis* focuses on Butler's treatment of difference and on "issues of interspecies breeding and human-alien power relations" (Doerksen 24).[1] But *Xenogenesis* can also be read in terms of communication. In the Afterword to her short story "Speech Sounds," Butler wonders "whether the human species would ever grow up enough to learn to communicate without using fists of one kind or another" (*Bloodchild* 110). The Oankali offer a model of such evolved, nonviolent communicators, who use their bodies and senses to connect in ways unattainable through words alone.

Butler's plea for a new, more communicative language is reminiscent of the language theories of Romantic thinkers like Wordsworth and Rousseau. Interestingly, reading the Oankali in light of the Romantics helps us consider the possibility that the Oankali may actually communicate *too* well. The aliens produce a more egalitarian and sustainable society based on increased levels of intimacy and empathy made possible through forms of bodily contact. And yet, such immediate and transparent interactions also produce a universally legible discourse that collapses differences by making the other part of the self. By absorbing others into themselves, Oankali methods of incorporation serve to limit subject positions. Rather than improving on the limitations of human languages, Oankali communication eliminates difference and enables colonization.

Although they eschew violence and competition, leading to one view that they "value the diversification of life over certain forms of expansion and growth" (Greenwald 548), a closer look at Oankali forms of interaction will reveal that beyond their engineered flora and fauna, Oankali do not promote diversity. In this light, we should question the view that Butler's subjects "improve on the available human models" (Spillers 4) as we reconsider the extent that community requires empathy and that empathy depends on complete, unmediated understanding. While Butler posits a dichotomy between a society that is egalitarian but homogeneous, and one that is diverse but hierarchical, I hope to challenge this dualism to consider the possibility for equality predicated on diversity, in which difference allows for equality through the proliferation of unranked multiplicities.

Dealing with Difference

The Oankali save humanity from complete extinction, but their benevolence exacts a price. They give humans an offer they cannot refuse: life, at the expense of their cultures, communities, and biological makeup. Biologically compelled to crossbreed with other species and exchange genetic material in a process they call "trade," the Oankali merge their genes with other beings to produce new species better adapted to their environments. They protect humanity on the premise that the existing humans will participate in this trade and birth new beings who are neither fully human nor Oankali. In *Dawn* (1987), Lilith Iyapo, the first person "awakened" from suspended animation aboard the Oankali ship, teaches the first group of humans to resettle in the Amazon basin. The subsequent novels, *Adulthood Rites* (1988) and *Imago* (1989), take place on Earth and follow Lilith's children, the first "constructs," or human–Oankali hybrids, to be born. The Oankali identify a phenomenon they call the "human contradiction," a deadly combination of hierarchical impulses and intelligence that caused humanity to self-destruct. Humans that agree to reproduce with the Oankali breed out this contradiction, which also means eliminating defining features of humanity. Most humans refuse this arrangement and become "resisters," whom the Oankali sterilize so as not to reproduce a race that will destroy itself again.

Although humans fear the loss of reproductive autonomy and species purity, they are also losing their language.² I read the biological differences between humans and Oankali as principally differences in their forms of communication. The Oankali are covered in writhing masses of sensory tentacles that burrow into other bodies to see, touch, and taste—a form of "reading" the available cellular makeup to discern the truth about an object. Oankali males and females have tentacles patterned over their bodies, and the Oankali's third gender, known as ooloi and referred to as "it," also has retractable sensory "hands" used for reproduction. Communication occurs primarily through penetration by these tentacles and hands. Within Oankali logic, bodily interaction produces knowledge by revealing the internal structure and thus inner nature of another object or being.

While humans order difference through realms of inclusion and exclusion, the Oankali incorporate difference into their bodies. Whenever they find something new, they use their tentacles to store its cellular makeup in an organ near the heart, literally making internal what was once outside. As Lilith notes, "Humans persecute their different ones, yet they need them to give themselves definition and status. Oankali seek difference and collect it" (329). "Collecting" lets the aliens "abolish the dualism of self and other" (White 404) by bringing external objects into themselves. But Oankali transgressions of bodily boundaries do not create sites where "the search for homogeneity is resisted," as Jenny Wolmark claims happens in Butler's "transitional states in which the boundaries between self and other become fluid" (29). Instead, incorporating difference within makes it no longer Other but integral to the self, addressing difference by eliminating its very differentness. Both species seek difference, but only humans maintain heterogeneity by allowing the Other to maintain its difference and integrity.

The human compulsion to categorize and the Oankali to merge are rooted in their linguistic structures. Peter Sands identifies two ways the Oankali mediate a self/other divide: taking in the body of the other—which he identifies as a form of cannibalism, a "violent transgression of bodily boundaries" (2)—and language. I consider the penetration of the "skin boundary" a form of communication akin to but also distinct from specifically linguistic forms of communication. Cannibalism and language are not two separate considerations in the text, for the Oankali version of cannibalism *is* a language—the physical act of their communication. If the Oankali bring the Other into the self, and this cannibalistic transgression is the same way the body communicates, then communication also eliminates difference by eliminating the self/other divide. Without this divide, there is no disconnect between communicative bodies, such that listening and speaking subjects experience each other absolutely through unmediated bodily connectedness.

Romanticism and the Oankali

Although Butler's science fiction may seem to posit a unique conception of language, it actually harkens back to a well-established vision of ideal communication. Understanding this history helps us see how the Oankali reiterate pervasive views of language instead of developing different systems. In directly transmitting experience, the Oankali reenact a central tenet of Romanticism: the development of a language that fully aligns with its referent in order to convey an inner self. Wordsworth's intention in the Preface to *Lyrical Ballads* to write "in a selection of language really used by man" connects language to lived experience. He argues that rustic language "arising out of repeated experience and regular feelings" represents humanity more accurately than the elevated language through which neoclassical poets "separate themselves from the sympathies of men." If poetry is "the spontaneous overflow of powerful feelings," then its language must tap into those feelings directly, without distancing writer or reader. This emphasis on feeling, "the essential passions of the heart," implies an underlying state that language expresses and reveals, like the inner natures the Oankali can discern. In both cases, forms of direct communication access and convey an essential interiority (597–598).

Wordsworth doesn't suggest this inner nature exists prior or external to language. Instead, "we know objects only as they are grasped by the mind in a creative though private act, and the nature of this act can be communicated only in the socially shared words of language" (Aarsleff 374). In this view, the mind brings significance to the object, such that meaning happens through perception and is not inherent to the object itself. This perspective is also evident in Rousseau, who, like Wordsworth, links the original site of language to primal emotion. In his *Essay on the Origin of Languages*, Rousseau imagines savage man's first encounter with other men. The fearful savage initially perceives the others as larger than himself and calls them "giants." But as the savage becomes more familiar with them, he realizes they are not giants at all:

> After much experience he will have recognized that since these supposed Giants are neither bigger nor stronger than he, their stature did not fit the idea he had initially attached to the word Giant. He will therefore invent another name common both to them and to himself, for example the name *man*, and he will restrict the name *Giant* to the false object that had struck him during his illusion [254].

The word "giant" is based on the savage's perception, not on a concrete state inherent to the object being described. A giant can become a man when greater proximity allows for familiarity and a concomitant shift in perspective. The Oankali, upon first contact with new beings, undergo no such perceptual change, until and unless their corresponding biologies also change through genetic trade. Their knowledge of the man/giant is only evinced through deep physical contact; attaching a word like giant or man to the body in question would not produce meaning for the Oankali. And while the words produce meaning for human communicators — our vision of another is different depending on whether we think of him as a giant or a man — this meaning is held within the viewer's perceptual capacities and does not speak to the nature of the object beheld.

Butler's aliens recognize that perception does not indicate certainty, and their bodily communication is not subject to "the sad incompetence of human speech" (1850 Prelude 6.593). Recapitulating this Romantic search for (and belief in) direct communication attempts to redress these problems inherent to language: for Wordsworth, Locke, Condillac, and others, only language can "mediate between the subjective and private world of the individual and the public world" (Aarsleff 377), even if this language is necessarily imperfect. *Xenogenesis* compensates for the problems of linguistic (in)communicability by imagining an alternative way of mediating the relationship between individuals and society, so that communicators directly tap into each others' innermost thoughts and experiences.

The Oankali develop their egalitarian society through this fuller access to interiority. Rousseau's example shows how the society that human language makes possible is contingent upon the capacity to compare and then rank. We make meaning out of recognizing difference and creating hierarchy to order this difference, as giant only makes sense relative to man.[3] Those with human bodies and human languages cannot rid themselves of hierarchy, because they have no other way of creating and expressing order. Conversely, the Oankali do not rely on hierarchy as a foundational principle of social organizing, not because they are inherently egalitarian, but because their communication is not based on differentiation or rank. Bodily communication eliminates the separation between the bodies in contact, such that the message passes unchanged and uninterpreted between communicative vessels. There is no signifying chain, no gap between bodies and between words, no fact of difference between two things. Oankali society has no miscommunication, privacy, secrecy, or dishonesty, for no thought, feeling, or state of being can be withheld.

This Romantic fantasy of direct transmission makes writing particularly threatening to the social order because it relies on the mediation of sound and symbol, disconnecting message sent from message received. The Oankali "are suspicious of writing and speech because it transmits a contingent view of reality that runs counter to their own ability to directly transmit both experience and genetic knowledge" (Sands 5). When Lilith tries to learn the Oankali language, she asks to write it down. The Oankali, however, deny her any writing implement and instead change her neurological functions to improve her memory. They make bodies, not words, the primary vehicles for knowledge and communication (although they don't directly change humans' genes to make them nonhierarchical). Humans maintain difference through the intervention of external mediators that affirm the separateness of the associating entities. The Oankali adapt their bodies to perform activities humans need technological mediators to perform, eliminating any distance — any difference — between self and other and between self and environment.

Colonialist Knowledge

This absence of division proves highly threatening to human's sense of self and order, suggesting that human communication requires a degree of alienation through differentiation. When ooloi enter to meet the first group of awakened humans, they sedate the humans to help them overcome their natural fear of the unknown, expecting those disturbed by aesthetic aspects of difference to habituate to the unfamiliar. But the humans' deeper fear is of the permeating aspects of bodily communication. While one man, Peter, accepts his ooloi while he is drugged, he later feels the drugs caused him to "demean himself in alien perversions. His humanity was profaned. His manhood was taken away" (192). For Peter, the invasiveness of bodily communication and its disruption of gender norms are more problematic than the physical differences between alien and human. Humans resist having their capacity for language taken away, as the ooloi read their bodies instead of heeding their words.

Replacing language with the body is a theme Butler introduces earlier: in *Wild Seed* (1980), from the *Patternist* series, a shape-shifter named Anyanwu learns about the nature of a dolphin by transforming into one. She tells her companion, Doro, that messages of the flesh are clearer than those in books: "It seems that you could misunderstand your books.... Other men made them. Other men can lie or make mistakes. But the flesh can only tell me what it Is" (80). Madhu Dubey uses this passage to contrast Anyanwu's system of knowing to rational, distant scientific knowledge. I would add that Anyanwu's epistemology is posited as superior not simply because she "heals the dichotomy between mind and body" (Dubey 37) in a form of merging elaborated by the Oankali, but because she engages in an entirely different mode of communication with her environment. Anyanwu suggests, like the Oankali, that language, constructed by people and subject to interpretation, can never be as specific as the information contained in a cell, associating certainty with biology and a superior form of knowledge.

The dangers of this celebrated transmission become clear as the *Patternist* series progresses and Anyanwu's offspring become enmeshed in a telekinetic web that controls their thoughts and feelings directly, without opportunities for agency made possible through the inconstancies of language. Here, direct biological control becomes enslaving and bodily knowledge does not guarantee more humane forms of living. Likewise, we must be critical of the stance in *Xenogenesis* that biology is the best or only viable communicator.

Anyanwu's and the Oankali's hierarchy of biological over linguistic epistemologies points to Foucault's formulation of ranked knowledges. According to Foucault, there are both erudite and disqualified knowledges, so categorized by those whose dominance depends on their power to determine what counts as knowledge. In contemporary Western society, Oankali knowledge of how to live in sync with the environment, without the use of synthetics or machines, is generally considered native, low-hierarchy knowledge. Yet in the novels, as in Butler's *Parable* series, this knowledge becomes erudite and necessary for survival. Oankali knowledge of the body, like Anyanwu's knowledge of the dolphin, is also categorized as erudite, more accurate and discerning than what could be determined by human knowledges that retain a self/other divide through language and physical touch. Humans' insights into their own selves and bodies is shown to be disqualified knowledge, subjugated or naïve knowledge that is "located low down on the hierarchy, beneath the required level of cognition or scientificity" (Foucault 82).

The claim to know others and discount their knowledges leads Gayatri Spivak to ask, "Can the subaltern speak?" (28). Can those who have been disqualified have a voice or be heard, especially by those whose claim to knowledge enacts this silencing? In *Xenogenesis*, humans are discoursing subjects to the extent that the novels renarrativize the process of colonialism from the perspective of the colonized subject, making Lilith the central speaking subject, followed by her construct children. But they are only heard to the degree they remain legible to the Oankali. As Saidiya Hartman suggests, the body comes to speak when the voice of the colonized is refused recognition, and it speaks only what the colonizer interprets: "To the degree that the body speaks it is made to speak the master's truth and augments his power" (22). Although the Oankali can fully read the humans' internal makeup, this encompassing knowledge is not reciprocal. Humans cannot listen, hear, know, or absorb Oankali thoughts and systems in the same way that their own bodies are mined for knowledge.

Instead, this asymmetry remains central to maintaining the human-alien imbalance, as the human body is posited as the site of colonization through which the Oankali enact their genetic trade. By arriving at a claim to knowledge through penetrating, cannibalizing, or taking in the body of another, the Oankali enact the conception of incorporation theory, largely discredited in human law, whereby "external things become property by being brought into the body" (Munzon 61). A claim to know another through communicative acts thus takes on a colonialist dimension when such knowledge is a way of exerting property rights over the body and subjectivity of another. The Oankali's interpretations of what human bodies are speaking suggest that the dominant's claim to know the Other is a way of appropriating the colonized subject's attempts at speech.

Lilith's human lover Joseph, who mates with her and an ooloi named Nikanj, struggles to understand how he could enjoy being penetrated. He stammers, "Then how can they.... How can they make us feel ... what I felt?" Lilith responds, "By pushing the right electrochemical buttons. I don't claim to understand it. It's *like a language* that they have a special gift for. They know our bodies *better than we do*" (169 emphasis mine). Nikanj penetrates Lilith to heal her and make genetic alterations that eliminate her predisposition for cancer and strengthen her body against aging and disease. It gives pleasure through its touch and through erotic neural stimulation she shares with Joseph. It also penetrates her to determine something fundamental about who she is that she may not even know herself. It is telling that Lilith understands all these aspects of her bodily interactions with Nikanj as a language and prioritizes its knowledge of her body over her own.

Nikanj's erudite knowledge characterizes human self-knowledge as lesser than its awareness of their internal subjectivities. That the Oankali can know humans so fully through their bodies, such that Nikanj knows Joseph wants to have sex with it before Joseph admits this to himself, leads humans to think the aliens can read their minds or manipulate them into thinking, feeling, and doing things at odds with their "real" interests. Joseph's knowledge of his own self is dismissed as a subjugated knowledge lesser than Nikanj's penetrative, more discerning comprehension. But Nikanj justifies his advancements by considering desire in terms of consensus: although the mind may say one thing, if the body truly wants another, the Oankali can pleasurably guide the human to fulfill what the self "really" wants but won't let itself articulate. Because the Oankali claim to infer humans' real interests based on their bodies and not words, when humans try to establish boundaries around what they do not desire, the Oankali disregard the speech act in favor of their own interpretations of biological statements.

This view of consensus between conflicting wants suggests that what we say to others and ourselves may be hollow words. We can be unknowable to ourselves, more unknowable to others, and we can lie — all of which are unknown to the Oankali. To them, the body is the final arbiter of truth. The body never lies; if it says one thing and the voice another, the Oankali never consider that it may be the body that is out of sync with the mind, or that the body's wants may not ultimately be desirable. These divisions are meaningless within an Oankali worldview because an integrated being wouldn't act against its own self-interests. In seeking consensus, the Oankali cannot understand internal contradictions because they have no mind/body divide. Explaining its capacity to read other bodies, especially during sex, Nikanj tells Joseph, "I won't hurt you. And I offer a oneness that your people strive for, dream of, but can't truly attain alone" (189). Oankali methods of penetrative discourse allow for a deeper connection than what can be realized through human physical and linguistic contact alone. Yet it is precisely this ability to connect that fuels the Oankali's disturbing claim to know the colonized subject better than he knows himself.

Colonialist Discourses

Butler shows the complexities of colonization by making human survival dependent on an imperfect relationship with its saviors. Through the Oankali, humans are able to survive and develop a more peaceful, sustainable, and egalitarian society, with hope for the future. Yet this perspective that the Oankali offer a better future casts human knowledge as secondary to alien erudition and justifies their coercive acts. As Erin Ackerman points out regarding the genetic trade, "Despite being repulsed by such an intimate trade with such un-human creatures, the humans have very little choice in the matter, Awakening as they do on the Oankali ship" (24). Does it matter that these "un-human creatures" save people that otherwise would have died on the inhospitable Earth? Human reliance on and indebtedness to the Oankali may revise this question of agency, but at the same time, the fact that humans need the Oankali reinforces a colonial fantasy that assures the colonizers their presence is necessary for the betterment of a backward race that could not survive without their intervention. To what extent does the lack of human agency — no matter the extenuating circumstances surrounding that lack — problematize attempts to rationalize the benefits of colonialism to the colonized subject? Or does the suggestion that humans are better off for being colonized (since otherwise they would be dead) imply that colonization benefits the colonized, despite or because of the ways those in power can coerce consent from those with "very little choice in the matter"?

The assumption that the colonized subjects are better off for their subjugation is repeated in the insistence that the resisters, who elect not to reproduce with the Oankali, are being left behind as the rest of civilization progresses. Alyson Buckman writes, "Butler depicts those who attempt to maintain stasis and contemporary normative injunctions concerning behavior, sexuality, and human physicalness as stagnant, sterile, and obsolete" (204). But the novels do not in fact portray such stagnation. The first construct child, Akin, eventually persuades the other Oankali to let the resisters establish their own colony on Mars, so that they will not die when the construct generation eventually leaves Earth and life on the planet fades.[4] Another critic echoes Buckman's view, stating that resisters "exist unchanged on Mars" (Belk 379). But the fact that resisters have to adapt to life on Mars (thus enacting their own extraterrestrial colonization) suggests they are neither stagnant nor obsolete. The novel intentionally leaves unresolved how the humans fare but suggests a continued process of adaptation and change that, significantly, also requires the Oankali to change as they are compelled by the new constructs to consider human views.

The resisters' vision of humanity and their own species integrity is already defunct, regardless of their refusal to participate in the colonizer's breeding program. Resisters think they can recolonize Earth without the Oankali, but all of the plants and animals they depend on for survival are Oankali creations, produced from genetic blueprints the Oankali gathered from the wreckage of post-apocalyptic Earth and changed to become stronger and more resilient. Their attachment to homeland as they associate their identities with humanity and their humanity with Earth is based on a false premise, for the Earth has been altered by the Oankali presence and can't be said to constitute a pure human space. The Mars settlement, although not polluted with Oankali genes, is also dependent on the Oankali for its existence and survival. The conviction that the group's humanity is not changing ignores how the novels call into question basic conceptions of humanity such as "humans live on Earth."

The ways the resisters are forced to adapt to the Oankali even without consenting to these changes suggest that consent is never really possible when it comes to adaptation, for as Butler continually shows, survival requires change.[5] In this sense, critics are right to point out the problems of stagnancy within human populations. But the assertion that the resisters do not change at all discounts the extent to which change happens whether or not we dictate its course. Butler reinvests the abject subject with the agency denied by colonization, in the form of this capacity for change. Lilith survives, in an altered form, because she chooses life over death, deciding not to ask an ooloi to kill her when offered an out. Challenging the argument that this choice does not represent a free and informed decision, Lilith herself says, "I chose to live" (672). To deny Lilith this decision is to further force her abjection by refusing her a say in her own life. Butler does enact forms of resistance, then, by refusing to reproduce in its entirety a colonial discourse that maintains clear power dynamics and identity boundaries between colonized and colonizer. Or rather she, like her characters, reproduces with a difference more conventional narratives of encounter — to adapt Cathy Peppers's observation that *Xenogenesis* describes "the production of offspring different from either of its parents" (47). Both colonized and colonizer are altered by their meeting, debunking the myth that the colonized exist in an unchanging prehistory while colonizers remain stable and untouched by change.

Other Ways

My point is not just that the novels enact a complicated view of colonization, suggesting that contact across differences, while potentially beneficial, implicates bodies and knowledges in preexisting power relations. Rather, I call attention to the contradictions within Butler's recapitulation of Romanticism and its implication for colonial discourses to ask what kinds of equalities are constructed through forms of connectivity engendered via alternate means of communication. The peaceful Oankali society predicated on a valuation of difference is preferable to humans' xenophobia and war, but the seductiveness of the Oankali world order should not blind us to the fact that their incorporation of difference is also an eradication. We are familiar with horrific attempts at creating a world without difference, whether totalitarian eradications of alternative subjectivities from the social and political body or genocidal injustices perpetuated to create a false sense of unity through purification.[6]

Difference and differentiation are necessary for the perpetuation of life, because without difference we lose ourselves completely. When a construct ooloi named Aaor is unable to find human mates with whom it can bond, it disintegrates into a barely-conscious sea slug. In becoming less genetically complex, it grows closer to its origins and its environment, enacting a more extreme form of Oankali interconnectivity. Aaor cannot survive without a separate physical and mental self, revealing the dangers of eliminating distinctions between self and surroundings. Aaor's need for connection does not simply signal that "community and companionship is necessary to avoid dissolution" (Buckman 211), but reveals that life forms, no matter their drive for connection, must also maintain differentiation to exist.[7] The merging of subjectivities is necessarily a failed project, a form of self-annihilation through the elimination of the other.

Aaor's near-suicide reveals the necessity, even within Oankali society, of preserving what we can think of in terms of Levinasian ethics as the Other's actual otherness. Considering face-to-face interactions, Emmanuel Levinas develops an ethics of responsibility that allows the Other to remain an unknowable entity whose very unknowability allows for multiplicity within society. If goals of the Oankali include longer, healthier, more sustainable existences, they also show us through the erasure of ontological distinctions the necessity of diversity, not simply through naturalized social categories but though the respect for and promulgation of distinct subjectivities that resist being subsumed into a larger, dominant whole. This does not mean that all forms of difference are equally attractive; I do not claim a more equitable society is undesirable because such fairness somehow eliminates the divisions necessary to maintain difference. Rather, I mean that the elimination of difference down to the level of the subject's interiority, through claims that this interiority can be accessed by a more dominant power, promotes a centralized, disciplined subjectivity at odds with the diversity that Butler otherwise seems to promote.

A world without division, in speech and subjectivity, serves the totalitarian interests of a universal governance that eliminates the very subjectivities it seeks to collapse. Levinas worries that in this dystopic scenario, "in becoming a discourse universally coherent, language would at the same time realize the universal State, in which multiplicity is reabsorbed and discourse comes to an end, for lack of interlocutors" (217). Language without multiplicity is meaningless, for a universal connectivity eliminates the wholeness and singularity of the discoursing subject. Thus the liberation that seems promised by communicative possibility is prevented when the social is formed by tethering individuals to the majority and ensuring their equality by eliminating their distinctions. The idea that there exists an essential self accessible through language — an underlying reality that we could reach if only we could contact it — makes absolute knowledge the aim of communication and assumes that knowledge is foundational to empathy, understanding, and community. This produces a false dichotomy in which the choices for being are egalitarian homogeneity or hierarchical diversity.

There must be other ways to conceptualize equality, such as the possibility for empathy and equality *without* complete understanding and connection. As Claire Curtis notes, "Butler's discomfort with utopia is a discomfort with an ideologically pure utopia," and she challenges her readers "to embrace ambiguity and uncertainty" (366). More specifically, the discomfort with the colonialist ramifications of the Oankali's claim to empathetic connectivity should open us up to other forms of connection, namely those that allow for the preservation of the other's selfhood. It can be precisely the distance — the difference — between individuals that allows for community to exist as a necessary plurality. In "the human community instituted by language, where the interlocutors remain absolutely separated," it is possible to experience equality "where the other commands the same and reveals himself to the same responsibility" (Levinas 213–214). True equality in action and not abstraction not only demands others, but encounters others in all their unknowablity. Such a form of subjectivity that seeks to maintain difference would allow humans to overcome the limitations of fully communicable interactions and live more peacefully, without losing the differences that allow us to live in the first place.

Notes

1. See Bonner, Jacobs, Michaels, Peppers, Sands, Tucker, and Zaki.
2. On the importance of language diversity within postcolonial power relations, see Ashcroft pp. 8–11.
3. A well-known structuralist and poststructuralist point is that meaning requires difference; I am concerned with the role of hierarchy in this aspect of speech.
4. The Oankali also preserve their own ur-species, the Akjai, which does not participate in trades. This suggests the Oankali do value species purity—but only in their species. It takes significant convincing for most Oankali to concede that a strain of humanity should be allowed to endure without cross-breeding.
5. Compromise is a constant theme in Butler's work; see the *Patternist* and *Parable* series; *Kindred* (1979); and *Fledgling* (2005).
6. See Rouvillois, "Utopia and Totalitarianism."
7. An opposite reading of Aaor could be that it breaks down out of a failure to properly colonize and incorporate, but this interpretation would still counter the idea that Aaor and the Oankali exemplify egalitarian, communal bonds.

Works Cited

Aarsleff, Hans. "Wordsworth, Language, and Romanticism." In *From Locke to Saussure: Essays on the Study of Language and Intellectual History,* edited by Hans Aarsleff, 372–381. Minneapolis: University of Minnesota Press, 1982.
Ackerman, Erin. "Becoming and Belonging: The Productivity of Pleasures and Desires in Octavia Butler's *Xenogenesis* Trilogy." *Extrapolation: A Journal of Science Fiction and Fantasy.* 49.1 (Spring 2008): 24–43.
Ashcroft, Bill, Gareth Griffiths, and Helen Tiffin. *The Empire Writes Back: Theory and Practice in Post-Colonial Literatures.* New York: Routledge, 2002.
Belk, Nolan. "The Certainty of the Flesh: Octavia Butler's Use of the Erotic in the *Xenogenesis* Trilogy." *Utopian Studies* 19.3 (2008): 369–389.
Bonner, Frances. "Difference and Desire, Slavery and Seduction: Octavia Butler's *Xenogenesis.*" *Foundation* 48 (Spring 1990) 50–62.
Buckman, Alyson. "'What Good Is All This to Black People?': Octavia Butler's Reconstruction of Corporeality." *FEMSPEC* 4.2 (2004): 201–218.

Butler, Octavia. *Lilith's Brood: Dawn, Adulthood Rites, Imago.* New York: Grand Central, 1989.
_____. *Seed to Harvest: Wild Seed, Mind of My Mind, Clay's Ark, Patternmaster.* New York: Warner, 2007.
_____. "Speech Sounds." *Bloodchild and Other Stories.* New York: Seven Stories, 1996.
Curtis, Claire. "Editorial." *Utopian Studies* 19.3 (2008): 365–367.
Doerksen, Teri Ann. "Octavia E. Butler: Parables of Race and Difference." In *Into Darkness Peering: Race and Color in the Fantastic*, edited by Elisabeth Anne Leonard, 21–34. Westport, CT: Greenwood, 1997.
Dubey, Madhu. "Becoming Animal in Black Women's Science Fiction." In *Afro-Future Females: Black Writers Chart Science Fiction's Newest New-Wave Trajectory*, edited by Marlene S. Barr, 31–51. Columbus: Ohio State University Press, 2008.
Foucault, Michel. "Two Lectures." *Power/Knowledge: Selected Interviews and Other Writings 1972–1977.* Colin Gordon, ed. New York: Pantheon, 1980. 78–108.
Greenwald, Rachel. "Ecology Beyond Ecology: Life After the Accident in Octavia Butler's *Xenogenesis* Trilogy." *Modern Fiction Studies.* 55.3 (Fall 2009): 545–565.
Hartman, Saidiya. *Scenes of Subjection: Terror, Slavery, and Self-Making in Nineteenth-Century America.* New York: Oxford University Press, 1997.
Jacobs, Naomi. "Posthuman Bodies and Agency in Octavia Butler's *Xenogenesis.*" In *Dark Horizons: Science Fiction and the Dystopian Imagination*, edited by Tom Moylan and Raffaella Baccolini, 91–112. New York: Routledge, 2003.
Levinas, Emmanuel. *Totality and Infinity: An Essay on Exteriority.* Trans. Alphonso Lingis. Pittsburgh: Dusquesne University Press, 1969.
Michaels, Walter Benn. "Political Science Fictions." *New Literary History* 31.4 (2000): 649–64.
Munzer, Stephen. *A Theory of Property.* New York: Cambridge University Press, 1990.
Peppers, Cathy. "Dialogic Origins and Alien Identities in Butler's *Xenogenesis.*" *Science Fiction Studies* 22 (1995): 47–62.
Rousseau, Jean-Jacques. "Discourse on the Origin and Foundations or Inequality Among Men *or* Second Discourse." In *Rousseau: The Discourses and Other Early Political Writings*, edited and translated by Victor Gourevitch, 111–231. New York: Cambridge University Press, 1997.
_____. "Essay on the Origin of Languages." In *Rousseau: The Discourses and Other Early Political Writings*, edited and translated by Victor Gourevitch, 247–299. New York: Cambridge University Press, 1997.
Rouvillois, Frédéric. "Utopia and Totalitarianism." Trans. Nadia Benabid. In *Utopia: The Search for the Ideal Society in the Western World*, edited by Roland Schaer, Gregory Claeys, and Lyman Tower Sarvent, 316–332. New York: New York Public Library/Oxford University Press, 2000.
Sands, Peter. "Octavia Butler's Chiastic Cannibalistics." *Utopian Studies* 14.1 (2003): 1–14.
Spillers, Hortense. "Imaginative Encounters." In *Afro-Future Females: Black Writers Chart Science Fiction's Newest New-Wave Trajectory*, edited by Marlene S. Barr, 3–5. Columbus: Ohio State University Press, 2008.
Spivak, Gayatri. "Can the Subaltern Speak?" In *The Post-colonial Studies Reader*, edited by Bill Ashcroft, Garreth Griffiths, and Helen Tiffin, 28–37. New York: Routledge, 1995.
Tucker, Jeffrey. "'The Human Contradiction': Identity and/as Essence in Octavia Butler's *Xenogenesis* Trilogy." *Yearbook of English Studies* 37.2 (2007): 164–181.

White, Eric. "The Erotics of Becoming: *Xenogenesis* and 'The Thing.'" *Science Fiction Studies* 20.3 (1993): 394–408.
Wolmark, Jenny. *Aliens and Others: Science Fiction, Feminism and Postmodernism.* Iowa City: University of Iowa Press, 1994.
Wordsworth, William. *Preface to* Lyrical Ballads. New York: Oxford University, 1984. 595–615.
_____. *The Prelude: 1799, 1805, 1850.* Ed. Abrams, M.H, Stephen Gill, and Jonathan Wordsworth. New York: Norton, 1979.
Zaki, Hoda. "Utopia, Dystopia, and Ideology in the Science Fiction of Octavia Butler." *Science Fiction Studies* 17.2 (1990): 239–251.

10

Engineering a Cosmopolitan Future
Race, Nation, and World of Warcraft
Jason W. Ellis

Many scholars, technologists, and futurists agree that the Internet, as an open and neutral network that facilitates the unrestricted flow of information, communication, and virtual presence, breaks down the real world barriers to human interaction separated by natural and political barriers.[1] An established and increasingly popular Internet-based video game, more specifically, a massively multiplayer online role-playing game (MMORPG), called *World of Warcraft*,[2] inventively brings people together in the virtual fantasy world of Azeroth, which is a postmodern mashup of recognized fantasy and science fiction tropes with real-world people, ethnicities, and cultures.[3] According to the most recent press release from Blizzard Entertainment, the company responsible for its creation, 11.5 million subscribers[4] from around the world play within the insanely successful virtual world — an imagined space made real on the computer screen thanks to 3D graphics technologies.[5] Obviously, something significant is taking place when people from different parts of the planet Earth meet to role-play a unique character that is not required to match the player's ethnicity, gender, or appearance.[6] Furthermore, gamers' characters generally veil their real-world identity and its culturally constructed characteristics, such as race or gender,[7] to the extent that human beings in the physical world meet each other within the game world on an equal playing field; each as a character that he or she creates to play the game and interact antagonistically or cooperatively with other players.[8]

Given this brief synopsis of the number of *WoW* players and the equalizing space of the game for people from a variety of geographical places associated with nation-state boundaries and representing numerous ethnicities and cultures, it seems that the game, which is overtly about war, death, and defense of one's own race and faction, carries an implicit cosmopolitanism hidden within the game's mechanics (quests), in-game achievements (associated with travel and exploring the entire world of Azeroth), and the over-arching game narrative in which the two opposing factions, which are comprised of the only playable races, tentatively cooperate against the subversively encroaching Burning Legion.[9] Furthermore, it is these cosmopolitan imbued in-game elements that may serve an educational and pedagogical function for game players. In this essay, I argue that *WoW* not only represents cosmopolitan ideals, but it also teaches players how to be more cosmopolitan in the physical world.

The most significant emblem of the cosmopolitanism of *WoW* is character travel through friendly and non-friendly geo-political regions within the game world of Azeroth. Characters must walk, ride animals or magical/mechanical vehicles, and most importantly, board ships that traverse a dividing ocean between the three largest landmasses: Kalimdor, the Eastern Kingdoms, and Northrend. It is the signification of the ship as a transport for people, commodities, and culture — a signification that predates Paul Gilroy's *The Black Atlantic* in regard to cosmopolitan theory — that provides a constructive point of departure for the next phase of this essay in which I will briefly chart the genealogies of cosmopolitan thought, establish how important the ship plays in modern cosmopolitan theory, and in turn, reveal how indebted cosmopolitan theory is to the experiences of people of the African diaspora.

As a guide, I will begin by offering a few definitions of cosmopolitanism, which may be constructive for getting a grasp on this big idea before proceeding to a discussion of its modern reascension from antiquity. However, it should be noted that, as Bruce Robbins writes, "Situating cosmopolitanism means taking a risk" (2). It is a risky business, because there are stakeholders for and against what cosmopolitanism means and what it might mean for our future. The Oxford English Dictionary offers this definition to cosmopolitanism: "Cosmopolitan character; adherence to cosmopolitan principles." This OED entry helpfully points to "cosmoplite," or "A 'citizen of the world'; one who regards or treats the whole world as his country; one who has no national attachments or prejudices." These definitions of cosmopolitanism and cosmoplites are a beginning, but they lack an ethical dimension that is an important aspect of cosmopolitanism debates today. Tania Friedel offers some direction on this when she writes: "Cosmopolitanism allows for the possibility of inter-ethnic subjectivities, intercultural affiliations, and change in any given mode of identification. It also recognizes democratic common ground as an imagined or theoretical space, on that requires active, willed participation for its very existence" (2). Cosmopolitanism is like a tapestry woven of all of the exquisite representations of peoples and cultures. It recognizes the value and promise of all human beings, and it depends on the involvement of others to enjoy and carry the weight of its responsibilities. My working definition of cosmopolitanism is world citizenship with all the rewards of multicultural engagement and the responsibilities as an invested citizen among all of humanity.

Looking backwards, cosmopolitan theory and practice is often traced genealogically back to Greek, Cynic, and later Stoic philosophers. In Rome, philosophers including Cicero, Seneca, and Epictetus formulated what Thomas J. Schlereth calls "the most mature cosmopolitanism of antiquity" (xix). These philosophers promoted an early intellectual elitist identity as "citizens of the world" (Schlereth xix). In the West, cosmopolitan theory and ideals were rekindled during the Enlightenment among the intelligentsia including, but not limited to Benjamin Franklin, David Hume, Voltaire, and Immanuel Kant. Of these proto-cosmopolites, cosmopolitanism was, as Schlereth writes, "more symbolic and theoretical than actual and practical" (xii). Generally, Schlereth defines that era's cosmopolitanism as:

> Enlightenment cosmopolitanism possessed a number of distinguishing characteristics. First, it was an attitude of mind that attempted to transcend chauvinistic national loyalties or parochial prejudices in its intellectual interests and pursuits. In the ideal, the "cosmopolite," or "citizen of the world," sought to be identified by an interest in, a familiarity with, or appreciation of many parts and peoples of the world; he wished to be distinguished by a readiness to borrow from other lands or civilizations in the formation of his intellectual, cultural, and artistic patterns. Therefore, the typical Enlightenment cosmopolite aspired to be — although he did not always succeed in being — eclectic in his philosophical and scientific outlook, synergistic in his religious perspective, and international in his economic and political thought [xi–xii].

For Schlereth, Enlightenment cosmopolitanism was a way of seeing and imagining other peoples and their culture and history, which allowed one to reflect on the culture of others and incorporate those aspects that were considered useful, unique, or compelling.[10] The Enlightenment proto-cosmopolites did maintain their own culturally derived and invented racisms, but the theoretical ground work, especially that of Kant, cannot be jettisoned in whole, because there are important ideas that can be employed and rehabilitated for a continued promotion of cosmopolitan ideals.[11]

It is important that this theorization of cosmopolitanism is Kant's often repeated and cited essay from 1795, "Toward Perpetual Peace: A Philosophical

Sketch."[12] Kant argues in this essay for a juridical constitution that establishes individual citizen rights, rights for states among all states to arrive out of a state of nature (i.e., war), and what he terms "cosmopolitan right," which would make individuals citizens of humanity and therefore free from external—meaning from a citizen of another state—physical influence. Kant's cosmopolitan theory fits into his overall theory of history through human progress arising from Nature's creation toward the production of culture. However, he notes in his later work, *Metaphysics of Morals, Doctrine of Right* (1797, second edition 1798) that perpetual peace is a utopian goal that we are obligated to work toward:

> Since one ought to emerge from the state of nature among peoples in order to enter into a legal condition just as much as one ought to do so in the state of nature among individuals, therefore, before this happens, all right of peoples and all that can be acquired through war or preserved as external "mine" and "yours" among states are merely *provisional*, and only in a general *union of states* can this become *peremptorily* valid (analogous to the union through which a people becomes a state) and can a true *condition of peace* be attained. But since too great an expansion of such a state of peoples over vast regions would ultimately make governance of the same, and hence the protection of each member, impossible, whereas a number of such corporations would in turn lead to a condition of war, *perpetual peace* (the ultimate end of all of international right) is admittedly an idea that cannot be realized. Yet the political principles that aim at this idea, namely, those that direct us to enter into such relations as serve a continual *approach* toward perpetual peace are indeed, to that extent that they are a task grounded in duty and hence in the right of human beings and states, realizable [145].

It is the approach toward perpetual peace that is as important as its being asymptotically out of reach. For Kant, perpetual peace may be a utopian goal, but it is a goal worth striving towards. Returning to Kant's "Toward Perpetual Peace," he further elaborates on the problems inherent in its achievement:

> The growing prevalence of a (narrower or wider) community among the peoples of the earth has now reached a point at which the violation of right at any *one* place on earth is felt in *all* places. For this reason, the idea of cosmopolitan right is no fantastic or exaggerated conception of right. Rather it is a necessary supplement to the unwritten code of constitutional and international right, for public human right in general, and hence for perpetual peace. Only under this condition can one flatter oneself to be continually progressing toward perpetual peace [84–85].

In progressing towards perpetual peace, cosmopolitan right depends on its universal application to all places and all people.[13]

The scope of Kant's cosmopolitan theory depends upon the following important passage from the section titled, "Third Definitive Article of Perpetual Peace: *Cosmopolitan Right* Shall Be Limited to the Condition of Universal Hospitality":

As in the previous articles, we are concerned here with right, not with philanthropy, and in this context hospitality (a host's conduct to his guest) means the right of a stranger not to be treated in a hostile manner by another upon his arrival on the other's territory. If it can be done without causing his death, the stranger can be turned away, yet as long as the stranger behaves peacefully where he happens to be, his host may not treat him with hostility. It is not the *right of a guest* that the stranger has a claim to (which would require a special, charitable contract stipulating that he be made a member of the household for a certain period of time), but rather a right to visit, to which all human beings have a claim, to present oneself to society by virtue of the right of common possession of the surface of the earth. Since it is the surface of a sphere, they cannot scatter themselves on it without limit, but they must rather ultimately tolerate one another as neighbors, and originally no one has more of a right to be at a given place on earth than anyone else.—Uninhabitable parts of this surface, the sea and the deserts, separate this community, but in such a way that the *ship* or the *camel* (the ship of the desert) makes it possible to come into contact with one another across these regions that belong to no one, and to use the right to the *surface*, which is common to the human species, to establish commerce with one another. The inhospitableness of the sea coastlines (for example, of the Barbary Coast), where ships in nearby seas are pirated or stranded sailors are made into slaves, or the inhospitableness of the sand deserts (of the Arabic Bedouins), where contact with the nomadic tribes is regarded as a right to plunder them, is contrary to natural right. The right of hospitality, that is, the right of foreign arrivals, pertains, however, only to conditions of the possibility of *attempting* interaction with the old inhabitants.—In this way, remote parts of the world can establish relations peacefully with one another, relations which ultimately become regulated by public laws and can thus finally bring the human species ever closer to a cosmopolitan constitution [82].

In this passage, Kant addresses the connection between travel and commerce, and its significance to the development of cosmopolitan right. Notably, the word that Kant uses for "commerce" is "*Verkehr*," which has a variety of meanings including association, commerce, communication, dealings, intercourse, traffic, and transportation. Taking the translator's employment of Kant's term to mean commerce, it is important to consider the variety of meanings of this word in English. According to the OED, commerce may mean "exchange between men of the products of nature or art; buying and selling together; trading; exchange of merchandise," "intercourse in the affairs of life; dealings," "interchange (esp. of letters, ideas, etc.)," and "communication, means to free intercourse." Taking the broad spectrum of meanings for *Verkehr* and commerce together, this one word paints a very vivid picture of the kind of cosmopolitanism that Kant formulated. For Kant, cosmopolitanism is about the exchange of culture between peoples, which is made possible by the cosmopolitan right to hospitality. Furthermore, it is in the above passage, at the modern establishment and theorization of cosmopolitanism that along with the idea that all people have an equal right to habitation of the world and the promise of interaction with other cultures that the metaphor of the ship and camel — modes of transportation across vast distances and geo-political barriers — are paramount to understanding and fully engaging what cosmopolitanism really is. Thus, the technologies of travel, which bring together cultures, are integral to our understanding of cosmopolitanism, and this technological characteristic of cosmopolitanism will have more importance in the later discussion of "cosmopolitan patriotism" and *WoW*.

Before continuing to trace the technological aspects of cosmopolitanism, it is essential to connect Kant's ideas with the pragmatic cosmopolitanism of one of his near-contemporaries — an emancipated former African slave who would live a large part of his life on the water as a seaman who transcended the idea of a rooted existence by traveling and reversing the Middle Passage many times in his voyages. This individual used travel technologies to traverse the network of shipping lanes and commercial transaction. Also, he traveled nearly all over the globe during his time as a sailor when he voyaged to Europe, the Middle East, the Caribbean, and North, Central, and South America during his tenure on the high seas (Costanzo 257). The person to whom I am referring is Olaudah Equiano (1745–1797).

Equiano traveled the world as a slave and a free man, and he left a record of his experiences and personal reflections that place his travels in a unique light. Unlike Kant who I characterize as a proto-cosmopolite, or one who thinks and theorized the ideals of such a world citizen, Equiano was a cosmopolitan citizen of the world both in thought and deed — notably to an extent.[14] To better understand Equiano's world citizenship, it would be useful to consider a more contemporary engagement of the African diaspora, the middle passage, and the ship as symbol in Paul Gilroy's *The Black Atlantic: Modernity and Double Consciousness* (1993).

Gilroy argues in *The Black Atlantic* for a reevaluation of the Western post–Enlightenment view of modernity that isolates European history and cultural development from that of the peoples of Africa. He establishes the necessity of rethinking the relationship between Europe, Africa, and the Americas from the slave trade era to the present through the use of ships to traverse the Atlantic with people, ideas, and cultures. The diverse people of Africa did not intrude upon the European project of modernity, but instead the history and development of modern European history and culture is inextricably linked, tied, and united with that of Africa. Europe and Africa co-evolved such that modernity emerged for both as a result of the European imperialist incursions into African and the forceful enslavement and dispersal of African peoples into the Caribbean and the Americas. Obviously, peoples from all of the geographical areas involved intermixed, interacted, and smashed together like the infinite crash of waves on the rocks of history. Power of knowing and understanding the past and current milieu comes from the realization that history is not a monolithic structure, but a rhizomic network of resistances and power effects that culminate in a shared, organic history that points the way to future cooperation through mutual understanding. Furthermore, he defines the black Atlantic as:

> The specificity of the modern political and cultural formation I want to call the black Atlantic can be defined, on one level, through this desire to transcend both the structures of the nation state and the constraints of ethnicity and national particularity. These desires are relevant to understanding political organising and cultural criticism. They have always sat uneasily alongside the strategic choices forced on black movements and individuals embedded in national political cultures and nation states in America, the Caribbean, and Europe [19].

The black Atlantic is a broad theory, but it has the power of contraction or expansion in regard to studying what I call black cultures, or dispersed, local, imagined, or other shared Pan-African identities linked by an imagined cultural archive. I will elaborate further on parallels between this imagined cultural archive and *WoW* in the final phase of this essay.

Gilroy further delves into the contradictions inherent to European conceptions of modernity, and explicitly engages the discounted fact that slavery was necessary to developing the European Enlightenment. Furthermore, he resists and challenges essentializing and universalizing theories of race and identity in modernity. He complicates things in order to reveal the inherent beauty in networks, cross pollination, and a shared history. In his use of the black Atlantic as an emblem of fractal exchanges of culture, Gilroy is making a gesture towards cosmopolitanism without explicitly using the word.

Gilroy's theory of the black Atlantic breaks down the traditional historical barriers raised to encapsulate national and geographic narratives. He qualifies his theory as, harkening back to Deleuze and Guattari, "the rhizomorphic, fractal structure of the transcultural, international formation I call the black Atlantic" (4). The black Atlantic is the cross-pollination, transplantation, and circulation of language and culture that ignores historic and legal ideas of national and ethnic boundaries. It is a hybridization of cultures and languages that were a part of the cybernetic feedback loop of modernity. The black Atlantic cultures formed and were formed by modernity — they are inextricably linked through, using Gilroy's image, "the ship," which "immediately [focuses] attention on the middle passage, on the various projects for redemptive return to an African homeland, on the circulation of ideas and activists as well as the movement of key cultural and political artifacts: tracts, books, gramophone records, and choirs" (4). It is the movement of people and ideas that lends Gilroy's theory to a cosmopolitan reading in all of the disputed meanings of that word — morally, economically, culturally, and politically. Without naming it as such, Gilroy's theory is cosmopolitan in nature, because it is based on a transcendence of boundaries and a sharing of ideas conveyed by individuals and their creative works.

Olaudah Equiano represents a cosmopolitan figure within Gilroy's black Atlantic theoretical framework via his autobiography, *The Interesting Narrative of the Life of Olaudah Equiano, Gustavus Vassa, the African* (1789). Equiano, a trained and well-regarded seaman, traveled the world aboard ships as a slave and later as an emancipated freeman. He purchases his freedom from his master, Robert King. Recalling his day of emancipation, Equiano writes:

> When I got to the office and acquainted the Register with my errand, he congratulated me on the occasion, and told me he would draw up my manumission for half-price, which was a guinea.... Accordingly he signed the manumission that day; so that, before night, I who had been a slave in the morning, trembling at the will of another, was become my own master, and completely free" [Equiano 144].

There were two exchanges of capital in Equiano's attaining freedom. First, he had to pay King for himself, and then he had to pay the Register for drafting his manumission papers. With these things done, and the manumission papers signed by King, Equiano's status from slave to freeman shifts as from morning to evening; within the space of a day, he "becomes" free, but there is nothing about his person that has changed.[15] What has changed is the quasi-legitimate status as a freeman. I use the modifier "quasi," because we learn through the remainder of the narrative that having manumission papers were not absolutely respected by "free" whites.

The black Atlantic, as a network of relationships and movement of people and ideas, made Equiano a hybrid identity that was in part of African descent with a particular ethnic and cultural past. Also, there are significant moments of signifyin' in his autobiography evidenced by his veiled sarcasms and dealing with the white hegemonic world in the eighteenth century. Another part of his hybrid identity is his Englishness. He understands how to use the English language as a tool, and he recognizes English ways aboard ship and within personal relationships. Furthermore, the isolated world of the ship presents another set of codes that Equiano mastered in order to negotiate his way in a world diametrically opposed to his personhood as a free and cosmopolitan individual who enjoys encountering other cultures in his far travels abroad. Furthermore, he makes compelling arguments for opening trade between England and Africa instead of relegating Africa as a place for colonial rapaciousness. Equiano sought to engage his world as a cosmopolitan rather than take from it following the anti-cosmopolitan post–Enlightenment European model. What is most intriguing about his narrative is that the anthropological study of his homeland is not the only cultural observations taking place. As a cosmopolite, he observes, critiques, and incorporates what he feels will improve him as a citizen of the world.

The cosmopolitan ideas of Kant, Gilroy, and Equiano together add up to a cosmopolitanism that is founded on the importance of travel and direct engagement of other peoples and their cultures.[16] It is not enough to merely imagine the Other from a distance, but as Equiano demonstrated in his life and Gilroy develops theoretically for the Pan-African movement, it is necessary to be on the margins and meeting spaces in person. There is a particular fearlessness and steadfast courage that is required of people, particularly those of the African diaspora, to voyage to places that are new and potentially estranging from their cultural point of view. Equiano led the way in this kind of cosmopolitanism grounded in first hand engagement of other cultures. His freedom was tenuous and fragile, and he had to resist the power of the whites with the diabolical tenacity to claim emancipated Blacks as their escaped property. Despite his trials, Equiano held fast to his ways as a seaman and reflected on his interaction with people in various parts of the world, particularly in regard to slavery.

Equiano is an early cosmopolite who bridges the Enlightenment to the nineteenth century. In doing so, he revealed that persons of African descent who were enslaved as part of the progression and promotion of modernity were singularly capable and enlightened to the importance of understanding and engaging the Other when he, as the Other within the West and particularly the Americas, was violently expelled without regard to compassion or sympathy. Additionally, many other cosmopolitans of the Black diaspora followed this pioneer. A very brief survey of these cosmopolitans includes the following examples: Martin R. Delany (1812–1885) traveled to Africa and returned to promote his conception of Black nationalism; Frederick Douglass (1818–1895) toured England, Ireland, and Scotland and obtained a new perspective on the way people might be treated with greater equality and hospitality; W.E.B. Du Bois (1868–1963) supported Pan-African ideals and immigrated to Ghana; Langston Hughes (1902–1967), originally from the heart of America in Lawrence, Kansas, incorporated ideas from the Soviet Union into his philosophy following his return to the United States; Richard Wright (1908–1960) moved to France to experience life without the post–Civil Rights oppressions in America; Martin Luther King, Jr. (1929–1968) traveled abroad to India and Jamaica, and incorporated the ideas of Mahatma Gandhi (1869–1948) and Marcus Garvey (1887–1940) into his personal philosophy for civil rights;

and, Bob Marley (1945–1981) overcame the racial prejudice directed at his hybrid identity, and traveled the world sharing his Pan-African ideas through his music. Each of these cosmopolites reversed the middle passage to share with and learn from the cultures they encountered. Furthermore, each of these cosmopolitans deeply identified themselves as loyal to others within a group rooted in a sense of community or place. These people were patriotic to a place or a sense of community in addition to their cosmopolitan work and travel, but it is necessary to navigate the tension between global and local allegiances. It is this idea that leads to the final phase of this essay on "cosmopolitan patriots" and how *WoW* engineers future cosmopolites.

In his essay, "Cosmopolitan Patriots," Kwame Anthony Appiah's attempts to reconcile cosmopolitanism with local, regional, and national patriotism.[17] It is very much about the pragmatic and practical cosmopolitanism inaugurated by members of the African diaspora such as Olaudah Equiano and continued by countless others to the present day. In this work, Appiah invokes Kantian ideas of human progress through excerpts from letters from his deceased father. For his father, to be a citizen of the world means that "we could surely choose to live anywhere — we should make sure we left that place 'better than [we] found it'" (Appiah, "Cosmopolitan Patriots" 91). This sentiment contrasts sharply with the "conversational" cosmopolitanism that we see in his later work (*Cosmopolitanism* xxi). However, it suffices to say that the interaction among cultures and cosmopolites with cultures (theirs and others) is beyond conversational discourse. There are material and ideological exchanges taking place, some with penalties ranging from prestige to pecuniary to mortality, that cannot be avoided, and others that are actively encouraged. As such, it is equally important for each of us to assert our Kantian cosmopolitan right to equal access and occupancy of our humble world, as it is to constructively engage others with our ideas, ways, and deeply held convictions. Therefore, I assert that Appiah's theorization of the cosmopolitan patriot is a more practical and engaged ideal of the cosmopolitan citizen, and as such, it better represents the cosmopolitan lineage that began with Olaudah Equiano.

With these qualifications in mind, Appiah defines the cosmopolitan patriot as:

> The answer is straightforward: the cosmopolitan patriot can entertain the possibility of a world in which everyone is a rooted cosmopolitan, attached to a home of his or her own, with its own cultural particularities, but taking pleasure from the presence of other, different, places that are home to other, different, people. The cosmopolitan also imagines that in such a world not everyone will find it best to stay in a natal patria, so that the circulation of people among different localities will involve not only cultural tourism (which the cosmopolitan admits to enjoying) but migration, nomadism, diaspora [Appiah, "Cosmopolitan Politics" 91–92].

The cosmopolitan patriot need not be detached from one's own cultural heritage, but instead carry one's roots with him or her while enjoying the diversity bounded only by the extent of our world. Furthermore, the cosmopolitan patriot is committed to circulation and the acknowledgement that the circulation of people may take a variety of forms. Appiah goes on to elaborate on the kind of world most hospitable to cosmopolitan patriots:

> In a world of cosmopolitan patriots, people would accept the citizens' responsibility to nurture the culture and the politics of their homes. Many would, no doubt, spend their lives in the places that shaped them, and that is one of the reasons local cultural practices would be sustained and transmitted. But many would move, and that would mean that cultural practices would travel also (as they have always traveled). The result would be a world in which each local form of human life is the result of long-term and persistent processes of cultural hybridization — a world, in that respect, much like the world we live in now [92].

The key aspect of the cosmopolitan patriot's world is that the movement of these people supports cultural hybridization and not homogenization or universalization. At the margins where meetings between cultures takes places, new forms and ideas will blossom from the interaction of cosmopolitan patriots, and this is not to mean that these things will necessarily lead to a flattening of culture. Instead, it is the culmination of Kantian progress combined with a variegated production of culture in the same vein of the remix and mashup.[18]

What about the patriot aspect of Appiah's cosmopolitan patriot? He argues "Patriotism, as communitarians have spent much time reminding us recently, is about the responsibilities as well as the privileges of citizenship. But it is also and above all, as I have been suggesting, not so much a matter of action — of practical morality — as of sentiment" (Appiah, "Cosmopolitan Politcs" 95). Instead of patriotism being a matter of duty followed by action, as lauded in the United States of America following the September 11 terrorist attacks, Appiah grounds the concept in feeling and sentiment. Recognizing that patriotism is a sentiment rather than an action is important for understanding where patriotism comes from and how it can be reconciled with cosmopolitanism. As I discussed above, patriotism is something that can be carried with the cosmopolite, but need not be something that is performative only. Appiah continues: "We cosmopolitans *can* be patriots, loving our homelands (not only the states where we were born but the states where we grew up, the states where we live); our loyalty to humankind — so vast, so abstract, a unity — does *not* deprive us of the capacity to care for lives nearer by" ("Appiah, "Cosmopolitan Politcs" 95). Thus, one may be patriotic without pledging allegiance to a flag or remaining on the particular patch of land that is identified as within the geopolitical border of one's country; instead, one may feel patriotic in a variety of ways in regard to a number of allegiances, and that is enough. One may be a cosmopolitan and a patriot, forming a network of alliances and allegiances bound by ethically derived duties to one's fellow human beings and maintaining sentiments of patriotism to one's original, adopted, or both homelands. Obviously, there are parallels between real world patriotism and in-game patriotism within *WoW*, which does not obviate one's adherence to cosmopolitan ideals.

It is with the example set by cosmopolitans of the Black diaspora combined with Appiah's theorization of cosmopolitan patriots that I wish to demonstrate the promise and potential of engineering future cosmopolites through the MMORPG world of *WoW*. In the introduction, I alluded to the travel aspect of the game. The walking, riding, and sailing that all characters must do in order to move about the game on various official game missions and other independently derived goals (e.g., sight seeing within the game world of Azeroth) strongly connects the game to the cosmopolitan theories of Kant and Gilroy and the practical cosmopolitan example of Olaudah Equiano. To play the game means to travel the whole world of Azeroth, including those lands and territories that are controlled by peoples hostile to your character's race and faction.

In the final phase of the essay, I will discuss the three concrete aspects of *WoW* related to engineering cosmopolitan patriots: quests, achievements, and the required cooperation of the two factions against the Burning Legion, as well as the function of travel and commerce in relation to *WoW* and the Internet in general. Following this, I will conclude the essay by offering some thoughts about how *WoW* can be further developed to foster stronger cosmopolitan ideals, which may translate into gamers with a stronger cosmopolitan sentiment and hopefully an assumed cosmopolitan identity.

Challenging quests within *WoW* are the most obvious trajectory for engineering cosmopolitan patriots. Quests are missions that characters endeavor to complete in return for a reward and experience points, which accumulate over time in order to raise the character's level. Characters collect quests from non-playable characters (NPCs) and may work on a number of them simultaneously in order to more efficiently level up. Quests are important for building cosmopolitan ideals, because they are one of the first ways in which players are encouraged to take their characters into so-called contested or controlled (by the other faction) territories. This movement places the character directly in harm's way, because on player versus player (PvP) servers, this flags the character as a valid target for battle. Contested territories and neutral cities serve a central role in the game after a player reaches level 30, which forces higher level characters from both factions into the same restricted space to quest and play.

In-game achievements supplement the questing architecture of *WoW*. Achievements are a form of meta-quests. Instead of going to an NPC for what can be called an "achievement quest," one merely has to complete the requirements for a given achievement to have its reward automatically bestowed on the character. In this sense, achievements are awarded from the game rather from within the game as with NPC derived quests. The rewards for achievements are various, but include vanity items, titles, and the opportunity to learn new profession recipes. Achievements are important to the idea of educating players to cosmopolitan patriot ideals, because the (relatively) easier achievements to obtain are those dealing with world exploration. Again, as in the quest example above, the player must navigate each region and dungeon with their character despite the possibility of harm and death in order to see and explore the totality of Azeroth. This makes the player experience and observe areas very different than those of his or her character's home and factionally controlled areas. One of the more stark contrasts afforded by this achievement has to do with Horde factional characters, which are largely tied to magic and older technologies, visiting the human and gnomish areas, which feature the Deeprun Tram (a train that runs above ground, under ground, and underwater — obviously an engineering feat) connecting Ironforge and Stormwind City.

Another significant cosmopolitan gesture in *WoW* has to do with the lore of the Burning Legion. This group, largely comprised of demonic races, exists elsewhere in the Warcraft universe, and it is notorious for invading and destroying worlds. It has invaded Azeroth on three occasions in the past, and it represents a unifying threat to both the Horde and Alliance. However, it is part of the background story within *WoW*, and while there are quests related to the lore, the Burning Legion remains a story of unity that lacks the impetus to actually bring together characters from the two factions in battle against this foe.

Through the above examples, it is evident that *WoW* carefully places lessons in cosmopolitan patriotism that may go unnoticed overtly, but are ever present nonetheless. It is this constant presence that may serve to promote cosmopolitan ideals in the game as it now stands. However, I would like to offer a few of my ideas regarding how *WoW* may be augmented and improved to continue its traditional narrative while furthering pedagogy of cosmopolitan patriotism. The first suggestion builds on the fact that Undead characters of the Horde faction may communicate with Human characters of the Alliance faction. The reasoning behind this is that the Undead are merely reanimated deceased Humans, and as former Humans, they have retained their knowledge of Common language used by Humans. I believe that Blizzard could add a new profession like Enchanting or Inscription, or a level-oriented skill set like First Aid or Cooking that allows a character of one faction to learn the languages used by races of the other faction. This learning could involve quests that inculcate the language, culture, and lore of other races, which would automatically imply a certain kind of cosmopolitanism for the character endeavoring to communicate with the Other. Additionally, the quests required for this skill could involve having the character relocate for some time under a banner of friendship (cf. Kant's cosmopolitan right to hospitality) to learn from teachers or trainers in the major cities of the opposite faction. Another suggestion would be to implement instances or dungeons that require the cooperation of Horde and Alliance characters to complete an objective or quest that cannot be done by one factional group alone. Furthermore, the communication between the two groups could be facilitated by the above mentioned culture and language specialists, who will serve a purpose much like healers — they provide a service for the group as a whole instead of meting out damage to threats within the dungeon. It would require little work to integrate these suggestions into the *WoW* narrative that spans earlier strategy-based video games, comic books, and novels.

Finally, the most interesting cosmopolitan work is taking place outside the in-game world of Azeroth. *WoW* is a technology that facilitates travel across vast spaces via the Internet such that individual world citizens may come together to play within cyberspace. The Internet is a network of interconnected points or nodes that correspond to individuals on their personal computers and the semi-autonomous servers that make Internet technologies possible, ranging from those that move packets from point-to-point to the servers that make MMORPGs like *WoW* possible. *WoW*, as much as the ships and modes of transportation within the game, is a technology of travel that brings human beings together from around the world to a singular meeting place within the scope of its fantastic world. Additionally, the game makes possible conversations between players via typing and voice-over-ip technology. However, those in-game conversations extend beyond *WoW* into other virtual domains. The game is one locus of meeting, conversation, and play, but it is only the beginning of further cultural encounters and exchanges. The meta-game exchanges between players on both sides of the Horde-Alliance divide create a space of cooperation and sharing of experiences. These meta-game exchanges outside of *WoW* take place via email, message boards, instant messaging, and social networking websites including Facebook and Twitter. Some of these are positive while others are negative depending on the content of the particular message. However, the meta-exchanges generally do not recreate the destructive encounters between Factions found within the game. Instead, player communication outside of the game and constructive projects including public databases such as Thottbot and *WoW*head and the community driven

WoW Wiki where players construct informative compendiums for other players to publicly share, contribute to, and enjoy. These bring seemingly Othered in-game players together in meta-spaces beyond the confines of the game. Online culture in the Web 2.0 era of dynamic content and social networking has facilitated a new kind of responsibility that players within *WoW* develop on their own outside the confines of the corporate-controlled game space. It remains to be seen how much in-game time versus meta-game time influences players and in what ways. However, the responsibilities assumed by some players to participate in multicultural exchanges about the MMORPG so many people play seems to indicate that there is the beginning of responsibilities and duties of the game player to others. Certainly there are ulterior motives at work here, because players utilize these shared communications to have a more successful and fulfilling in-game experience, but these players choose to do this on their own and they do it regardless of the other players and where they are from who may join them within or without Azeroth.

Notes

1. Three significant works on this subject include: Lawrence Lessig's *The Future of Ideas: The Fate of the Commons in a Connected World* (2001), Manuel Castells' *The Internet Galaxy: Reflections on the Internet, Business, and Society* (2001), and James Boyle's *Shamans, Software and Spleens : Law and the Construction of the Information Society* (1997).
2. I will refer to *World of Warcraft* as *WoW* in the remainder of the essay.
3. In this essay, I discuss *World of Warcraft* (2004) as a single game, but it is in fact comprised of the original game and two add-ons or upgrades titled *World of Warcraft: The Burning Crusade* (2008) and *World of Warcraft: Wrath of the Lich King* (2008).
4. Admittedly, WoW players have to invest in computer hardware, an Internet connection, and pay Blizzard's monthly fee to play WoW. This means that the 11.5 million players are automatically elitist in regard to the material condition and relative wealth needed to play the game. What this means for the democratic ideals of cosmopolitanism as formulated by Appiah and others I cannot address in the space of this essay, but suffice it to say that even though this has an appearance of technocratic and bourgeois elitism, this must have some good toward teaching cosmopolitanism.
5. Unfortunately, we do not have access to Blizzard's player billing information, which would establish the distribution of game players around the world. Additionally, it is obvious that Blizzard has this information, but it is surprising that they do not capitalize on this more in their advertising and press releases.
6. Race in WoW derives from its terminological usage in fantasy, but popularized by J.R.R. Tolkien in his *Lord of the Rings* trilogy and extended into gaming through role-playing games (RPGs) such as the eponymous *Dungeons & Dragons*. For Tolkien and other fantasists, race equates with species and ethnic group identification. There are exceptions to miscegenation and the species rule, but overwhelmingly, races represent a people with a shared culture, heritage, and history. Since world building in fantasy is one of the first tasks for a fantasist, it follows that these so-called races are a shorthand

for constructing self-contained groups of people without the realistic complications of the margins, interaction, etc.

    7. Different players assume different roles for their characters within WoW. Some strictly role-play the character as an identity within the game world and divorced from his or her real life identity. Other players strongly link their game character with their real life identity. Ways to do this include designing a character that looks like the player, incorporating some aspect of their name or identity (ethnicity or gender for example) into the character's name. This naming also extends to the naming of a guild, or collective of characters that work together such that the player's real life affinities are reflected as a whole within the game. More on the tension between playing the game and role playing can be found in Esther MacCallum-Stewart and Justin Parsler's "Role-play vs. Gameplay: The Difficulties of Playing a Role in *World of Warcraft*" in *Digital Culture, Play, and Identity: A World of Warcraft Reader* (2008).

    8. According to the Entertainment Software Association, the leading video game industry group in the United States and responsible for the video game rating system, 65 percent of American households have video game players, and the average age of game players is 35. Of those players, 40 percent are female and 60 percent are male. Additionally, women age 18 or over represent a larger portion (33 percent) of game players than boys 17 or younger (only 18 percent). This data can be found in the ESA's *Essential Facts About the Computer and Video Game Industry* available here: <http://www.theesa.com/facts/pdfs/ESA_EF_2008.pdf>.

    9. The genesis of this essay began as a response to Jessica Langer's essay, "The Familiar and the Foreign: Playing (Post)Colonialism in *World of Warcraft*," in which she argues that the in-game character races are divided along an axis of familiarity and otherness, which she extrapolates to have real world meaning making. Langer's reading of *WoW* assumes a singular tact that ignores positive in-game phenomena and the extensive online communities for everyone that exist on the Internet at large. It bears noting that her observational point of view within the game was primarily from that of a female human character and not from the point of view of a character that she identifies as Othered. In effect, she participated in the very thing she argued was wrong in Azeroth rather than performing a more extensive reading of the game from the viewpoint of multiple races in both factions.

    10. For a more thorough historical examination of cosmopolitan thought see Derek Heater's *World Citizenship and Government: Cosmopolitan Ideas in the History of Western Political Thought* (1996), Samuel Scheffler's "Conceptions of Cosmopolitanism" in his volume *Boundaries and Allegiances* (2001), and the introduction to Thomas J. Schlereth's *The Cosmopolitan Ideal in Enlightenment Thought: Its Form and Function in the Ideas of Franklin, Hume, and Voltaire, 1694–1790* (1977).

    11. For more on the connections between the Enlightenment and racism, see Tzvetan Todorov's "Race, Writing, and Culture," in *"Race," Writing and Difference* (1986), edited by Henry Louis Gates, Jr.

    12. I am relying on David L. Colclasure's translation of Kant's works contained in *Kants gesammelte Schriften*, edited by the Royal Prussian (later German) Academy of Sciences (Berlin: Georg Reimer, subsequently Walter de Gruyter, 1902–), or what is also known as the Akademie edition. Colclasure's translation is from the collection edited by Pauline Kleingeld: *Toward Perpetual Peace and Other Writings on Politics, Peace, and History*.

    13. Universal application is not the same as universalism. For Kant, universal application means that the rights of all cosmopolitan citizens are assured the world over.

This does not mean that there is some homogenized and universalized set of moral and ethical beliefs that must be imposed on all peoples as part of cosmopolitan right.

14. Equiano's life as a seaman was not without its problems and questions. One notable scene involves his working on a slave ship. He writes, "After our vessel was discharged, we soon got her ready, and took in, as usual, some of the poor oppressed natives of Africa, and other negroes; we then set off again for Georgia and Charlestown. We arrived at Georgia, and having landed part of our cargo, proceeded to Charlestown with the remainder" (135). Reiterating my earlier point, but more emphatically now, I believe that Equiano had to be very pragmatic about his precarious situation in order to navigate the interpersonal dangers of being a black man in the Americas on the trans–Atlantic shipping routes. Additionally, the tension between "poor oppressed natives of Africa," and "cargo" may be an abolitionist maneuver to alert the reader to the dehumanization of people of the African diaspora, and not as one may read it as Equiano's lack of sympathy for slaves equated to the status of cargo.

15. This is a kind of "commerce" that I am not sure Kant would have considered in regard to his theory of cosmopolitanism. However, here is bold evidence where the commerce conducted to the emancipation of one's self from bondage results in an early, modern cosmopolitan.

16. It is important to remember that within any group of people there are multiple cultures that correspond in any number of ways to various in-groups and marginalized identities along with any notion of an über-culture encompassing the group as a whole.

17. Appiah draws on Martha Nussbaum's "Cosmopolitanism and Patriotism" from *Boston Review* 19:5 (1994) available here: <http://bostonreview.net/BR19.5/nussbaum.html>.

18. A remix is the use of sampling to augment or change a singular work, and a mashup is the overlay and juxtaposition of two or more works to create a new derivative work that is something unlike the original works alone. One of the leading proponents of less restrictive copyright and what is called the creative commons is professor of law at Stanford Law School Lawrence Lessig. See his works: *Remix: Making Art and Commerce Thrive in the Hybrid Economy* (2008) and *Free Culture: The Nature and Future of Creativity* (2004).

Works Cited

Appiah, Kwame Anthony. "Cosmopolitan Patriots." In *Cosmopolitics: Thinking and Feeling Beyond the Nation,* edited by Pheng Cheah and Bruce Robbins, 91–114. Minneapolis: University of Minnesota Press, 1998.
_____. *Cosmopolitanism: Ethics in a World of Strangers.* New York: W.W. Norton, 2006.
Blizzard Entertainment. *World of Warcraft.* Video Game. November 23, 2004 <http://www.worldofwarcraft.com/>.
_____. *World of Warcraft: The Burning Crusade.* Video Game. January 16, 2007 <http://www.worldofwarcraft.com/>.
_____. *World of Warcraft: Wrath of the Lich King.* Video Game. November 13, 2008 <http://www.worldofwarcraft.com/>.
_____. "World Of Warcraft Subscriber Base Reaches 11.5 Million Worldwide." Irvine, CA: Blizzard, 23 December 2008. 2 May 2009 <http://www.blizzard.com/us/press/081121.html>.

Costanzo, Angelo. "Equiano, Olaudah." In *The Oxford Companion to African American Literature*, edited by Eds. William L. Andrews, Frances Smith Foster, and Trudier Harris, 257–258. New York: Oxford University Press, 1997.
Entertainment Software Association. Essential Facts About the Computer and Video Game Industry: 2008 Sales, Demographic, and Usage Data. Washington, DC: ESA, 2008. 2 May 2009 <http://www.theesa.com/facts/pdfs/ESA_EF_2008.pdf>.
Equiano, Olaudah. *The Interesting Narrative of the Life of Olaudah Equiano, or Gustavus Vassa, the African. The Classic Slave Narratives*. Ed. Henry Louis Gates, Jr. New York: Signet Classics, 2002. 15–248.
Friedel, Tania. *Racial Discourse and Cosmopolitanism in Twentieth-Century African American Writing*. New York: Routledge, 2008.
Gilroy, Paul. *The Black Atlantic: Modernity and Double Consciousness*. Cambridge, MA: Harvard University Press, 1993.
Kant, Immanuel. *Toward Perpetual Peace and Other Writings on Politics, Peace, and History*. Ed. Pauline Kleingeld. Trans. David L. Colclasure. New Haven: Yale University Press, 2006.
Langer, Jessica. "The Familiar and the Foreign: Playing (Post)Colonialism in *World of Warcraft*." In *Digital Culture, Play, and Identity: A World of Warcraft Reader*, edited by Hilde Ge. Corneliussen and Jill Walker Rettberg. Cambridge, MA: MIT Press, 2008.
Robbins, Bruce. "Introduction Part I." In *Cosmopolitics: Thinking and Feeling Beyond the Nation*, edited by Pheng Cheah and Bruce Robbins, 1–19. Minneapolis: University of Minnesota Press, 1998.
Schlereth, Thomas J. *The Cosmopolitan Ideal in Enlightenment Thought: Its Form and Function in the Ideas of Franklin, Hume, and Voltaire, 1694–1790*. Notre Dame: University of Notre Dame Press, 1977.

11

When "Nation" Stops Making Sense
Mexico and Giorgio Agamben's "State of Exception" *in* Children of Men
STACY SCHMITT RUSNAK

Introduction: Post-NAFTA Mexico

This investigation proposes a reading of Giorgio Agamben's work on the *state of exception* in an attempt to examine Mexican identity as a transnational cosmopolitanism in the post–NAFTA and post–PRI (Institutional Revolutionary Party) context. I explore how Alfonso Cuarón's 2006 film *Children of Men,* in spite of being set in Britain, functions as an allegory of the current Mexican State as it struggles to define what it means to be both "Mexican" (local) and global. Mexico is a unique case because it presents us with an early model of hybridity. From Aztec domination, Spanish colonialism, and neocolonial subjectivity, Mexico has balanced a local and global identity since its inception. After the loss of the PRI party presidency to the PAN (National Party) candidate Vicente Fox, debates over *mexicanidad* have turned to twenty-first century questions of the politics of regionalism, the diaspora, and globalization to define a more cosmopolitan identity. Calling for change, the PAN government rejects the outdated PRI revolutionary ideology preferring instead to promote a climate of private self-interest as the motivator of "national progress."[1] Citizens are urged to take an active role in promoting and maintaining Mexico's status as a market competitor. *Children of Men* both encourages the notion of Mexico as integral to the world market while also highlighting the dangers of the U.S. liberal model of democracy.

A close analysis of the film reveals gaps in the film's fabric that open up sites to call into question the categories of nation-state and citizenship. In *Homo Sacer,* Agamben reveals that the state of exception occurs in supposed times of crisis that coincide with increasing power structures employed by governments. In these times, citizenship and individual rights are diminished and rejected.[2] *Children of Men* addresses how migration, exile, diaspora, political asylum, terrorism and technology influence these crises and impact identity formation. In the post–NAFTA period, the crisis of defining "Mexicanness" has been framed as a "national" crisis brought on by the dizzying processes of globalization and the individual's attempt to negotiate these processes and locate their own positionality in the global framework. The generic term "national" is inadequate for expressing the contemporary experience. Rather than an "identity crisis," the new global citizen is a mobile subject who is comfortably always on the move and at home anywhere. The "crisis" as such lies in the hegemony and the fear of losing power. Agamben's state of exception helps us see how and why the state institutionalizes particular notions of identity as the "norm" in moments of crisis to ensure control over the masses. The purpose of this paper is fourfold: (1) introduce the state of exception as a tool into postcolonial theory; (2) offer a theoretical understanding of the role that globalization plays in the shift from a "national" to a transnational Mexican culture in terms of biopolitcs and biopower; (3) investigate the term "citizenship" through the figure of the refugee as it pertains to the Mexican experience of migration; and (4) propose ways in which biopower can be resisted.

The State of Exception, Postcolonialism and the Postnational

This paper suggests that postcolonial theory has reached an impasse. Opening up the theory and extending it into the science fiction genre however opens up new possibilities. What other genre is so fascinated by the encounter with the "other" and issues of identity politics? SF presents us with an arena in which the binary opposition between good vs. evil must be dealt with in terms of difference. More often than not, the "good" entity is connected to humanity and the "evil alien" is the force that threatens the survival of the human race. The figure of "the alien" in SF shifts throughout history but is generally coded in terms of difference. For instance, "the alien" has been a communist threat (*Invasion of the Body Snatchers* 1956), a "monstrous female" (*Aliens* 1986), and a technological rogue (*I, Robot* 2004), to name a few examples. In no way do

I suggest that these binary relationships simplify the genre, nor do I suggest that SF is a straightforward morality tale of good vs. evil. Samuel Delany's work on SF[3] shows us that the moral outcome of the binary between good vs. evil has little to do with political correctness. Instead, we should be made to think about and confront the complex interactions between cultures and races that are revealed in the genre. As a result, the genre's recognizable conventions and attention to identity politics generates a mode of thinking that allows for a multifaceted and sophisticated response to the dynamics of difference through a popular idiom.

This attention to "difference" in SF lends itself to recent scholarship in postcolonial and postnational studies. As in most cases, scholars are not in complete agreement as to a single definition of either the postcolonial or the postnational. What SF, the postcolonial and postnational do share in common is an underlying exploration of representation and alterity. My concern here with the notion of the postcolonial is that it has not proven to be a flexible approach for charting media cultures of advanced capitalism. According to Ania Loomba, capitalism could not have taken place in Europe in the first place without colonial expansion (4). Colonies provided an abundance of labor and human resources that were valuable to the colonizers. Exploiting colonial subjects perpetuated a system of economic imbalance and uneven development that continues even today in the global context. Moreover, Kathleen Newman reminds us that capitalism "has always been a decentered practice" (4). However, in today's contemporary moment we are not dealing with direct rule by first world imperialist powers over third world nations. Instead, we must contend with how global capitalism "allow[s] the economic, cultural and (to varying degrees) political penetration of some countries by others" (Loomba 7), making it debatable whether "colonialism" has ended and "postcolonialism" begun.

Moreover, "postcolonialism" remains dependent on binary oppositions (colonizer/colonized) that often cloud over internal social and racial differences of some societies by failing to acknowledge the fragmentation, diversity and multiplicity of groups within societies wherein marginalized groups are still oppressed by "elitist" groups. For instance, in spite of its hybridity and emphasis on cosmopolitanism, much (if not all) of Mexico's indigenous populations continue to be ostracized and neglected because their presence serves as a reminder of the Old World / New World crisis of identity. Their alterity is blamed for holding Mexico back from completely integrating into the competitive market place. Consequently, "postcolonialism" is methodologically problematic because it does not apply to all citizens of a particular society; it does not take into account the uneven development between, and within, particular countries; and, it does not account for differences of class, race, gender or ethnicity. What remains to be seen is how other economic, social, cultural and historic factors impact how multiple individuals from diverse places across diverse times relate to and are impacted by the imbalances of global, multinational corporations and capital.

Alternately, the postnational offers a more multivalenced approach to investigate the impact of history on the contemporary experience. The "post" in postnational does not designate a specific temporal moment since the postnational and national have existed and continue to exist side by side. As such, the postnational allows for a "disjunctive temporality" (Bhabha 7) that interrupts the teleological relationship on which notions of the postcolonial approach are founded in an attempt to address colonial histories. Moreover, instead of hinging on binary formations of "otherness," the postnational allows for a fluidity that takes into consideration the issues of immigration, diasporic communities, exile, political asylum, terrorism, and technology as they increasingly impact culture and politics. The postnational need not be an alternative or rejection of postcolonialism, but rather it has the potential to build on and extend the usefulness of postcolonial theory. Furthermore, it is here in the postnational where the state of exception becomes the norm and takes on a significance of its own. Today, a growing indistinction between outside and inside the law exists, where the law suspends its ordinary functioning and determines how to control particular marginal populations under the rubric of "Homeland Security." Understanding how the state of exception functions and considering ways of resisting the powers that instantiate such states is at stake if we wish to propose alternative solutions within and under the current liberal state.

Children of Men: *The State of Exception, Biopolitics and Biopower*

Beginning in London in 2027, *Children of Men* is an apocalyptic representation of what is potentially in store for the entire world in the future. Women everywhere have become infertile. Anarchy reigns everywhere with the exception of Britain, where some order is maintained by the army and a paramilitary police force referred to as "Homeland Security." London has become an urban war zone full of unwanted refugees. The upper class separate themselves by relocating to the periphery where they pop pills and surround themselves with art and classical music in an attempt to connect to some historic sense of "civilization." Moreover, terrorist attacks have become daily events throughout the city and billboards liter the landscape with slogans such as:

"Suspicious? Report any suspicious activity. Report all illegal Immigrants." One Fugee (refugee), Kee, is pregnant and has come to Britain for asylum. She finds shelter with a resistance group, the "Fishes," who demand equal rights for refugees. They attempt to get Kee on a boat called the *Tomorrow* belonging to the "Human Project," a humanitarian organization researching the infertility crisis. It is believed that her pregnancy may somehow shed light on the crisis at hand. Theo, a former political activist turned disillusioned alcoholic after the death of his son to influenza, is recruited by the Fishes to get transit papers for Kee and to accompany her to the pick-up point. The mission is compromised during a shootout between the police and the Fishes and the group must take cover at a farmhouse. During a Fish meeting, it is revealed that the group is divided about whether to hand Kee and the baby over to the Human Project, or keep the baby for their own political purposes. Theo overhears a plot to steal the baby and thus escapes with Kee to a detainment camp in Bexhill-on-Sea. The camp resembles the Warsaw Ghetto, Nazi camps, contemporary war zones, political prisons like Guantánamo Bay and Abu Ghraib. Bexhill is horrific—full of military abuse and torture. Migrants of all ethnicities are killed and different groups start uprisings that elicit brutal military intervention. Bexhill is also the place where Kee gives birth to the first child born in 18 years.

The film raises questions regarding the ways in which political bodies define the nation state. In this case, the film is undoubtedly set in Britain. Is this an "authentic" image of Britain? What does "authentic" even mean in late capitalism? The film specifically tells us it is set in London with an intertitle and we recognize the British accent and the double-decker buses. Certain visual images, spaces, and languages emerge as national markers. As the text progresses, these markers are destabilized as the film moves from the urban center outwards towards the ghetto, where multiple ethnicities converge and a "strange sense of freedom prevails" (Zizek 25) amongst the different groups of people who manage to co-exist there. In this manner, the film takes on a multi-valenced level of cultural signification that is characteristic of recent New Mexican Cinema by Cuarón, Alejandro González Iñárritu (*Babel* 2006) and Guillermo Del Toro *(Pan's Labyrinth* 2006). Therefore, my proposed theoretical understanding of Mexican identity as transnational comes from a shift away from culturally coded landscapes that many citizens no longer identify with, towards themes about crossing borders, interrogating political policies, questioning national allegiance and negotiating human mobility across both physical and metaphorical spaces. As *Children of Men* illustrates, the paradigm of Mexican national identity is inadequate for addressing the contemporary experience of Mexico in the post–NAFTA climate. The place of Mexico and Mexicans in a transnationalized culture and economy provide evidence of neoliberal hegemony as well as an unsettled tension between U.S.-led globalization and Mexican popular sentiment. Biopolitics and biopower help us address this tension as we move away from rigid notions of "national" defined by "the principle of nativity and the principle of sovereignty" (Agamben 128), towards more flexible paradigms of identity formation.

Giorgio Agamben puts forth in his work on the state of exception that the "paradox of sovereignty consists in the fact that the sovereign is, at the same time, outside and inside the juridical order" (15). The sovereign, as the power of the law, executes the law and decides what is inside and outside of the law. What is external to the law is not abandoned but rather maintained in the very possibility of sovereignty. This paradox can be laid out as: "the law is outside itself," or "I, the sovereign, who am outside the law, declare that there is nothing outside the law" (Agamben 128). This is so because the sovereign alone can declare an exception to the law allowing the sovereign to suspend the validity of the law. As a result, the sovereign cannot be accused of injury to a subject because his (or her) role in the state of exception is to preserve "peace" and "security" at any cost. In *Children of Men*, the law has been suspended by the government in an attempt to protect British nationalism. This gesture allows the army and the paramilitary troops the ability to harass, torture and murder any individual, British or not, who interferes with their effort to maintain sovereignty. As the film begins, an acousmatique voice (a voice heard without an image) pierces through the film's fabric as a British newscast reports: "The Homeland Security Bill is ratified. After 8 years, British borders will remain closed. The deportation of illegal immigrants will continue." According to Michel Chion, this voice is the acousmetre, which produces the richest of voice-image relations. If the voice remains unseen it becomes "invested with magical powers, however slightly, in the image. The powers are usually malevolent, occasionally tutelary" (Chion 23). The space opened up by the news reporter's voice is like a harbinger declaring outright a state of exception.

The border closings are instituted in an effort to maintain sovereignty and to stop the flow of migration. The continued erection of "borders" in *Children of Men* finds its real world application on the border between the U.S. and Mexico. In the aftermath of 9/11, the U.S. Republican Party dismissed Vicente Fox's proposals for liberalized U.S.-Mexico border controls. NAFTA had already demonstrated the need for open borders to facilitate the flow of goods. In the years leading up to 9/11, the two governments had seemingly worked hard to renegotiate the border to also include greater movement of people between the two countries. However, in the post–9/11 climate, these discussions closed down in the name of "national security." The renewed restrictions to the permeability of the border substantiated a state of exception and called for increased surveillance and suspicion.⁴

In *Children of Men*, the state of exception manifests and becomes the rule when the cages of immigrants, camps and ghettos appear. In each of these spaces certain populations are excluded from political life reducing them to *bare life* defined as 'life stripped of all political guarantees, outside of the political community" (Shaw 124). In the state of exception, any marginal population can be removed from the political community on the sovereign's whim making anyone a potential *homer sacer*, a human being who may be killed but not sacrificed. *Children of Men* illustrates how easily one can be reduced to bare life by the hegemony. For instance, Theo, the disillusioned alcoholic in the film, and the epitome of British nationalism (since he is the only one who has the power to get transit papers), appears peacefully at rest on a train. Monitors flash images of the chaos worldwide in New York, Rome, Singapore ... etc., until the image of a British flag flashes up on the screen with the message, "Only Britain soldiers on." As the camera pans away from the screen it stops on Theo and we hear an alternating series of male and female acousmatique voices begin to speak from the TV: "He's my dentist." "She's my housekeeper." "He's the waiter." "She's my cousin." "They are illegal immigrants. To hire, feed, or shelter illegal immigrants is a crime." Theo pays little attention to the droning announcements. He believes he is exempt from their messages because he is a British citizen. However, a gap appears in the text that reveals his vulnerability in the hegemonic order. Theo is startled from his reverie when angry youths throw rocks at the train. In the background slogans on a wall speed by: "Avoiding Fertility Testing Is a Crime." "Last One to Die, Turn Out the Light." Regardless of his national allegiance, Theo, whether he recognizes it or not, is impacted by the events taking place around him. The poignancy of this moment, which is perhaps presented too subtly, is that we are all impacted by the new global order.

Theo reaches his destination and descends from the train. He passes a set of heavily guarded cages housing Europeans, Africans, and Asians. He walks by as if he does not even notice the spectacle. He chooses to ignore the events unfolding around him. His disregard for the obvious comes from the fetishist disavowal of, "'I know, but I don't want to know that I know, so I don't know.' I know it, but I refuse to fully assume the consequence of this knowledge, so that I can continue acting as if I don't know it" (Zizek 45–46). Theo fails to understand that in the state of exception the law arbitrarily decides who is inside and outside the law. When he agrees to accompany Kee to the Human Project, he transgresses the "law" and is reduced to bare life. Theo misrecognizes this transgression because of his fetishistic disavowal. However, when two police officers are gunned down in the transit process, Theo completely falls outside of the law and becomes as vulnerable to the law as the immigrants. Moreover, Theo has been reduced to a *homo sacer* in the Fishes plan. They intend to kill Theo after he transports Kee to the Human Project. As such, political life and biological life have been put into question and biopolitics extends into the *polis* of everyday life affecting anyone and everyone.

According to Foucault, a shift from classical sovereignty to biopolitics occurs when life becomes a political question. The investment of power and knowledge into life makes the hierarchization of living populations a norm (Foucault 144). Biopolitics determines the administration of a population to ensure its production, reproduction and security. Going a step further, Slavoj Zizek suggests that "bio-politics is ultimately a politics of fear" (34) and is used to mobilize people. We can interpret "fear" in two ways. First it is the emotional state of the citizen that fears his/her existence within the political community. There are numerous accounts of this type of fear in *Children of Men*. For instance, on a bus headed to Bexhill Refugee Camp Kee starts to have contractions and moan uncontrollably. As the bus pulls into the camp, the camera follows the moving vehicle and then enters into the bus giving the spectator the sense of being part of the ride. The camera swishes down the set of interior windows and shows caged immigrants outside being beaten, tortured and humiliated. Loud buzzing sounds are heard over screaming voices. Rows of immigrants line up with their hands on their heads and are shot execution style. The bus stops and a guard enters with a German shepherd. Kee's moaning alerts the guard who approaches her snarling, "What's wrong with you?" At the same time, Theo shouts: "Caca! Caca! Piss. Smell. Girl." In spite of the audible British accent, Theo's mimicking of the broken speech of a foreigner demonstrates the instability of language as a national marker. The guard yells profanities at the pair and moves on. Theo has successfully passed as the "other." Theo's speech act articulates "the narrative of cultural difference which can never let the national history look at itself narcissistically in the eye" (Bhabha 168). Motivated by fear, Theo comes to recognize his precarious place within the hegemonic order in spite of his "nationality."

Fear can also come from the state when it fears the loss of control of the masses. This is the type of fear employed by the state in *Children of Men* to keep the masses oppressed. Although the goal of the state is to administer, multiply and protect a population, its policy for doing so is based on the notion of an arbitrary exclusion. Choosing what populations must be privileged to reproduce becomes a biological issue. Racism puts forth a way to divide groups of people and justifies the exclusion of "other" marginal groups that threaten the state's sovereignty.

In *Children of Men*, the first type of fear is felt most poignantly by the viewer because of the violent visual images. However, the second type of fear recalls Mexico's most stringent adversary to NAFTA — the Zapatistas. On January 1, 1994, the year the NAFTA agreement was put into place, the Zapatista (EZLN — Ejército Zapatista de Liberación Nacional) uprising in Chiapas illustrated the group's disagreement with the treaty. The EZLN attacked government and military facilities in San Cristóbal de Las Casas. The army was sent in to crush the uprising which did not come easy. In the end, President Salinas' administration was made to look incompetent in front of the entire world. In an attempt to counter the blow to the administration, Salinas addressed the nation on 6 January, where he stated about the Zapatistas: "this is not an Indian uprising, but the action of a violent, armed group against the peace of the communities, public peace and the government ... it is an action against the national interest ... this group is against Mexico" (Montemayor 54). In spite of the government's attempt to soil the image of the Zapatista movement, "Zapatismo" emerged as a populist discourse (de la Garza 123) that greatly impacted popular sentiment regarding NAFTA and the neoliberalization of the country. The group's emphasis on "the restoration of the boundaries of 'revolutionary' nationalism" (de la Garza 126), the same nationalism on which the PRI built its hegemony, further complicated the tension between neoliberal policy and national identity. Salinas' attempt to separate the rest of Mexico from the EZLN in the name of "national security" is a biopolitical move instantiated by the EZLN's overt criticism of NAFTA. It demonstrates how the state responded to the fear of losing control by instituting a state of exception to quell the impact made by the EZLN.

The Refugee as Symptom: The Crisis of "Citizenship"

The figure of the refugee represents a crisis in both human rights and the nation-state. Agamben states about the refugee:

> If refugees (whose number has continued to grow in our century, to the point of including a significant part of humanity today) represent such a disquieting element in the order of the modern nation-state, this is above all because by breaking the continuity between man and citizen, *nativity* and *nationality*, they put the originary fiction of modern sovereignty in crisis. Bringing to light the difference between birth and nation, the refugee causes the secret presupposition of the political domain — bare life — to appear for an instant within that domain [131].

The problem here comes from the guarantee of the instituted system of law that offers man "sacred and inalienable rights" (Agamben 126). The figure of the refugee (who should embody "the rights of man") is left outside the law and signals both the crisis of these rights and the fact that these rights have always been linked to sovereignty and the nation-state. In instances where humanitarian groups pop up as advocates for refugees, we expect to see a humanitarian turn on the part of hegemonic powers. Instead, we witness the opposite and the rights of man become radically separated from those of the citizen (this is why, for instance bombing Iraq into "freedom" is justified). Agamben encourages us to look critically at the refugee and the potential of marginal populations to question rigid categories of national identity:

> The refugee must be considered for what he is: nothing less that a limit concept that radically calls into question the fundamental categories of the nation-state to the man-citizen link, and ... thereby makes it possible to clear the way for a long-overdue renewal of categories in the service of a politics in which bare life is no longer separated and excepted, either in the state order or in the figure of human rights [134].

In *Children of Men*, Kee's status as a refugee reduces her to bare life; however, her pregnancy establishes a direct link to the question of national identity and sovereignty. On one hand, the state has made it clear that Kee has no rights. She is neither a national subject nor a naturalized citizen. Her liminality places her outside the law as a *homo sacer*, excluding her from all political life. On the other hand, the Fishes attempt to reassert the birth-nation link by avoiding the refugee question all together and instead focusing on how the birth of the baby can unite Britain: "She [Kee] belongs here and this baby is the flag that could unite us all!" Both of these perspectives take us outside of the biological question of infertility and return us to the political. Ultimately, the film is not about infertility but rather the tyranny of democracy and the impact of globalization. The film puts forward that societies worldwide are in chaos and are unable to regenerate themselves out of their own resources leading to mass migrations. People like Kee who are unwilling to accept their culture the way it is are willing to move to find a better life. These people will survive economic and environmental changes better than those that attempt to revert to traditional notions of place and identity. For this reason, the final scene of the film ends with Kee floating on a small boat in the ocean with her newborn baby girl Dylan (blurring the gender line) wrapped in her arms. The bobbing of the boat reinforces their lack of roots and marks the possibility of a new identity that has nothing to do with the principle of nativity or the principle of sovereignty.[5]

The role of the refugee is not meant to valorize the nomadic possibilities brought on by globalization. Undoubtedly, *Children of Men* has a dystopian feel to it that (although the credits role over a black screen and we hear children's voices laughing) is meant to criticize the processes of globalization that led to the political, economic and environmental issues in the first place. Instead, the refugee bares witness to how previous marginalized exceptions to citizenship extend to the center of the political sphere. Although Theo and Kee are both well-developed characters, it is Kee who might ensure the future of Britain and the whole world, placing her center stage in the political question of nationality.

A real-world example of Kee's extension into the political by a minority occurred in 2005, when the Mexican migrant vote became a hot political issue. The migrant vote allows Mexicans living abroad the ability to participant in their home country's elections from afar. Critics of the vote stated that migrants living abroad lacked true links to Mexico and should be barred from casting their vote because they would not have to live with the consequences. Proponents however disagreed. They declared that the "migrants constituted a 'new political subject' living substantively and simultaneously in the U.S. and Mexico" (Smith 724). Moreover, many argued that the democratic transition in Mexico would never fully happen without migrants (Smith 724). In June 2005, Mexicans in the U.S. celebrated the passage of the migrant vote. Although the turnout was small for the July, 2006 election, the passage of the vote marked a gradual step towards full inclusion in political life for Mexicans abroad. It also marks a new way of conceptualizing citizenship and belonging that is not tied to specific geographic notions of national allegiance.

Resistance: Concluding Remarks

This paper reveals that biopolitics is inscribed in the functions of the state that infiltrate life and society. Biopolitics is not only a totalitarian mechanism. It cannot be avoided in liberal democratic forms of government. Since Mexico's model of democracy piggybacks on that of the U.S., and, since U.S.-led globalization has had such an impact on Mexican identity, we can make the conjecture that biopolitcs has also played a key role in creating a transnational identity in Mexico. When Vicente Fox won the Mexican presidential elections on the PAN platform and seventy years of PRI party politics was crushed, Mexico's place in the global network seemed ensured. High on Fox's agenda was the creation of a new "equal" relationship with the U.S. However, any headway Fox had made with the Bush administration was quickly halted by the 9/11 attacks and the subsequent tightening of the border. Moreover, Mexico's refusal to aid the U.S. invasion of Iraq further drove a wedge in between the two countries. Clearly, Mexico's shifting allegiance to a U.S. democratic model had not evened the playing field between the two countries at all. The U.S. still asserted itself as the imperial power it had always been. The problem remains that the discourse on rights is consistently recast within the global political order when ideological notions shift and need to be re-assessed in the wake of new events. Therefore, there is no reformist project for biopolitics because it is the democratic space that masks the fact that any particular individual or group can be reduced to bare life.

Instead, we are confronted by two alternatives: (1) that we first reject the ideological components of liberal democracy, and (2) that we maintain a place in our minds and in our practice, for the concept of the "event." The first call to change requires us to reject involvement in state policy that we do not believe in. This means going against the government during times of war (Iraq, for instance), even if comes back to bite us, because it is not up to us to fight the hegemonic powers' battles for them. Slavoj Zizek shares a similar perspective in *Welcome to the Desert of the Real* when he states, "even if terrorism burns us all, the U.S. 'war on terrorism' is not our struggle, but a struggle internal to the capitalist universe" (55). Furthermore, in terms of Mexican cinema, we witness a similar rejection of the ideological powers put into practice. For the directors of the New Mexican Cinema, like Cuarón, Del Toro and Iñárritu, there proved to be little opportunity for young, forward thinking talent in the national film industry. Instead, this group of "Tres Amigos" sought opportunities in Hollywood that allowed them to gain the necessary skills, money and prestige to impact the nepotistic infrastructure that is characteristic of the Mexican industry. After the success of their 2006 films (*Children of Men*, *Pan's Labyrinth*, *Babel*—respectively) the trio started the Cha Cha Cha production company which has no phone number or office. Like Kee floating around in the boat, the Cha Cha Cha company is rootless — connected to no one space nor to any bureaucratic red tape. Having joined forces with Universal as its distribution company, the directors shoulder the bulk of the financial risk for production. In exchange, they receive creative independence. Combining their talents has given them a bargaining power never witnessed before in the Hollywood system. As such, the creation of Cha Cha Cha is a step towards rejecting the traditional model of filmmaking and as such, opens up the space for new ways of engaging and relating to Hollywood.

Agamben's second alternative relates to the "event." Although vague, the notion of the "event" is at least as important as any reformist gesture or intellectual philosophizing found in today's political theory. An example of Agamben's "event" might be the "Battle of Seattle" in 1999, an event that *Children of Men's* opening line references when the acousmatique news reporter's voice states, "Day 1,000 of the siege of Seattle." At the 1999 event, large numbers of demonstrators descended on the Washington State Convention and Trade Center in Seattle to protest the World Trade Organization's Ministerial Conference. Like the Zapatista's uprising in Chiapas in 1994, this protest was part of a larger anti-globalization movement. Both events represent a collective rejection of biopolitical subjectivation and capitalist globalization. Only large scale collective events of this magnitude can break the cycle of the liberal democratic ideology that utilizes biopower to motivate and maintain its hegemonic power.

Notes

1. See Bruce Campbell, ¡Viva la historieta! Mexican Comics, NAFTA, and the Politics of Globalization (Jackson: University Press of Mississippi, 2009). Campbell gives insight into the tension between maintaining a national specificity of Mexican culture while also reflecting an image of cosmopolitanism. The problem with Campbell's work is that it tends to cite NAFTA as the main cause for this tension instead of taking into account the other political, social and cultural factors at stake in redefining "Mexicanness."
2. Giorgio Agamben, Homo Sacer, trans. Daniel Heller-Roazen (Stanford, CA: Stanford University Press, 1998).
3. See Adam Roberts, Science Fiction (New York: Routledge, 2006).
4. In the special feature on the DVD titled "The Possibility of Hope," Saskia Sassen discusses how border crossers are looked at suspiciously no matter what their reasons for crossing. The tension produced by this paranoia and fear results in a feeling of guilt on the part of the crosser. In today's increasing fragmentation and increasing mobility between communities, this relationship is problematic and demands more attention.
5. In the special features of the DVD, Zizek makes the suggestion that this lack of "roots" is the solution to the ideological despair that the individual is currently subject to in late capitalism. He suggests that contemporary subjects have lost their relationship to history but that they continue to cling to empty notions of the past in order to make sense of their place in an increasingly uncertain global system. Zizek puts forth the idea that one must severe this clinging to roots in order to move forward and renew the future.

Works Cited

Adams, Robert. *Science Fiction*. New York: Routledge, 2006.
Agamben, Giorgio. *Homo Sacer*. Trans. Daniel Heller-Roazen. Stanford: Stanford University Press, 1998.
Bhabha, Homi. *The Location of Culture*. New York: Routledge, 1994.
Campbell, Bruce. *¡Viva la historieta! Mexican Comics, NAFTA, and the Politics of Globalization*. Jackson: University Press of Mississippi, 2009.
Children of Men. Dir. Alfonso Cuarón. Universal Pictures, 2006.

Chion, Michel. *The Voice in Cinema*. Trans. Claudia Gorbman. New York: Columbia University Press, 1999.
De la Garza, Armida. *Mexico on Film: National Identity and International Relations*. LaVergne: Arena, 2006.
Foucault, Michel. *The History of Sexuality*. Trans. Robert Hurley. New York: Vintage, 1990.
Loomba, Ania. *Colonialism/Postcolonialism*. New York: Routledge, 1998.
Montemayor, Carlos. *Chiapas, la Rebelión Indígena de México*. Mexico D.F.: Joaquín Mortiz, 1997.
Newman, Kathleen. "Notes on Transnational Film Theory: Decentered Subjectivity, Decentered Capitalism." In *World Cinemas, Transnational Perspectives*, edited by Natasa Durovicová and Kathleen Newman, 3–11. New York: Routledge, 2010.
Shaw, Devin Zane. "The Absence of Evidence is Not the Evidence of Absence: Biopolitics and the State of Exception." In *Philosophy Against Empire*, edited by Tony Smith and Harry van der Linden, 123–138. Radical Philosophy Today, Vol. 4. Charlottesville: Philosophy Documentation Center, 2006.
Smith, Robert. "Contradictions of Diasporic Institutionalization in Mexican Politics: The 2006 Migrant Vote and Other Forms of Inclusion and Control." *Ethnic and Racial Studies* 31.4 (2008): 708–741.
Zizek, Slavoj. *Violence*. London: Profile, 2008.
_____. *Welcome to the Desert of the Real!* London: Verso, 2002.

12

Fantastic Language/ Political Reporting
The Postcolonial Science Fiction Illocutionary Force Is with Us
MARLEEN S. BARR

We have been approaching this presidential race the wrong way. It's not political science. It's science fiction. Something is amiss in the space-time continuum. The candidates running now are not the same ones we started out with. It's *Invasion of the Body Snatchers* all over again. We're watching the clash of the pod people. The first hint that things were not what they seemed came when Barack Obama turned into Hillary Clinton. We believe this was engineered by Hillary fans who had seen that early *Star Trek* episode about the woman who wanted to be a starship commander so bad that she figured out a way to switch brains with Captain Kirk.
Gail Collins, "Cloned Candidates"

Have the worlds of science fiction and presidential politics ever been more closely aligned than they were in 2007? This was the year when Rudolph Giuliani told a young questioner on the campaign trail that "we'll be prepared" if the United States is attacked by aliens from another planet; when Dennis Kucinich blithely confessed during a Democratic debate that he'd seen a U.F.O.; and when Mitt Romney revealed in an interview that L. Ron Hubbard's *Battlefield Earth* was one of his favorite novels. But really, is it all that remarkable that Romney would identify with the story of a virtuous hero who saves Earth from a foreign invasion force? Or that several candidates have embraced science fiction when so many of them could benefit from its lessons?
Dave Itzkoff, "Planetary Politics"

Dave Itzkoff notes that science fiction and presidential politics are closely aligned worlds. Gail Collins' piece, which is replete with science fiction contexts and references to science fiction texts, exemplifies how science fiction parlance permeates *New York Times* op-ed page columnists' prose. In order fully to understand Collins, readers must be fluent in fantastic language and cognizant of the science fiction canon. They must immediately recognize "space-time continuum" and "pod people"; they must be familiar with *The Invasion of the Body Snatchers* and *Star Trek*. By stressing science fiction language's political communicative effectiveness, Itzkoff complements Collins' content which indicates that this language is a political presence. He points to how Giuliani, Kucinich, and Romney use science fiction tropes to describe their individual agendas. My purpose is to apply Samuel R. Delany's notion of "the language of science fiction" to the pervasive use of science fiction's linguistic presence and resonance in current political reporting parlance. I will closely read *New York Times* political opinion writers as well as other political commentators with an eye toward showing that the language of science fiction has become a post colonial illocutionary force that exemplifies how to do political things with science fiction words.

Delany's discussion of "the language of science fiction" emphasizes that science fiction language is a distinct communicative system and, in order to understand science fiction, science fiction readers must be fluent in this system. In the manner of Creole and American black dialect, science fiction language has been positioned as a linguistic Other — a silenced, colonized, and marginalized discourse practice. Collins and Itzkoff indicate that this is no longer true. Science fiction language, in the manner of postcolonial discourse, now speaks as a major force at the nexus of current debates about national politics; it serves as an instantaneously recognizable metaphor, which challenges, normalizes, and contests political debates. Postcolonial science fiction language has become the United States' new national language for navigating the political landscape.

I will explain the affective value of the new postcolonial language of science fiction and its connotation in the context of national and, by implication, global politics. I will accomplish this objective by analyzing how postcolonial science fiction language functions as a major communicative force used by political opinion writers (especially *Times* columnists publishing between 2006 and 2010). Maureen Dowd's following description of George W. Bush's last departure from the White House via presidential helicopter exemplifies what I mean by the political presence of science fiction language as text: "It was the Instant the Earth Stood Still. Not since Klaatu landed in a flying saucer on the Ellipse has Washington been so mesmerized by an object whirring through the sky" (Dowd "Exit"). In order best to understand Dowd, readers must comprehend her science fiction language. Klaatu has joined, say, such household word names as Kleenex, Khrushchev, and King Cheops as garden variety *Times* readers' expected immediately recognizable lexicon.

Itzkoff's suggested reading for Hillary Clinton and Barack Obama exemplifies what I mean by the political resonance of science fiction language as context. For Clinton, Itzkoff says that Frank Herbert's *Dune* is appropriate: "Left adrift to wander in a desert wasteland, the scion of a deposed dynasty retakes the family's lost throne in thrilling and violent fashion" (Itzkoff). For Obama, Itzkoff says that Michael Moorcock's *Behold the Man* is appropriate: "Obsessed with Messianic ideas, a man with issues about his lineage travels back in time to discover he is actually the Messiah" (Itzkoff). To respond to the hilarity Itzkoff generates, readers must instantaneously understand science fiction culture — the fact that Herbert's and Moorcock's science fiction scenarios describe political reality.

I have briefly cited Collins, Dowd, and Itzkoff to ground my primary argument: no longer a linguistic subaltern, the postcolonial force of science fiction language (and imagery) is with us as the lingua franca of twenty first century America's political terrain. In what follows, I substantiate this claim in the following three sections: 1) "Beyond BEMS and Boobs": Samuel Delany's "The Language of Science Fiction," 2) "Learning from Other Worlds": Science Fiction Language's Political Presence, and 3) "Storming the Reality Studio": Science Fiction Language's Political Resonance.[1] I will, for example, explain the importance of picturing Obama attired in a Starfleet uniform with Vulcan ears extending from his head. (Illustrator Shan Carter created a comic image of Obama pictured as a Vulcan which accompanied Maureen Dowd's "Put Aside Logic.") I will, in short, argue that it is necessary to be fluent in the language of science fiction to comprehend political reporting discourse. In the science fiction world Americans currently inhabit, "science fiction" is becoming ever more synonymous with "political science."

"Beyond BEMS and Boobs": Samuel Delany's "The Language of Science Fiction"

James Gunn states that "the way we read science fiction differs from the way we read other genres or categories." He concurs with Delany's point and describes it. "Three decades ago ... Samuel R. Delany, gave a talk at a Modern Language Association meeting in which he said that he had visited many universities and had discovered that people who said they didn't read science fiction or didn't like science fiction actually couldn't read science fiction.... To the question of whether science fiction works in the same way as other categories of writing, he answers: 'no. Science fiction works differently from other written categories, particularly those categories traditionally called literary. It works the same way only in that, like all categories of writing, it has its specific conventions, unique focuses, areas of interest and excellence, as well as its own particular ways of making sense out of language. To ignore any of these constitutes a major misreading — an obliviousness to the play of meanings that makes up the SF text.'" Gunn continues: "Earlier in the essay, Delany writes that 'the conventions of poetry or drama or mundane fiction — or science fiction — are in themselves separate languages,' and in other essays, he called the process by which one approaches and reads those languages 'protocols'" (Gunn 160). Reading science fiction, then, involves engaging in a specific reading practice which necessitates learning particular language protocols. Delany and Gunn focus on reading science fiction genre texts. To my mind, the language of science fiction has broken out of its generic boundaries and invaded political reporting prose. In order to be fully cognizant of this prose's meanings — to avoid misreading — it is necessary to understand science fiction's separate language traits.

Delany and Gunn list many representative texts to explain their points. Following their example, I include specific examples of how diverse *New York Times* political commentators pervasively use the same science fiction language:

GAIL COLLINS: "Hillary now lives in a Golden alternative universe" (Collins "Misery").

DAVID BROOKS: "I went ... in the White House to hear President Bush answer questions on the same subject [Iraq]. It was like entering a different universe" (Brooks "Heroes").

BOB HERBERT: I find myself speculating on what might have been if the man who got the most votes in 2000 had actually become president. It's like imagining an alternative universe" (Herbert "Passion").

MAUREEN DOWD: "While W. and Dick conjured an alternative reality about Iraq, our avaricious bankers created an alternative reality about our financial system" (Dowd "Dark").

UNSIGNED *NEW YORK TIMES* EDITORIAL: "Watching the [Republican presidential] debate, it felt as if these candidates ... were living in an alternative universe" (*Times* "Worry").

FRANK RICH: "But the brazenness of Bush's alternative-reality history is itself revelatory" (Rich "Forgotten").

FRANK RICH: "What was the most striking about the Obama speech in Berlin was not anything he said so much as the alternative reality it fostered" (Rich "Acting").

BOB HERBERT (article title): "Palin's Alternate Universe" (Herbert).

Any *Times* reader who does not understand the science fiction genre protocols of "alternative reality" and "alternative universe" comes from another planet in relation to reading the *Times*. The *Times*' political writers turn to science fiction language to comment upon a political reality which is ever more unreal. Science fiction language is the best parlance to address, for instance, Iraq's nonexistent weapons of mass destruction — the unreal reality which constituted George W. Bush's pretext for going to war. For example, Dennis Kucinich's science fiction language utterance aptly described Washington: "Around Washington, the truth is an unidentified flying object" (Solomon). No wonder political writers use science fiction language to comment upon political truth cast as a U.F.O.

"Heeeeere's" how Jay Leno describes the science fictionesque juxtaposition of the real and unreal: "Dick Cheney had an awkward moment tonight at the White House Halloween party. He went dressed as Darth Vader. And at the party, he ran into the real Darth Vader, who was dressed as Dick Cheney" ("Laugh Lines"). Dowd, who has also characterized Dick as Darth, stands corrected by a stellar science fiction community practitioner: "[George] Lucas ... had told me that I had gotten Dick Cheney completely wrong, that Cheney was no Darth Vader.... Lucas explained ... Anakin Skywalker is the promising young man who is turned to the dark side by an older politician and becomes Darth Vader. 'George Bush is Darth Vader,' he said. 'Cheney is the emperor.' I was relieved. In 'Star Wars' terms, Dick Cheney was more evil than Darth Vader" (Dowd "Aura"). In the days of mundane political old speak, in that 1988 galaxy far far away when political reality and unreality were distinct genres, Lloyd Bentsen famously told Dan Quayle that he was "no Jack Kennedy." In today's real/unreal political universe, Lucas exemplifies the new science fiction language political lexicon when he authoritatively states that Cheney is no Darth Vader. "*Star Wars* terms"— and all science fiction terms of its ilk — are the definitive political descriptors of our time. Science fiction language has drastically morphed in that it has gone from marginalized colonized language to postcolonial postmodern political parlance par excellence. Dan Quayle never became a John F. Kennedy clone. But Cheney as Darth Vader White House denizen has been superseded by a new political illocutionary force: the young man who has fulfilled his promise, the new American leader who makes "Mr. President" synonymous with "Mr. Spock." Washington political truth is an unidentified flying object; the old Cheney-as-Vader has given way to the new president-as-Vulcan. Science fiction language has become politically important to the extent that Obama, during his inauguration speech, could have lifted his hand from the bible, spread his fingers, and told the nation to "live long and prosper."

This science fiction language scenario did not happen. Obama is not really a Vulcan; Dowd explains that he merely plays one on TV. But the frightening fact is that Sarah Palin really does speak a science fictional version of standard English: "Sometimes, her sentences have a Yoda-like —'When 900 years old you reach, look as good you will not'— splendor.... Then she uttered yet another sentence that defies diagramming: 'It is from Alaska that we send those out to make sure that an eye is being kept on this very powerful nation, Russia, because they are right there" (Dowd "Pompom"). Palin uses language that is fantastic to the extent that comprehending its protocols are beyond the powers and abilities of science fiction scholars. Her sentences are linguistically science fictional in that, like the unearthly language invented for James Cameron's Na'vi, humans who encounter it need to resort to subtitles. Before further applying Delany's terms to the complexity that is science fiction language's representation of the real/unreal contemporary political world, I will briefly go back to the future — to a brief close reading of his description of the language of science fiction.

Matthew Cheney, in his introduction to Delany's *The Jewel-Hinged Jaw*, concurs with Gunn's observation that the language of science fiction works differently from other language and uses its own protocols. According to Cheney, Delany says that science fiction "was special because of its language, and the assumptions and techniques readers used to interpret that language, and the ways writers' knowledge of those assumptions and techniques affected the stories they wrote" (Cheney xv). He seems to address Palin's "Yoda-like' failure correctly to parse when he emphasizes that "*science fiction is another language*" (Cheney xix). He explains Delany's "protocol" when he states that though science fiction "uses many of the same words that mundane fiction uses, it uses them differently. To be able to understand science fiction, you must be able to crack its codes" (Cheney xix). The notion of science fiction using words "differently" grounds my understanding of science fiction language as a predominant cultural code for understanding political reporting discourse. In order to read the *Times* op-ed page most effectively, it is necessary to use science fiction reading practices, to be able to crack science fiction cultural codes.

Delany situates communicating via science fiction language in terms of Marshall McLuhan and states that science fiction influenced McLuhan. His comments about McLuhan point to why political reporters adopt science fiction language. Delany says:

> McLuhan explains that any manmade object, and a good many natural ones, as they express or reflect aspects of our inner consciousness, become factors in the equations governing communication as soon as they come into our perception. But well before McLuhan had put this so succinctly — indeed, SF was to prompt McLuhan to this statement, another example of influence across boundaries — American SF writers, freed from the strictures of the probable ... sat contemplating marvelous objects in the theater of the mind.... Editor Campbell was astute enough to see that this was perhaps the most powerful tool in the realization of these marvelous inventions.... As the writers followed Campbell, SF began to grow up [Delany "Critical" 24].

Grown-up science fiction language — or, postcolonial science fiction language that progressed to childhood's end — came into the perception of political reporting commentators. These commentators intuited that science fiction language most efficiently expresses and reflects the nation's inner conscious understanding of the at once real and unreal political environment. The commentators, then, speak in terms of a juxtaposition between postcolonial science fiction language and media ecology. Iraq's supposed ability to generate a "mushroom cloud" exemplifies one reason why this juxtaposition became necessary. The mushroom cloud was nothing more than a marvelous object which existed solely in the theater of the minds of Bush, Cheney and Condoleezza Rice. Political opinion writers use science fiction writers' powerful linguistic tools to communicate their ideas regarding the mushroom cloud and other fictions of its ilk. The pervasive presence of science fiction language in the *Times* shows that this parlance has matured into a communicative force of universal perception. Science fiction influenced McLuhan's statement — and McLuhan's statement, combined with Delany's "protocol," explains why science fiction language has become such an important factor in the media ecology equations governing how political opinion writers communicate.

The revelations about John Edwards' relationship with Rielle Hunter indicate why science fiction language is such a potent communicative tool for political writers. We now know that Edwards' forthright family values persona was as unreal as the stage set human zoo cage located on Kurt Vonnegut's planet Tralfamadore. Together with his wife Elizabeth, the entire electorate learned that there was no such thing as the John Edwards they thought they knew. Like the major human protagonists of *Avatar*, this simultaneous husband and philanderer lived in two separate cultural spheres. Elizabeth Edwards abruptly learned that her marriage was a close encounter with an androidesque fake human whose dual roles as loyal husband and honest politician were constructed forgeries; John tried to hide Hunter from Elizabeth in general and from the world in particular. Delany's description of science fiction language can describe John Edwards' actions. Delany says: "Mundane fiction can get by with a clear and accurate portrayal of behavior *that* occurs merely *because* it occurs. Science fiction can not" (Delany "Read" 128). Edwards' behavior was not something that occurs because it occurs. It was, from the point of view of observers, a fake, a forgery, a story. In other words, from Elizabeth Edwards' and the media's perspective, his relationship with Hunter belonged in an alternative universe. No one believes in Tralfamadorians; everyone (with the exception of a few confidantes) believed that Edwards was not the father of Hunter's daughter. Edwards was not mundane; he reconfigured himself as unreal, alien. He existed in what Delany calls an "alien culture": "In an alien culture ... we are obliged to speculate on the reason behind any behavior; and this speculation, whether implicit or explicit, must leave signs on the texts" (Delany "Read" 128). It has become necessary to reread Edwards, to go back and ask this question: what did he know about Hunter's daughter's paternity and when did he know it? When political writers describe the unreality Edwards created, they speculate and this speculation leave signs on their texts.

What is a nice discourse like political journalism doing in a subgeneric sodden communicative place like this — one replete with such words as "warp drive," "zap gun," and "Klingon?" Delany's definition of science fiction language addresses the answer. He explains that the "particular *manner* in which the inmixing of syntagm and signifier occurs in science fiction, whether at the level of term, sentence, or plot to create something *more than* and *different from* what those syntagms and signifiers yield separately is what makes science fiction.... The language with which SF accomplishes its particular mode of inmixing must frequently use unusual verbal juxtapositions, by which certain words are estranged from their more usual, extrageneric contexts. But the process we are trying to fix is that by which we recognize these new and different images, rather than how we later recognize them as structures" (Delany "Read" 144). Lying politicians confront the electorate with signifiers gone awry. A rose is a rose is a rose; the Bush team's mushroom cloud, is not a mushroom cloud, is not a mushroom cloud. Because politicians who eschew the reality-based world place their words within a system of unreal contexts, mundane language fails vis-à-vis political reporting. If, as Saussure tells us, language is a system and words derive their meaning from other components in that system, meaning in the mundane sense fails in the face of "truthiness." Bill Clinton's assertion "I did not have sex with that woman Monica Lewinsky" communicates nothing; in a world made as a false construction, we do not know what "the meaning of is is." Or, to turn to Darko Suvin's understanding of the relationship between "cognitive estrangement" and science fiction, we cannot generate accurate cognition in a political world, which represents itself in terms of "untruth."

People are not estranged from the language of science fiction; it is the best language to use when reporting on our brave new real/unreal political world. In other words, Delany explains that supposedly inadequate science fiction language has the "analytic energy"— or illocutionary force — to write the present political world: "As a genre, it [science fiction] so frequently begins as a discourse that appears inadequate to discourse on anything at all, but which, by auctorial application to it of a certain analytic energy among its visions, ends up writing much more of the world than, certainly, any description of the discourse can say" (Delany "Read" 144). In the present real/unreal political environment, science fiction has the right media ecology stuff. The illocutionary force is with science fiction language.

"Learning from Other Worlds": Science Fiction Language's Political Presence

My epigram quotes Gail Collins saying that that 2008 presidential election is "not political science. It's science fiction" (Collins "Year"). The candidates who participated in this science fiction election are positioned as science fiction characters. Pamela Sargent's "Hillary Orbits Venus" recasts Hillary Clinton as a science fiction story hero. Many political commentators act in kind when describing Hillary. For example, Anne E. Kornblut, in *Notes from the Cracked Ceiling: Hillary Clinton, Sarah Palin, and What It Will Take for a Woman to Win*, argues that women candidates are alien in relation to the presidential election process. And Collins wonders if Hillary is secretly an extraterrestrial. "What if she has a secret life as a French undercover agent or a space alien?" (Collins "Unwelcome"). The new generation of female candidates is seen as being no less science fictional than their predecessors. Kornblut focuses on Hillary and Sarah Palin. Even though Collins calls New York's post–Hillary senator Kirsten Gillibrand the "New Hillary," Gillibrand is just as science fictional to Collins as the Old Hillary. Move over Sigourney Weaver; here comes Hillary's successor cast as a science fiction movie star: "the new senator's politics are evolving at a rate previously seen only in science-fiction movies" (Collins "New"). Collins implies that Gillibrand would be appropriate critical fodder for such science fiction film critics as Scott Bukatman or Vivian Sobcheck. *The New Adventures of the Old Christine* is a sitcom set in the real world; the new adventures of Kirsten the old Hillary's successor happen faster than a speeding bullet. New York's old and new female senators are described as science fiction Super Senators. Dowd imbues Hillary with super powers: "Hillary has created a regal force field that can be breached only with permission" (Dowd "Blood"). Hillary's force field really works. The science fiction illocutionary force *is* with Hillary.

Superhero powers and abilities are attributed to other politicians as well. Collins opines that "[m]aybe Rudy [Giuliani] has a secret grip, like the Vulcan mind-meld" (Collins "Loves"). Dowd imagines that Dick Cheney, who she often calls Dr. No, is evil and powerful to the extent that even science fiction accoutrements cannot prevail against him. Immersing Cheney within J. K. Rowling's world, she imagines that he could wack Harry Potter: "It's hard to imagine how Dick Cheney could get more dastardly, unless J. K. Rowling has

12. Fantastic Language/Political Reporting (Barr) 197

him knock off Harry Potter.... Harry's cloak of invisibility would be no match for Vice's culture of invisibility" (Dowd "Vice"). Paul Krugman, seeking a means to express his disdain for Republican party dastardly doings, also turns to science fiction. He asks if Sarah Palin can really portray herself as running against the Washington elite if the Republicans, "borg-like, assimilated much of the D.C. lobbying industry into itself" (Krugman "Resentment").

Science fiction imagery can be appropriately applied to John McCain as well as to Palin. Collins notes that when the economy began to consist of things falling apart, "McCain appeared to be a loopy visitor from the Planet of the Overwrought" (Collins "Grievance"). When Collins is not positioning McCain as a John orbits Venus equivalent of Sargent's story about Hillary, she posits that "he's an android." She worries "you always worry that when they [McCain and Mitt Romney] appear in the same place, there'll be a rift in the space-time continuum" (Collins "Guide").

Obama as android? Is he or isn't he? Only political writers know for sure — and they are aligning themselves with the public superhero option. Dowd, in the pieces she calls "Less Spocky, More Rocky" (Dowd "Spocky"), announces that Obama should eschew his extraterrestrial emotionless guise in favor of an earthly hero's boxing ring prowess. Leonard Nimoy famously contemplated whether or not he is Spock. Dowd announces that Obama should be less Spocky. Whether or not Obama chooses to adopt a Rocky-esque persona, he is not immune to the implications of geology. A specific science fiction rock functions as the hero president's Achilles heal: "The legislative process is like Kryptonite to the existential hero; it is designed, somewhat ingeniously, to expose even the most powerful president for the mortal that he is" (Bai 44). Obama's political base at once knows that he is mortal and elevates him to superhero status. In a piece called "Can He Unleash the Force?," Dowd states that "[i]n mythic tales from 'Superman' to 'Star Wars' to 'Spider-Man,' there comes a moment when the young superhero has to learn to harness his powers. That's the challenge Barack Obama faces now." Obama would do well to proclaim that the science fiction illocutionary force is with himself.

Obama, in a revelation that would cause the Birthers' heads to explode, actually did state that he was indeed born on another planet. "Obama joked that he was not the messiah but Superman. 'Contrary to the rumors you've heard, I was not born in a manager. I was actually born on Krypton'" (Blow). Charles M. Blow responds to this news by concurring with Dowd's "less Spocky, more Rocky" point: "[O]ur mild mannered president is in desperate need of a telephone booth. He needs to summon his inner Superman who knows how to pair optimism with force when responding to a crisis, a Man of Steel who's more than a silver tongue with a tin ear" (Blow). Blow asserts that Obama needs less linguistic force and more science fiction superhero mode. Obama's illocutionary force — his "Spocky" ability to do legislative things with silver tongue words — is rendered impotent in the presence of the literally rocky: the red, green, blue or gold legislative Kryptonite the Republican Party routinely throws in the path of his political agenda.

In addition to Dowd and Blow, political humorist Andy Borowitz also turns to science fiction to describe Obama's response to the Republicans' incessant efforts to derail his legislative effectiveness. Obama, according to Borowitz, steels himself against Republicans who gleefully enact an H. G. Wells plot. Borowitz's time travel scenario called "GOP Launch Time Travel Machine to Disagree with Obama in Future" would do Wells proud: "[K]ey congressional Republicans launched themselves in a state-of-the-art time machine today to complete an important mission: traveling to the future to disagree with President Barack Obama....' My colleagues and I have traveled four days into the future and listened to everything the President will say,' he [House Minority Leader John Boehner] told reporters at the Capitol. 'And it will suck'" (Borowitz). No matter that The Great Recession precludes financing time machine construction and available funds would be more fruitfully directed toward tackling present infrastructure problems. Borowitz creates a Vulcan mind meld between his political commentary and Wells' classic science fiction scenario. His humorous text is science fiction; when creating it he becomes a science fiction writer. Borowitz's turn toward science fiction provides the perfect point to move from noting the presence of science fiction terms within political commentary to discussing the implications of how science fiction scenarios resonate when political commentators incorporate them as a stylistic component.

"Storming the Reality Studio": Science Fiction Language's Political Resonance

Multi-media journalist Farai Chideya, when she cites China Mieville's science fiction novel *The Scar*, illustrates that in addition to specific science fiction terms, entire science fiction texts resonate politically. Chideya says, "'For every factual attack, there are a thousand possibilities — and all of them strike down together.' ... [i]t's a line from China Mieville's speculative novel *The Scar*, but it could easily describe today's politics" (Chideya). Mieville's words are exceedingly applicable to the Bush administration's attacks against facts, its "strike down" of what it disparagingly called the reality based community. As I have written elsewhere, George W. Bush authored alternative reality science fiction. Science fiction language, then, does more than describe politics. Science fiction language becomes politics. During the Bush years, for example, science fiction was positioned as a substitute for real world truth.

A citizen observer seems to address this point in a letter to the *New York Times*, which compares watching the Republican National Convention to reading a science fiction text: "[W]ith all its [the Convention's] sarcastic references to the Washington elite, I thought I had entered some kind of alternative universe. In this universe, John McCain isn't a four-term senator, and there hasn't been a Republican in the White House for almost eight years. Just because the name George W. Bush was conspicuously absent from the evening's oratory does not mean that he does not exist in our universe. Nor is it like that the voters ... are going to forget that they live in the real world" (Weiss). This writer can differentiate between fact and science fiction as surely as David Lindsay's readers are absolutely aware that they are not voyaging to Arcturus. But, Washington we have a problem: conservatives have become adept at substituting science fictional versions of reality for reality to the extent that voters have difficulty distinguishing between facts and the political alternative realities politicians author. For example, many people did not know that Iraq's purported weapons of mass destruction, no part of reality, are akin to a Harry Turtledove alternative reality science fiction novel.

Bush responded to political adversity by digging his heels ever more firmly within science fiction terrain: "With the American public in despair over the Iraq war and key members of his own party deserting him, Bush is still trying to twist reality to claim that his failed effort is worth sticking with" ("No Progress"). He dug himself into a science fiction hole that has turned out to be no more secure than the real hole that served as Saddam Hussein's hiding place. Despite the power of Bush double speak, the former president could not talk himself into really being able to follow Alice down the rabbit hole.

The now widespread understanding of Bush's executive decision making failures is due in no small part to political satirist Jon Stewart. Stewart fought Bush's science fiction language with science fiction language. Like a twenty-first-century male incarnation of Betty Friedan defining sexism as the problem that has no name, he was able "to name things [Bush's lies] that don't seem to have a name" (Kakutani). Stewart's particular language successfully nullified Bush's science fiction based locutionary obfuscations. He made it increasingly difficult for Bush to do science fiction things with science fiction words. He accomplished this public good through his "ferocious exposes of the [Bush] administration's Orwellian manipulations: ... [such as] its efforts to redefine the meaning of the word 'torture'" (Kakutani 19). Stewart, in other words, deployed a verbal force field, which repelled Bush's science fiction language. His tactic was most effective when he repositioned Bush from science fiction writer to science fiction character. Stewart, unlike his colleagues who merely compare Obama to a superhero, literally repositioned Bush as a superhero. When the satirist created the cartoon strip called "The Decider," he recast Bush as a superhero replete with spandex suit, cape, and single letter emblazoned on his chest. Stewart's televised cartoon comic strip superhero version of Bush clearly revealed Bush's hidden science fiction agenda. Unreal news demystified politics rooted in the unreal. Stewart's television news science fiction language powers and abilities effectively outfoxed Bush — and the Fox Network.

Stewart, someone who describes a world located in a universe far far away from Walter Cronkite's broadcasting reality, is the current most trusted television newscaster in America. This faith in a fake news creator is appropriate; our political milieu deviates from reality to an almost unbelievable extent. Many *Times* op-ed columnists comment on this situation. Krugman notes that "reality has a clear liberal bias" (Krugman "Desperately"). For Thomas L. Friedman, both sides of the aisle are not realistic: "the various gradual, partial withdrawal [from Iraq] proposals by many Democrats and dissident Republicans are not realistic either" (Friedman "In"). Perhaps Judith Warner most startlingly shows the extent of just how far the unreal pervades politics. "[T]he dividing line between what's believable and what's not, between fantasy and reality, has become utterly permeable" (Warner). Warner refers to such reality as the destruction of the World Trade Center and Saddam Hussein's hole.

"Rules for the Real World" is the title of a *Times* editorial which argues that alleged illegal enemy combatants should not be subjected to abuses stemming from United States federal government power. Bob Herbert emphasizes that Republicans do not think that "rules for the real world" apply to them. He asserts that Bush's No Child Left Behind Law was written during "an era in which reality was left behind" (Herbert "High"). Further decrying the Republican flight from real world rules, in a piece called "Running from Reality," Herbert positions "deception" as "the pre-eminent characteristic of the Republican convention.... Words completely lost their meaning. Reality was turned upside down" (Herbert). He describes the Republican verbiage turn as an Orwellian amusement park ride, a decidedly unfunny political version of John Barth's description of postmodern language as being "lost in the funhouse."

Democrats are not innocent of being lost in unreal political verbiage space. David Brooks points out that Democratic political candidates sometimes run from reality when running for office. In his "When Reality Bites," Brooks, quoting Harvard Law Professor William J. Stuntz, notes that Democrats "have conducted their races amid unconstrained 'Yes We Can!' unreality."

Despite Brooks' observation that Democrats resort to unreal speak, Bush and Cheney are by far the most egregious practitioners of authoring an alternative reality which does not conform to real world rules. In an editorial called "The World According to Cheney" the *Times* (of course evoking John Irving's novel), positions Cheney as a fiction writer who constructs a reality all his own — the world according to alternative reality science fiction he authors: "[I]t must be exhausting to rewrite history as much as Mr. Cheney has done.... In Mr. Cheney's reality" ("World"). Cheney as alternative reality author must be exhausted; he, after all, spews alternative reality based verbiage to the extent that it is akin to Barth's "The Literature of Exhaustion." But it is Bush — not Cheney — who is the alternative reality science fiction writer and sometimes science fiction character extraordinaire. Bush could have been eligible to win the Nebula and Hugo Awards. Krugman proclaims that Bush "has lost touch with reality. Actually, it is not clear that he ever was in touch with reality" (Krugman "Enablers"). Bush creates and inhabits a world of his own. Like Arthur C. Clarke, Bush authored a science fiction space odyssey about 2001.

Dowd takes Bush to task for this science fiction writerly penchant and throws the rules of real world book at him. Bush's "conflation [of bin Laden and Al Qaeda] is contradicted by the fact that Al Qaeda in Mesopotamia, as the Sunni terrorist group is known, did not exist before 9/11 (Dowd "Hey"). Dowd's reality check demonstrates that "Bushworld" (Dowd's term) history exists in an alternative universe. Jacob Weisberg is so vehement about positioning Bush as a fictional character, he calls his very existence into question: Bush "remains an appealing character, but a largely fictional one. I wonder how the last seven years would have turned out if he had actually existed" (Weisberg). Unfortunately, according to real world rules, the Bush presidency did in fact exist. What planet were Bush and Cheney on? Not the Earth we know. Perhaps they are akin to the replicates Philip K. Dick imagined. According to Timothy Egan, the Bush team's version of the Iraq War resembles "a postapocalyptic sci-fi film like 'Blade Runner.' Here is a troubled super-power headed by a pair of delusional men, with a rag-tag army fighting a constant low-grade insurgency" (Egan). At least Bush greeted the Obama era by ceasing and desisting from inflicting his delusions upon us. Not so for Cheney's ongoing rewritten history.

Frank Rich describes Cheney's continuing alternative reality tall tale telling. In "The New Rove-Cheney Assault on Reality," he explains that members of the Bush coterie wish to go back to the future. "This gang's rewriting of history knows few bounds. To hear them tell it, 9/11 was so completely Bill Clinton's fault that it retroactively happened while he was still in office. The Bush White House is equally blameless for the post 9/11 resurgence of the

Taliban." If Bush is the master of what Rich calls "this non-reality based shtick stick," then Rich is the master of using science fiction language to reveal this penchant; Rich sticks it to Bush. "History will be repeated not only if we forget it, but also if we let it be rewritten by those whose ideological zealotry and boneheaded decisions have made America less safe to this day" (Rich "Assault"). I will conclude this section by looking back to Rich's efforts to protect our future; I will discuss how Rich uses science fiction language to counter the Bush speak science fiction language which described rewritten alternative reality history.

Rich, like the members of Starfleet Command who authored the Prime Directive against tampering with reality, routinely warns against the Bush Team's retelling of history penchant. In "Truthiness Stages a Comeback," Rich warns that "[a]s truthiness repeats itself, so may history, and not as farce" (Rich "Truthiness"). He routinely seems to shout "you lie" to the Bush team by railing against the science fiction alternative reality scenarios they generate. He turns to McLuhan to support his point that the team authors propagandistic genre fiction fables: "The medium is the message. This administration just loves to beguile us with a rollicking good story, truth be damned. The propagandistic fable exposed by the [Valerie Wilson] leak case — the apocalyptic imminence of Saddam's mushroom clouds — was only the first of its genre" (Rich "Tillman"). Rich's piece is about Pat Tillman, the Arizona Cardinals football player who sacrificed a multimillion dollar football contract to join the army. Counter to the Bush team fiction about how Tillman died heroically, Tillman was in truth killed as a result of friendly fire. Rich calls this cover-up one of "the official fictions that have corrupted every stage of this war" (Rich "Tillman"). Two years after commenting on the Tillman official fiction, Rich revisits the case and accuses Iraq war hawks of the "rewriting of history" (Rich "Patriots"). Pointing specifically to the Congressional hearings on Tillman's death, Rich states that "we still don't know who rewrote the witness statements of Tillman's cohort so that Pentagon propagandists could trumpet a fictionalized battle death to the public and his family" (Rich "Patriots"). This particular rewritten history is venal to the extreme; it turns one individual's personal sacrifice into a propaganda lie. Science fiction writers benignly fantasize about firing fictitious rockets; Bush team fabulists author vicious lies about the existence of friendly fire.

Bush team lies led to the firing of very real rockets which killed very real people. Or, in Rich's words, "Mr. Bush has become so reckless in his own denials of reality that he seems to think he can get away with saying anything" (Rich "Colonoscopy"). Bush, who has not been prosecuted for the consequences of the fictions he articulated, did get away with saying anything.

Rich, with McLuhanesque prescience, adroitly describes the implications of Bush's untruths when he equates them to Stephen King's horror fiction: "like the hand that suddenly pops out of the grave at the end of 'Carrie,' the past keeps coming back to haunt the Bush White House" (Rich "Thousand"). Rich describes Bush as being in a horror fiction mess. Specifically referring to the "discredited fictions" about the weapons of mass destruction, Rich continues: "The demons that keep rising up from the past to grab Mr. Bush are the fictional W.M.D. he wielded to take us into Iraq. They stalk him as relentlessly as Banquo's ghost did Macbeth. From that original sin, all else flows.... Mr. Bush's poll numbers wouldn't be in the toilet if American blood was not being spilled daily because of his fictions" (Rich "Thousand"). King's work is not sufficiently horrifying to describe Bush. Rich finds it necessary to add Banquo's ghost to the hand from hell King imagines. In addition to the popping hand, Rich mentions "flows" and "American blood. " His implication: like Lady Macbeth, Bush has blood on his hands which he cannot wash away. No amount of "out out brief spot"— no amount of alternative history writing — can remove the blot on American history he authored.

Or, in Rich's words: "The [Bush] White House's most accomplished artificial-reality Imagineers," "Orwellian incantation," and "a fresh round of White House fictions" cannot render "the reality-based world that our president [Bush] disdains" unreal (Rich "Shuffling"). Rich is not subtle when describing the Bush team's untruths, fictionalizing, and rewritten history,

> The untruths are flying so fast that untangling them can be a full-time job.... Ms. Rice rose to a whole new level of fictionalizing by wrapping a fresh layer of untruth around her most notorious previous fiction [about Saddam Hussein's ability to create a mushroom cloud].... She also rewrote history to imply that she had been talking broadly about the nexus between "terrorism and a nuclear device" back then — a rather deft verbal sleight-of-hand. Ms. Rice sets a high bar, but Mr. Bush, competitive as always, was not to be outdone in his Oval Office address. Even the billing of his appearance was fiction [Rich "Longer" 14].

Rich storms the Bush team's unreality studio. He positions the team as alternative history science fiction writers who construct fictitious American reality.

Conclusion

"The End" now applies to the Bush administration's fake American history. The faux cowboy president has faded into the Texas sunset. With his effusive title "It's a Bird, It's a Plane, It's Obama!," Rich uses science fiction language to express his joy about Obama's presence in general and his health care victory in particular: "Not since Clark Kent changed in a phone booth has there been an instant image makeover to match Barack Obama's in the aftermath of his health care victory" (Rich "Bird"). Obama's success has caused a Clark Kentesque change in relation to political science fiction rhetoric: conservatives are now accusing liberals of being the fabulators. Douglas Holtz-Eakin, the President of the American Action Forum Policy Institute, believes that the Democrats use fantasy accounting to imaginarily tackle the deficit. He states that they resort to using unreal arithmetic to mask health care reform legislation's impact on the federal deficit: "Could this [the budget office permitting the federal government committing itself to spending nearly $1 trillion more over the next decade] really be true? The answer, unfortunately, is that the budget office is required to take written legislation at face value and not second guess the plausibility of what it is handed. So fantasy in, fantasy out" (Holtz-Eakin "Real"). In the brave new Obama world in which Rich implies that the president is Superman, Republicans linguistically enter a Clark Kent phone booth; Republicans now change into the Frank Rich of Bushian yore. In the manner of so many Rich columns, conservative commentator Holtz-Eakin accuses the Democrats of authoring alternative reality untruth and replacing fact with fantasy.

This is not to say that Obama's election and health care victory has turned America into a political utopia for liberals. Even though Bush has sequestered himself within a non–ok corral, Cheney continues to shoot off his mouth. And, in a spinoff resembling an evil twin of *Star Trek: The Next Generation*, Cheney's daughter Liz now seeks political office. The rise of Liz Cheney positions liberals as swimmers who, thinking it is now safe to go back into the political water, closely encounter the attacking shark in *Jaws*. Accordingly, Bill Maher responds to Liz in terms of genre fiction language: "*Twilight* is bullshit. Elect a real vampire spawn. Liz Cheney" (*Real Time*). The specter of Liz Cheney as an elected official recasts vampire fantasy fiction into political reality.

Conservatives, in the face of their political defeats, have not desisted from creating fake reality. The Supreme Court's conservative justices (in January 2010) science fictionally expanded the definition of "human"; they ruled that, in relation to campaign advertising, corporations have the same rights as a person. The *Times* is not buying what it calls "The Court's Blow to Democracy": "Most wrongheaded of all is its [the Supreme Court's] insistence that corporations are just like people and entitled to the same First Amendment rights. It is an odd claim since companies are creations of the state that exist to make money.... It was a fundamental misreading of the Constitution to say that these artificial legal constructs have the same right to spend money on politics as ordinary Americans have to speak out in support of a candidate"

(Court's). Declaring that artificial legal constructs have the same rights as citizens is grounds for giving the Hugo and Nebula Awards to the Obama era conservative justices as well as to Bush and his team. Barbra Streisand, in this vein, uses science fiction language to respond to the Supreme Court's advocacy of having Pod People fund political candidates. "I felt like I was in suspended animation as I read the Supreme Court decision which essentially enables a corporate coup d'etat of American democracy" (Streisand internet). So, Pod People in, "suspended animation" out — of Streisand's mouth.

The *Times* Op-Ed page embraces science fiction to the extent that it includes Nick Pope's piece which advocates being more curious about U.F.O.'s. Pope (who was in charge of U.F.O. investigations for the British Ministry of Defense from 1991 to 1994) concludes that the "United States Air Force or the National Aeronautics and Space Administration should reopen investigations of U.F.O. phenomena. It would not imply that the country has suddenly started believing in little green men. It would simply recognize the possibility that radar alone cannot always tell us what's out there" (Pope). We live in a world in which science fiction routinely becomes real; Pope implies that the scientific tools we use to separate what we perceive to be fact from what we perceive to be science fiction are not always absolute. That which is off our radar screens can in fact exist.

In the face of this truth — the ever-tightening convergence of the fanciful and the factual — it is difficult to separate political reality from political alternative reality. Under Bush, many people believed in a little green men alternative reality mushroom cloud story. The science fiction language which political commentators used describe this situation focused our radar screens, our interpretative skills.

The science fiction, which became real when Apollo 8 astronaut Bill Anders created his "Earthrise" photograph, enhances viewing political reality in a positive and constructive way. Oliver Morton (the chief news and features editor of the journal *Nature*) explains why this is so: "'Earthrise' showed us where we are, what we can do and what we share. It showed us who we are, together; the people of a tough, long lasting world, shot through with the light of a continuous creation" (Morton). The no longer science fictional means to make and see "Earthrise" seems to address the "I see you" refrain in *Avatar*. Morton indicates that "you" are "us." Despite differing political opinions, all humans inhabit earth together. The Republicans, the party of no, should take another look again at "Earthrise."

Thomas L. Friedman politically recasts Morton's comments about "Earthrise" and, and when doing so, insinuates that Obama's "yes we can" is not science fiction language. Friedman says that "America has the right stuff to survive. We still have the most creative, diverse, innovative culture and open society — in a world where the ability to imagine and generate new ideas ... is the most important competitive advantage. John Kennedy led us on a journey to discover the moon. Obama needs to lead us on a journey to rediscover, rebuild and reinvent our own backyard" (Friedman "Reboot"). As Morton and Friedman point out, discovering the moon — turning what used to be science fiction into scientific reality — helps us to discover our own political reality. A *Times* editorial called "Earthstruck" states that the "real Earth seen from the Moon is surely as lovely as ever, even with thinner ice caps, smaller forests.... We are still brothers and sisters in the eternal cold, but increasingly connected by invisible threads — able to see — and hear and understand — one another as never before. That, at least, is reason for optimism" (Editorial A24). We all inhabit political reality together. "I see you," we can say to each other on a world made ever smaller by the communicative technology innovations which are no longer science fictional.

Friedman echoes Tom Wolfe when he states that Americans have the right stuff to long endure. According to Friedman, in the Obama era, as opposed to the Kennedy era, we have to do our imagining and new idea generating much closer to home; we need to turn our attention from the moon to our own backyard. This injunction does not necessarily mean that we must tighten our science fiction belts. Some of the rockets that people built in their backyards really did fly — and they flew high in the sky.

In terms of the blurring between science fiction and reality, we can read Rich in a manner indicating that Obama's relation to science fiction is not pie in the sky. Rich's "It's a Bird, It's a Plane, It's Obama!" effusive piece uses science fiction language to explain that Obama's post health care victory demeanor change is very real indeed: "But in the immediate aftermath of his health care victory ... there does seem to be real, not imagined, change in Obama's management modus operandi.... The pace has picked up — if not faster-than-a speeding-bullet Superman velocity, then at least as much as the inherent sclerosis of Washington will allow" (Rich "Bird"). Rich at last says that there is finally something real, not something imagined, emanating from the Oval Office.

If Obama's pace is not really comparable to Superman's pace, he is at least working as fast as any mortal president possibly can. Rich proposes that this new Obama working mode reality is in the president's best interest: "It [the speed with which Obama navigates America out of the recession] will be the moment of clarity that allows us to at last judge him, as we should all presidents, on what he's actually done rather than on who we imagine he is" (Rich "Bird"). In the manner of Leonard Nimoy — who when playing Mr. Spock, like Obama, is a tall thin man endowed with big ears — the figure we imagine Maureen

Dowd's "Spocky" Obama to be is open to interpretation. Nimoy, who wrote *I Am Spock* and *I Am Not Spock*, is unsure as to whether or not he really is science fictional. The same holds true in relation to our judgment of Obama. Is he science fictional? Is he not science fictional? How do we answer these questions in relation to what Rich and David Remnick — in his biography about Obama called *The Bridge*— view as our propensity to judge and imagine the president in terms of "the enigmatic, Rorschach-test" (Rich "Bird")?

Clarity is not generated when political science fiction language is used to judge Obama and to enable imagining who he is. Like the many demarcations Obama renders indistinct, he blurs the boundaries between science fiction and reality. On the one hand, yes he can't work faster than Superman. On the other hand, yes he can be the first black American president. And yes he can successfully enact health care reform.

In light of these very real accomplishments, according to the logic which Mr. Spock champions, the following statement is true: Barack Obama *is* Superman.

It is perfectly logical for America's president to be a real science fiction super hero. Jonathan Lethem, when participating in a PEN World Voices Festival panel called "Utopia and Dystopia: Geographies of the Possible," stated that manifest destiny in particular and America in general, like science fiction novels, are "conceptual projects." In terms of *truth*, justice, and the American way, Obama uses real and fantastic illocutionary force to unite the science fictional aspects America and its political conceptual projects share. The political science fiction illocutionary force is now with the Democrats.

Notes

1. These titles refer to the following works: Anderson, Susan Janice. "Introduction: Feminism and Science Fiction: Beyond BEMS and Boobs. In *Aurora: Beyond Equality*. Eds. Susan Janice Anderson and Vonda McIntyre. Greenwich, CT: Fawcett, 1976. McCaffery, Larry. *Storming the Reality Studio: A Casebook of Cyberpunk and Postmodern Science Fiction*. Durham, NC: Duke University Press, 1991. Parrinder, Patrick. *Learning from Other Worlds: Estrangement, Cognition, and the Politics of Science Fiction and Utopia*. Durham, NC: Duke University Press, 2000.

2. See Barr, Marleen S. "Science Fiction and the Cultural Logic of Early Post Postmodernism." *Socialism and Democracy* (November 2003): 167–186.

Works Cited

Avatar. Written and directed by James Cameron. With Sam Worthington, Zoe Saldana, and Sigourney Weaver. Twentieth Century–Fox, 2009.

Bai, Matt. "The Edge of Mystery." *New York Times Magazine*, January 18, 2009, pp. 37–38, 44.
Barr, Marleen. *Alien to Femininity: Speculative Fiction and Feminist Theory*. Westport, CT: Greenwood, 1987.
Barth, John. "The Literature of Exhaustion." *The Atlantic*, August 1967.
_____. *Lost In the Funhouse*. Garden City, NY: Doubleday, 1968.
Benchley, Peter. *Jaws*. Garden City, NY: Doubleday, 1974.
Blow, Charles M. "Crucible of Change." *New York Times*, February 13, 2010, p. A23.
Borowitz, Andy. "GOP Launch Time Travel Machine to Disagree with Obama in Future." *Huffington Post*. http://www.huffingtonpost.com/andy-borowitz/gop-launch-time-traavel-ma_b_471996.html, February 22, 2010.
Brooks, David. "When Reality Bites." *New York Times*, February 12, 2008, p. A21.
Cheney, Matthew. "Ethical Aesthetics: An Introduction to *The Jewel-Hinged Jaw*." Middletown, CT: Wesleyan University Press, 2009.
Chideya, Farai. "The Black President Trap." *Huffington Post*. http://www.huffingtonpost.com/farai-chideya/the-black-president-trap_b_470933.html, February 21, 2010.
Collins, Gail. "The Grievance Committee." *New York Times*, March 19, 2009, p. A31.
_____. "The New Hillary." *New York Times*, January 24, 2009, p. A21.
_____. "Pat Loves Rudy." *New York Times*, November 8, 2007, p. A33.
_____. "Unwelcome Surprises." *New York Times*, March 13, 2008, p. A25.
_____. "A Voter's Guide." *New York Times*, February 2, 2008, p. A19.
_____. "The Year of the Cloned Candidates." *New York Times*, September 13, 2008, p. A19.
"The Court's Blow to Democracy." Editorial. *New York Times*, January 22, 2010, p. A30.
Delany, Samuel R. "Critical Methods/Speculative Fiction." In *The Jewel Hinged Jaw: Notes on the Language of Science Fiction*. Middletown, CT: Wesleyan University Press, 2009. pp. 17–28.
_____. *The Jewel-Hinged Jaw: Notes on the Language of Science Fiction*. Middletown, CT: Wesleyan University Press, 2009.
_____. "To Read the Dispossessed." In *The Jewel Hinged Jaw: Notes on the Language of Science Fiction*. Middletown, CT: Wesleyan University Press, 2009. pp. 105–165.
Dowd, Maureen. "The Aura of Arugulance." *New York Times*, April 19, 2009, p. 11.
_____. *Bushworld: Enter At Your Own Risk*. New York: Putnam's, 2004.
_____. "Can He Unleash the Force?" *New York Times*, June 6, 2007, p. A23.
_____. "Exit the Boy King." *New York Times*, January 21, 2009, p. A31.
_____. "Hey W! Bin Laden (Still) Determined to Strike in U. S." *New York Times*, July 18, 2007, p. A19.
_____. "Less Spocky, More Rocky." *New York Times*, September 9, 2009, p. A29.
_____. "Put Aside Logic." *New York Time*, May 10, 2009, p. 9.
_____. "Sarah's Pompom Palaver." *New York Times*, October 5, 2008, p. 11.
_____. "There Will Be Blood." *New York Times*, February 3, 2008, p. 17.
_____. "A Vice President Without Borders, Bordering on Lunacy." *New York Times*, June 24, 2007, p. 15.
"Earthstruck." Editorial. *New York Times*, December 24, 2008, p. A24.
Egan, Timothy. "Courage without the Uniform." *New York Times*, June 30, 2007, p. A17.
Friedman, Thomas L. "In or Out." *New York Times*, July 11, 2007, p. A19.

___. "Time to Reboot America." *New York Times*, December 24, 2008, p. A25.
Gunn, James. "Reading Science Fiction as Science Fiction." In *Reading Science Fiction*, edited by James Gunn, Marleen S. Barr, and Matthew Candelaria, 159–167. London: Palgrave Macmillan, 2009.
Herbert, Bob. "High-Stakes Flimflam." *New York Times*, October 9, 2007, p. A31.
___. "Running From Reality." *New York Times*, September 6, 2008, p. A17.
Herbert, Frank. *Dune*. Philadelphia: Chilton, 1965.
Holtz-Eakin, Douglas. "The Real Arithmetic of Health Care Reform." *New York Times*, March 20, 2010, p. 12.
Invasion of the Body Snatchers. Directed by Don Siegel. Written by Daniel Mainwaring and Jack Finney. With Kevin MCCarthey and Dana Wynter. Walter Wanger Productions, 1956.
Irving, John. *The World According to Garp: A Novel*. New York: Dutton, 1978.
Itzkoff, Dave. "Planetary Politics." *New York Times*, December 16, 2007, Section 7, p. 16.
Kakutani, Michiko. "Is Jon Stewart the Most Trusted Man In America?" *New York Times*, August 17, 2008, pp. AR1, 18–19.
Kornblut, Anne E. *Notes from the Cracked Ceiling: Hillary Clinton, Sarah Palin, And What It Will Take For a Woman to Win*. New York: Crown, 2009.
Krugman, Paul. "All the President's Enablers." *New York Times*, July 20, 2007, p. A23.
___. "Desperately Seeking Seriousness." *New York Times*, October 26, 2008, p. 15.
___. "The Resentment Strategy." *New York Times*, September 5, 2008, p. A27.
"Laugh Lines." *New York Times*, November 4, 2007, Sect. 4, p.2.
Lethem, Jonathan. Panel. "Utopia and Dystopia: Geographies of the Possible." PEN World Voices Festival. CUNY Graduate Center, New York, April 30, 2010.
Lindsay, David. *Voyage to Arcturus*. London: Methuen, 1920.
Mieville, China. *The Scar*. London: Macmillan, 2002.
Morton, Oliver. "Not-So-Lonely Planet." *New York Times*, December 24, 2008, p. A25.
The New Adventures of the Old Christine. Created by Kari Lizer. With Julia Louis-Dreyfus, Clark Gregg, Hamish Linklater, and Wanda Sykes. CBS, March 2006.
Nimoy Leonard. *I Am Not Spock*. Milbrae, CA: Celestial Arts, 1975.
___. *I Am Spock*. New York: Hyperion, 1995.
"No Progress Report." Editorial. *New York Times*, July 13, 2007, p. A18.
Pope, Nick. "Unidentified Flying Threats." *New York Times*, July 29, 2008, p. A19.
Real Time with Bill Maher. HBO, March 19, 2010.
Remnick, David. *The Bridge: The Life and Rise of Barack Obama*. New York: Knopf, 2010.
Rich, Frank. "Bush of a Thousand Days." *New York Times*, April 30, 2006, p. 15.
___. "It's a Bird, It's a Plane, It's Obama!" *New York Times*, April 4, 2010, p. 9.
___. "The Longer the War, the Larger the Lies." *New York Times*, September 17, 2006, p. 14.
___. "The Mysterious Death of Pat Tillman." *New York Times*, November 6, 2005, p. 12.
___. "The New Rove-Cheney Assault on Reality." *New York Times*, March 14, 2010, p. 8.
___. "Patriots Who Love the Troops to Death." *New York Times*, August 5, 2007, p. 10.
___. "Shuffling Off to Crawford, 2007 Edition." *New York Times*, August 12, 2007, p. 11.

_____. "Truthiness Stages a Comeback." *New York Times,* September 21, 2008, p. 9.
_____. "Who Really Took Over During that Colonoscopy." *New York Times*, July 29, 2007, p. 10.
"Rules for the Real World." Editorial. *New York Times*, September 20, 2006, p. A26.
Sargent, Pamela. "Hillary Orbits Venus." *Amazing Stories*, Spring 1999.
Solomon, Deborah. "Questions for Dennis Kucinich: The Wild Card." *New York Times Magazine*, August 24, 2008, p. 13.
Streisand, Barbra. "We the Corporations? I Don't Think So." *Huffington Post,* January 28, 2010. *http://www.huffingtonpost.com/barbra-streisand/we-the-corporations-i-don_b_440748.htm.*
Vonnegut, Kurt. *Slaughterhouse Five*. New York: Delacorte, 1969.
Warner, Judith. "'24' As Reality Show." *New York Times*, July 31, 2007, p. A19.
Weisberg, Jacob. "The Bush Who Got Away." *New York Times*, January 28, 2008. p. A23.
Weiss, Russ. Letter to the Editor. *New York Times*, September 5, 2008, p. A26.
"The World According to Cheney." Editorial. *New York Times*, December 23, 2008, p. A28.

About the Contributors

Suparno Banerjee is an assistant professor in English at Texas State University, San Marcos, and is a scholar of science fiction and postcolonial literature, especially interested in postcolonial and international science fiction. Recent scholarly publications have been on Anglophone science fiction from India.

Marleen S. Barr is known for her pioneering work in feminist science fiction and teaches in the department of communication and media studies at Fordham University. She has won the Science Fiction Research Association Pilgrim Award for lifetime achievement in science fiction criticism. Barr is the author of *Alien to Femininity: Speculative Fiction and Feminist Theory*; *Lost in Space: Probing Feminist Science Fiction and Beyond*; *Feminist Fabulation: Space/Postmodern Fiction*; and *Genre Fission: A New Discourse Practice for Cultural Studies*.

Jenn Brandt is in the English Ph.D. program at the University of Rhode Island, where she is focusing on twenty-first century literature and theories of images and the body. In addition to teaching women's studies at the university. She is also a lecturer of English at the Rhode Island School of Design.

Michele Braun teaches writing and literature at Mount Royal University in Calgary. Her research looks at ways in which technology is represented in contemporary literature, particularly in genres like science fiction and fantasy, through figures like cyborgs and clones who question definitions of human nature.

Katherine R. Broad is a doctoral candidate in English at the City University of New York Graduate Center. She teaches at Lehman College.

Karen Cardozo is an assistant professor with Commonwealth (Honors) College at the University of Massachusetts Amherst. During the past decade she served intermittently as a dean of student and academic affairs at Mount Holyoke College and taught a range of cultural, ethnic, literary/film, and trauma studies courses. She is writing a book, *Generic Engineering: Reforming American Studies*, which argues that the diversification of academic norms and practices is necessary to revitalize higher education and maximize its democratic potential.

Jason W. Ellis is an English literature Ph.D. candidate at Kent State University and is Vice President of the Science Fiction Research Association. He has published on science fiction and online identities in the collection *Practicing Science Fiction: Critical Essays on Writing, Reading and Teaching the Genre*, and his writing on science fiction has also appeared in *Locus*, *Foundation*, and the *German Quarterly*.

Adam Frisch is a professor and the chair of English and writing at Briar Cliff University in Sioux City, Iowa. He is the immediate past president of the Science Fiction Research Association. He has published work on Ken MacLeod in *The True Knowledge of Ken MacLeod* and other articles on science fiction subjects.

Ángel Mateos-Aparicio Martín-Albo is an associate professor at the University of Castilla–La Mancha (Ciudad Real, Spain). His main research interests include the intersection of science fiction and mainstream postmodern literature/culture. Mr. Martín-Albo's recent publications include "Trespassers of Body Boundaries: The Cyborg and the Construction of a Hybrid Postgendered Posthuman Identity" in *Border Transits: Literature and Culture Across the Line*.

Swaralipi Nandi is an English literature Ph.D. candidate and teacher at Kent State University whose research focus is postcolonial literature and theory. She is the editor of a forthcoming volume on postcolonial films, *Gory Third Screen: Violence and Masculinity in Postcolonial Films*.

Chris Pak is completing a Ph.D. at the University of Liverpool, investigating the intersections between postcolonial and ecocritical theory in narratives of terraforming. He has been published in the journal *Green Letters*.

Masood A. Raja is an assistant professor of postcolonial literature and theory at University of North Texas and author of *Constructing Pakistan*. He is editor of *Pakistaniaat: A Journal of Pakistan Studies*. His critical essays have been published in journals including *South Asian Review*, *Digest of Middle East Studies*, *Caribbean Studies*, *Prose Studies*, and *Mosaic*.

Stacy Schmitt Rusnak is a Ph.D. student at Georgia State University in Atlanta. She is completing her dissertation on the cinema of Mexican directors Guillermo Del Toro, Alfonso Cuarón, and Alejandro González Iñárritu.

Banu Subramaniam is an associate professor of women's studies at the University of Massachusetts, Amherst. She received her Ph.D. in evolutionary biology/genetics from Duke University. Her research is at the intersections of feminist science studies, postcolonial studies and gender studies. She is co-editor of *Feminist Science Studies: A New Generation* and *Making Threats: Biofears and Environmental Anxieties*.

Index

adaptation 113–14, 150
Africa 12, 48, 88–90, 161, 163–4
Agamben, Georgio 175, 179, 183, 185–6
agribusiness, politics of 32, 37
agriculture, industrialized 32–3
alienation 17–18, 30, 146
alternative reality 191, 201
American culture 1, 103–4, 107, 110, 114, 117
American frontier 1–2, 105, 107, 110, 119
American frontier myth 108, 117–19, 123
American history 104, 124, 203
American Indians 111, 113
American melting pot 114, 116–17, 120
American West 20, 103–6, 108, 112, 120, 122–3
Anzaldúa, Gloria 103, 116–17, 120, 123
Appiah, Anthony 165–6, 170, 172
appropriation 49, 57–8, 67
Ashcroft, Bill 48, 55–6, 69, 153–4
assimilation 12, 64, 113–14

Bhabha, Homi 50, 52, 55, 57–8, 69, 113, 123, 177, 181, 186
biodiversity 33–4, 41–2
biofiction 10, 30–2, 35, 38–9, 42, 44
biopower 175, 177, 186
Bollywood 11, 73–4, 77, 80, 85–6
borderlands 103, 120, 123
Bose, Subhas Chandra 129–30, 135–7
Bradbury, Ray 77, 105, 111, 124
Britain 174, 177–8, 184
British nationalism 179–80
Burroughs, William S. 109–10, 123
"Bushworld" 201, 208

Calf Island 20–2, 25–8
capitalism 32–3, 38, 40, 53, 176
Cheney, Dick 192–3, 196, 201, 204, 208, 210
Children of Men 13, 174–5, 177–85, 187

cinema 73, 76, 85, 187, 212
circulation 40, 162, 165–6
citizens 34, 102, 114, 159, 164–6, 174, 176, 178, 181–3, 205
citizenship 11, 116, 166, 175, 182, 184
class 3, 5–6, 82, 108, 121, 123, 177
Clinton, Hillary 188, 190, 196, 209
colonial discourses 13, 77, 151
colonization 13, 50, 60, 79–80, 88–91, 94, 97–8, 104–5, 108, 121, 129, 142, 147, 149–51, 176; of other 57–8
communication 7, 13, 49, 121, 141, 143, 145–6, 151–2, 156, 160, 169, 193, 211; bodily 145–6
community, political 180–1
compassion 43–4, 51, 164
compromise 11, 46–7, 49, 51, 53, 55, 95, 98, 153
conceptual technology 24–7
conquest 89, 100, 102, 104, 107–8, 110, 122–3
consciousness 7, 17, 20–2, 41, 63, 67–8; national 7, 75
cosmopolitan ideal 157–8, 167
cosmopolitan patriotism 161, 165–8, 172
cosmopolitan theory 9, 157–8
cosmopolitanism 7–8, 10, 32, 38, 42, 64, 156–67, 169–73, 176, 186
cosmopolitics 7–8, 10–11, 14, 31, 34, 39, 172–3
cultural bias 102, 118, 120–1
cultural differences 50, 52, 55, 110–11, 114, 181
cultural identity 11, 50, 58, 61–2
cultural nationalisms 34, 136
cultural practices 18, 166
cultural productions 32, 110, 121
cultures: alien 194; cinematic 74–5; western 65, 113
cyborgs 9, 60, 102, 124, 211–12

213

Delhi 11, 58, 62–5, 67, 70, 86, 126–7
democracy 107, 131, 135–6, 175, 183, 204, 207–8
differentiation 145–6, 151
discourses 10–11, 31, 33, 40, 42, 45, 57–8, 65, 67–9, 75, 121, 134, 152, 154, 195
displacement 18, 52
diversity 32–3, 39, 41, 44, 52, 59, 142, 152, 166, 176
domination 84, 107, 113, 130–1
Dowd, Maureen 189–93, 196–8, 201, 207–8

empathy 141–2, 152
environment 25, 108, 127, 132, 142, 146–7, 151, 196
Equiano, Olaudah 161, 163–5, 167, 172–3
ethnicities 11, 50, 84, 156–7, 162, 171, 177–8
Europe 77, 91, 97, 111, 113, 161–2, 176
exception 102, 170, 174–5, 177, 179–80, 182, 187, 194
exchange 46, 50, 58, 61, 70, 76, 120, 160, 163, 169, 185
extratextual world 23, 25

Fable of Utopia 88–9, 99
Fanon, Frantz 7–8, 14
fantasy 1–2, 6, 9, 14, 20, 23, 30–1, 57, 70, 81, 153, 170, 200, 204, 211
Foucault, Michel 147, 154, 181, 187
frontier 1, 32, 100, 103, 106, 109–10, 112–13, 116, 119–20, 122, 124; new 1, 100, 107, 109, 114–15
frontier myth 12, 104, 106–7, 110, 112, 117, 119–24
frontier myth and racial politics 12, 100–1, 103, 105, 107, 109, 111, 113, 115, 117, 119, 121, 123

Gandhi, Indira 131, 136
gender 32, 36, 40–1, 93, 102, 108, 116–17, 121, 143, 156, 171, 177
Gilroy, Paul 161–4, 167, 173
globalization 2, 8–10, 14, 32, 39, 41, 78, 86, 119–21, 174–5, 179, 183–4, 186

Hindi films 73, 75–6, 86–7, 116, 128–9, 134, 136
Hollywood 73–4, 185
Huffington Post 208, 210
human beings 20, 26, 28, 36, 94, 101, 117, 156, 158–60, 167, 169, 180
human bodies 145, 147–8
Human Project 178, 181
human rights 136, 182–3

hybridity 12, 32–4, 40, 42, 44, 57–8, 125, 134, 174, 176
identity, hybrid 163, 165
identity politics 13, 34, 42, 175–6
ideologies 31, 34, 51, 106, 117–18, 123, 129, 131, 135–6, 155
India 3, 12, 63, 66, 73, 77–82, 85–6, 112, 125–31, 134–7, 164, 211
Indian films 74–6, 79, 85–6
Indian nation 12, 80, 82, 84, 125, 128
Iraq 185, 191, 194, 199–200, 203

Kant, Immanuel 158–61, 164, 167, 171–3
Kenya 88–91, 96, 98
Kikuyu 90–8
Kirinyaga 12, 88–99
Kolkata 125–8, 130, 134
Krishna 81–4

language: human 145; new national 13, 189; poetic 68
language of postnationality 11, 56–7, 59, 61, 63, 65, 67, 69
life: bare 180–3, 185; political 180–1, 183–4
London 2, 14, 29, 45, 55, 69–70, 86, 123–4, 177–8, 187, 209

MacLeod 11, 46–7, 52–3, 55
magic 10, 19–22, 22–9, 79, 81, 97, 157, 168
magical realism 18–21, 23–5
Mars 100, 103–11, 113–16, 118–23, 150; landscape 103–8, 111; settlers 107–8, 116
Martian Chronicles 105–6, 111, 123
Martians 103, 105–11, 115
Martín-Albo 101, 103, 105, 107, 109, 111, 113, 115, 117, 119, 121, 123, 212
massively multiplayer online role playing game *see* MMORPG
Megalopolis 132–3
megatext 57–8, 62, 65
melting pot 12, 102, 108–9, 113–14, 117–20
mestiza 103, 116–17
mestizos 103, 116–17, 122
metaphor 35, 62, 67, 69–70, 123, 161
Mexico 13, 174, 176, 178–9, 182, 184, 187
MMORPG 156, 167, 169, 170
Modern India 79, 86, 136
modernity 52, 85, 161–2, 164
multicultural 12, 102–3, 105, 115, 119
myth 19, 24–5, 27, 63, 76–7, 86, 102–3, 107, 110, 120–2, 124, 151
mythology 19, 24–5, 75, 76, 81, 83, 85, 132

NAFTA 179, 182, 186
nation 7–8, 10–14, 39, 45, 53, 56, 75, 78–82, 84, 91, 101, 117, 129–30, 172–3, 182

Index

nation states 8–10, 81, 84, 162, 175, 178, 182–3
national allegiance 178, 180, 184
national identity 7, 18, 20, 33, 64, 68, 75, 178, 182–3
nationalism 7–8, 10, 13–14, 30–1, 33–6, 39–40, 56, 85, 128–30, 141, 182
nationalities 84, 108, 113, 115, 121, 181–2, 184
nationhood 12, 73, 75
Native Americans 102, 109–10, 112–13
nature 9, 18–19, 26, 31, 33, 35–6, 89, 95, 97–8, 109, 112–13, 144–6, 159–60, 163, 172
naturecultures 31, 35–6
New York Times 14, 189, 199, 208–10
Nova 58–62, 69
novels 11, 17–22, 24, 28, 31–9, 41–2, 50–3, 105, 107–12, 114–15, 117–23, 125–8, 131–5, 150–1
novum 59, 63, 65

Oankali 141–50, 152–3
Obama, Barak 188, 190, 192, 197–8, 200, 203–9

Pakistan 127–8, 130–1, 135
Palin, Sarah 192, 196–7, 209
pedagogy 32, 36, 38–9, 44, 168
perception 21, 144–5, 193–4
perpetual peace 158–9, 171, 173
physics, quantum 19, 22–3
Popular Science 11, 73, 75, 77, 79, 81, 83, 85, 87
postcapitalist politics 35, 39, 44
postcolonialism 12–14, 31, 55–6, 58, 65, 85, 98, 123, 126, 137, 175–7, 187, 190, 211–12; discourses 13, 189; literature 12, 18, 30, 34, 56–7, 88–9, 211–12; Nation 12, 84, 125, 127, 129, 131, 133, 135, 137; Novel 10, 17–19, 21, 23, 25, 27, 29; studies 9–10, 30, 32; theory 7, 9, 48, 55–6, 175, 177
postnational discourse 12, 142, 144, 146, 148, 150, 152, 154, 158, 160, 162, 164, 166, 168
postnationalism 7–11, 13, 30, 56–61, 63–5, 67–9, 175–7
power: colonial 6, 80; hegemonic 183, 185–6
power dynamics 80, 84

racial politics 12, 100–1, 103, 105, 107, 109, 111, 113, 115, 117, 119, 121–3
recognition 12, 35, 63, 111–13

red planet 103–9, 111–14, 116, 119, 124
resistance 33, 35, 37–8, 42–3, 80, 150, 162, 184
rights 108, 111, 159, 171, 183, 185, 204–5; human 136, 182–3
Robbins, Bruce 7, 14, 157, 172–3
Rousseau, Jean-Jacques 141, 144, 154
Rushdie, Salman 10, 18–20, 22–9

science: discourse of 11–12, 73; empirical 77–8, 81–2, 85
science fiction: community 2–3; films 11, 74, 87; genre 20, 84, 175; illocutionary 196–7; language, postcolonial 189, 194; postcolonial 10, 12, 69, 76–7, 86; studies 9, 86, 124, 155
Science Fiction Research Association 211–12
science fictional modes 23, 25
science studies, feminist 30, 212
scientific knowledge 5–6, 9, 19, 79
self 5, 7, 11, 17–18, 66, 123, 141–3, 146–8, 151–2, 172
self-aware robots 48–50
Singapore 82–4, 180
slavery 153–4, 162, 164
sovereignty 179, 183
space, subterranean 64
space-time continuum 188–9, 197
species 1, 33, 102, 142–3, 153, 170; human 141, 160
Star Trek 1, 102, 104, 117, 204
state of exception 13, 174–5, 177, 179–80, 182, 187
subject, colonized 147–9
subjectivity 29, 123, 148, 151–3
Superman 74, 197, 207

technology, trope of 5, 10–11, 17–20, 24–9, 31, 45–6, 52, 59–60, 77–8, 82–6, 90, 92, 126–7, 161, 168–9

universe 23–4, 27, 61, 65, 101–2, 191, 199–200; alternative 191, 194, 199, 201
utopia 6–7, 9, 14, 34, 41–2, 88–91, 93–9, 107, 116, 119, 122–4, 133, 152, 154–5, 159, 207, 209; vision of 90, 94, 97
Utopian Studies 153–4

western landscapes 105, 107
Western world 77, 154
World of Warcraft 156–7, 167–170